THE RISING AMERICAN EMPIRE

The Author

Professor Richard W. Van Alstyne holds a B.A. from Harvard University, an M.A. from the University of Southern California, and a Ph.D. from Stanford University. In 1938 the French Government conferred upon him the honorary title of *Officier d'Académie*. He was Professor of History and Chairman of the Department of Social Studies at Chico State College, California, from 1935 to 1945, and in 1947 became Professor of History at the University of Southern California. He was Visiting Professor in 1950 at the Fletcher School of Law and Diplomacy and at the University of Michigan, in 1956 at the University of British Columbia, and in 1958 at Queen's University, Ontario, Canada. Professor Van Alstyne gave the Commonwealth Fund Lectures at University College, London, in 1956, and in 1960 returned there as a Fulbright Scholar and Honorary Research Associate. He was a Fellow of the Henry E. Huntington Library & Art Gallery in 1965–1966, and in 1967 came to his present post as Distinguished Professor of History at Callison College, the University of the Pacific, in Stockton, California.

The original edition of *The Rising American Empire* was published in 1960 by Basil Blackwell of Oxford. Aside from many articles, Professor Van Alstyne has written the following books: *American Diplomacy in Action* (first published in 1944, reissued in 1968), *American Crisis Diplomacy* (1952), *Empire and Independence: The International History of the American Revolution* (1965), *Genesis of American Nationalism* (1970), and *The United States and East Asia* (1973). He is also co-author of the book *From Colony to Empire: Essays in the History of American Foreign Relations* (1972), and a contributor to *The Times* (London) *Atlas of World History*.

THE RISING
AMERICAN EMPIRE

R. W. VAN ALSTYNE

The Norton Library

W·W·NORTON & COMPANY·INC·

NEW YORK

To Margaret

Books That Live
The Norton imprint on a book means that in the publisher's
estimation it is a book not for a single season but for the years.
W. W. Norton & Company, Inc.

Library of Congress Cataloging in Publication Data
Van Alstyne, Richard Warner, 1900–
    The rising American empire.
    (The Norton library)
    Reprint of the ed. published by B. Blackwell, Oxford.
    Bibliography: p.
    1. United States—Territorial expansion. 2. Imperialism.
3. United States—Foreign relations. I. Title.
E179.5.V32   1975   911'.73   74-10792
ISBN 0-393-00750-2

Printed in the United States of America
1 2 3 4 5 6 7 8 9 0

PREFACE

THIS book—an outgrowth of the Commonwealth Fund Lectures which I had the honour to deliver at University College London in 1956—is a study of the origins and the emergence of the United States as a national state and of its subsequent growth pattern. It views the United States relative to other national states, possessing like them (and being possessed by) clearly recognizable nationalist urges or drives. The entire course of American history coincides with the rise of modern nationalism; and, set in this frame of reference, the American Empire, as its founders so conceived it, provides an excellent introduction to the study of international history.

In these pages I have tried to convey a sense of direction and unbroken continuity in the history of the United States. The early colonies were no sooner established in the seventeenth century than expansionist impulses began to register in each of them. Imperial patterns took shape, and before the middle of the eighteenth century the concept of an empire that would take in the whole continent was fully formed. A drive south into the Spanish Caribbean was also in progress, with the ultimate goal in view of converting the Caribbean into an American lake. In the Revolution the spirit of conquest was a powerful force, and it took about a century thereafter to satisfy the territorial ambitions of the United States. Except for the internal dissension which was a constant factor during the first half of the nineteenth century, and which finally exploded into a civil war of vast proportions, it seems probable that these ambitions would have been pursued more persistently and energetically, that indeed they would have been pushed to the limit. But, by the time of the Mexican War, the controversy between North and South developed into an obsession; and further conquests became for the time being impossible. On the North American continent American expansion reached its maximum limits by 1867, the process of advance having been delayed long enough to enable the Canadians to develop the necessary counter-moves. The two related drives, south into the Caribbean and westward to China via Cape Horn, continued to the end of the century, when a burst of energy finished off the process in a war against Spain. From the island conquests of that war the United States emerged a satiated power, so that thereafter American statesmen could truthfully say, with Woodrow Wilson, that 'never again' would the United States 'seek one

additional foot of territory by conquest '. The sentiment became a
fixation, repeated on innumerable occasions, but it is irrelevant.

The structure of the American Empire thus was completed some
sixty years ago; and since my object in this book is to analyze the
construction process, I view my task as, in the main, finished with
the first decade of the present century. The process of empire-
building continues, of course, but thereafter it is more of a problem
of consolidation and rendering secure what has been gained. So
as to round out the book and emphasize this all-important factor
of historical continuity, I have tried in the concluding chapter, to
describe, with necessary brevity, this period of consolidation.

While this book is intended in part as an interpretation and as a
general synthesis, much of it nevertheless is based on original sources,
some of them hitherto unused. This is particularly true of the
second and third chapters, which are a study of the American quest
for foreign aid and alliances during the War for American Independence. The diplomatic history of this contest merits drastic
reconsideration and calls for new perspectives in which British viewpoints deserve a closer and fairer scrutiny than has yet been offered.
The subject is too large to be treated in full in the present volume
and, moreover, its historical importance is such as to justify a separate
book. This is a task which I am assigning to myself for the future.
Much research thus far completed had to be left out in the writing
of these two chapters. In connection with Chapters V and VI
certain hitherto unused correspondence in the George Bancroft
Collection of the Massachusetts Historical Society is remarkably
revealing with respect to the Oregon controversy and to the war with
Mexico. Full reference to my sources being found in the footnotes,
a separate bibliography is regarded as superfluous.

My acknowledgments and thanks are due to the following
libraries and repositories for their help: the William L. Clements
Library, Ann Arbor, Michigan; the Henry E. Huntington Library,
San Marino, California; the American Philosophical Society,
Philadelphia, Pennsylvania, to which I also am grateful for a research
grant in 1954; the Historical Society of Pennsylvania; the Alderman
Library of the University of Virginia; the New York Public Library;
the Massachusetts Historical Society, Boston, Massachusetts; the
University of Southern California Library, in which connection I
owe special appreciation to Miss Helen Azhderian and Mrs. Irmadean

Haberly for their help in obtaining valuable documents on loan; the
National Archives in Washington, D. C., and the Division of Manuscripts of the Library of Congress; the Public Record Office in
London; and the Sheffield City Libraries. For their support and
active interest I wish to repeat the thanks which I previously gave,
in the pamphlet on the American Empire issued in 1960 by the
Historical Association of Great Britain, to Professors Geoffrey Barra-
clough, H. C. Allen and R. A. Humphreys; and to include with them
Mr. H. L. Schollick, the director of Basil Blackwell of Oxford, the
original publisher of this volume.

R.W.V.A.

Los Angeles, California

CONTENTS

MAPS

CHAPTER I

INTRODUCTION

THE CONCEPTION OF AN AMERICAN EMPIRE

'Wheresoever the Roman conquers, he inhabits'

THE title of this book comes straight from George Washington.
Even as early as March 1783 the United States was, to Washington, a 'rising empire'. The phrase describes precisely what he and his
contemporaries had in mind, that is to say an *imperium*—a dominion,
state or sovereignty that would expand in population and territory,
and increase in strength and power. Benjamin Franklin had been
speaking and writing in terms like these for nearly forty years.[1] Nor
was the example of ancient Rome overlooked. Speaking with revolutionary fervour, William Henry Drayton, one of South Carolina's
leading planters who was also chief justice of that province, delivered
himself in 1776 of the following:

> Empires have their zenith—and their descension to a dissolu-
> tion. . . . Three and thirty years numbered the illustrious Days of
> the Roman greatness—Eight Years measure the Duration of the
> British Grandeur in meridian Lustre! How few are the Days of
> true Glory! . . . The British Period is from the Year 1758, when
> they victoriously pursued their Enemies into every Quarter of the
> Globe. . . . The Almighty . . . has made choice of the present
> generation to erect the American Empire. . . .
> And thus has suddenly arisen in the World, a new Empire,
> stiled the United States of America. An Empire that as soon as
> started into Existence, attracts the Attention of the Rest of the
> Universe; and bids fair, by the blessing of God, to be the most
> glorious of any upon Record.[2]

The contrast between Washington's matter-of-fact way of
expressing himself and Drayton's flamboyancy hardly needs a comment. Yet both men were moved by pride, and by a sense of

[1] For a penetrating discussion see Gerald Stourzh, *Benjamin Franklin and
American Foreign Policy*, Chicago, 1954, pp. 43–82.
[2] *A Charge on the Rise of the American Empire*, delivered by the Hon. William
Henry Drayton, esq., chief-justice of South Carolina: to the grand jury for the
District of Charlestown. (1776). Rare Book in the Henry E. Huntington Library,
San Marino, California.

future greatness, a conviction that the United States was the heir to, and the successor of, Britain in the New World. The declared purpose in fighting the War for Independence was to create a new empire or, to put the thought in words hardly familiar at the time, a new national state. Prior to the Seven Years War people had allowed to the term ' British Empire' only the limited meaning that the original Latin word ' imperium' conveyed, that is, a power or a sovereignty. But by 1760, under the influence of the sweeping victories over France, the meaning of the term had been broadened so that the emphasis was put upon territorial expanse and upon the people who inhabited it. This shift in meaning took place under the leadership of Chatham and the victorious Whigs, who desired to keep Canada; and Washington, Franklin and other Americans who had participated in this war and who ardently desired to eliminate the French and make North America a British continent, readily accepted the new interpretation. And so, with the coming of the Revolution and with the welding of the Thirteen Colonies into a new sovereign nation, the substitution of the phrase, 'American Empire', for British came easily and naturally. The Revolution also revived and strengthened the ancient Roman conception of patriotism and, through the zeal and passion of this feeling, it breathed life into the American imperium.[1]

[1] The Roman *imperium* went through the same evolution in usage as we have noted above for the British. The familiar phrase ' Roman Empire', as applied to a large territory inhabited by different peoples and ruled over by Rome, expresses a concept of the Middle Ages. See Richard Koebner, ' The Emergence of the Concept of Imperialism', *Cambridge Journal*, V, no. 12, Sept., 1952, pp. 726–41, and also his learned essay on ' Imperium: the Roman Heritage' in *Scripta Hierosolymitana*, vol. I, *Studies in Classics and Jewish Hellenism* (Jerusalem, The Hebrew University, 1954), pp. 120–44. ' Imperialism', which as a word was unknown to the eighteenth century, is purely emotive and has the attributes of a slogan; but the word ' empire' has both a substantive and an emotive sense. Koebner establishes that even in ancient Rome its use aroused controversy. ' The emotive significance of *imperium*', he remarks, ' and of all the expressions derived from it, was born on the Roman Forum.'

Benjamin Franklin, who learned at least some of his Roman history from Machiavelli's *Discourses*, regarded first the British Empire, and then the American, as Roman in conception; and he used the terms ' national' and ' imperial' interchangeably. His *imperium* was Augustan, but even more he stressed an expanding empire of territory and population. Koebner, *Scripta*; Stourzh, *op. cit.*, pp. 78–9, 101–2, 281–2. Machiavelli, it will be remembered, stressed the role of the Patriot, and Bolingbroke popularized it in the mid-eighteenth century. Herbert Butterfield, *The Statecraft of Machiavelli*, N.Y., 1956. See also Antonio Pace, ' Franklin and Machiavelli', *Symposium*, I, No. 2, 1947, pp. 36–42.

The term ' dominion', which I treated in the text above as an equivalent of ' empire', suffers too from confusion, but in a different way. If relative frequency of use in the King James Bible is an indication, one can only conclude that it

But the United States emerged from the war a loose federation of sovereign states, about whose future many capable observers, foreign and domestic, were less sanguine than was Washington. It took the Federal Constitution of 1787, with its emphasis on a central sovereign power, to clarify the objectives of the war. The framers of the Constitution intended a Leviathan type of state, as Thomas Hobbes conceived it—one that would be perpetual and not subject to revolution or withdrawal at the hands of its component parts. But this denial of the right of revolution, or secession, did not become clear until 1865, after the Southern States had failed in their attempts to secede. The Southern States, let us recall, rested their case on the theory that the Union was a compact from which the members might withdraw when, in their judgment, the central Government had violated their liberties. The philosophical position of the Southern States was repetitive of the arguments of the American rebels of 1775, who invoked John Locke to prove that the government of George III had violated the British Constitution. Thus the State of South Carolina, which in December 1860 led the procession of seceding states, deliberately employed the style of the Declaration of Independence, referred to that document by name, and charged that the Federal Government had violated the Constitution, which, it said, was a compact between the States.[1]

By its victory over the Southern Confederacy in 1865, the United States in effect repudiated Locke and assumed the mantle of Hobbes. The secession issue being no longer debatable, it was able to consolidate its power and to act thereafter as an integral national state. The right of revolution, sacred to eighteenth-century America and given homage repeatedly during the first half of the nineteenth, was renounced for ever. Such renunciation the founders of the Republic had desired to accomplish at the outset. There were two principal

enjoyed high favour over its rival in the seventeenth century. The ratio is 54:1. It was officially applied to political entities within the British Empire during that century, but it evidently dropped out of use during the eighteenth since it does not belong to American political terminology. But the Canadians in 1867 revived it effectively, and it has ever since enjoyed high priority in the terminology of the British Commonwealth. Reputedly the designation 'Dominion of Canada' comes from Psalms lxxii:8; but, except for the fact that the word 'empire' was again in disrepute, the Canadians might just as accurately have described themselves as the 'Empire of Canada'.

[1] 'Declaration of the Immediate Causes which induce and justify the Secession of South Carolina from the Federal Union,' reprinted in Louis M. Hacker, *The Shaping of the American Tradition*, N.Y., 1947, pp. 601–4.

' plans ', or drafts, of the Constitution: the Virginia Plan and the New Jersey Plan. Both of these plans set forth the principle of national supremacy over the states, and authorized the central Government to use force, if necessary, to compel the states to obey its laws. Realizing, however, that such candour would lead to the certain rejection of their instrument, the framers resorted instead to a formula that the Constitution, not the national government, was ' the supreme law of the land '. ' The judges in every State ', they added, ' shall be bound thereby, anything in the constitution or laws of any State to the contrary notwithstanding.' Moreover, the term ' federal ' was decided upon as descriptive of the new government in order to convey the idea of a compact, in place of the word ' national ', which at the time awakened doubts because it appealed to a novel type of loyalty. To express the point differently, the founders of the Republic succeeded in performing a political miracle: they created a Leviathan state, but clad it in the garments of the social compact. It took seventy-five years of controversy and four years of bloody warfare, however, to make good on this paradox.

Now, since it seems necessary to clarify terms and to analyse, however briefly, the nature of the American national state, there is one other matter which will bear mention. It goes without saying that a powerful central government cannot exist without an executive. The fathers of the Constitution knew this, and so they created the presidency. Moreover, they did so with the expectation that General Washington would be the first President and that he would mould the office to fit his own ideas. The written Constitution has much to say regarding the powers of the legislative branch, but it is singularly silent on the powers of the executive branch. It has often been pointed out that the presidency is a man-made office, which is some-times one thing and sometimes another depending upon the incum-bent and the times in which he is serving. In America there is an historic distinction between the few ' strong ' Presidents and the many ' weak ' ones. The ' strong ' ones have for the most part made the office, that is, they have used their initiative in the exercise of personal power. But the sole constitutional authority which justifies personal power is the simple statement in Article 2, section 1 to the effect that ' The executive power shall be vested in a President of the United States of America '. There is no attempt in the written Constitution to define the executive power, no elaboration or explanation of the phrase, and no limit placed upon its possible use. One can only surmise what meanings, if any, the authors of this phrase had in mind. Being students of Locke, as well as of Blackstone, it is highly probable, however, that they accepted his exposition of the phrase. ' Where the legislative and executive power are in distinct hands, as they are in all moderated monarchies and well-framed governments ', writes Locke, ' there the good of the society requires that several things should be left to the discretion of him that has the executive power '. This of course is the royal prerogative, which Locke goes on to define as the ' power to act according to discretion for the public good, without the prescription of the law and sometimes even against it '.[1]

President Washington had not been long in office when the occasion arose to put this matter to the test. With the outbreak of war between Britain and France, much of the American populace and its republican (or democratic) leaders ranged themselves violently on the side of the French. But the President saw the issue differently and dared to publish, on his own initiative, a proclamation of neutrality which, it was recognized, would hinder the war schemes of the French Republic. The act brought back to life all of the latent republican fervour against monarchy, especially since Alexander Hamilton seized the opportunity to expound the thesis that the Executive possessed virtually unlimited power in the sphere of foreign affairs. Urged on by Jefferson, James Madison undertook to develop an opposing thesis that power over foreign policy was vested in the legislative branch; and Madison hoped to silence his opponent by comparing Hamilton's claims for presidential power to the royal prerogative. The analogies which Madison drew were sound enough, but in suggesting alternatives he was ineffective. Washington's Neutrality Proclamation of 1793 established a firm precedent, and presidents have invoked the executive power many times since, in domestic but more especially in foreign affairs.

Actually the executive power is one of the most significant features of the *unwritten* American Constitution, though it seldom fails to arouse controversy when used. Legend and tradition require that the American Republic appear anti-monarchical and anti-imperial. Such is the legacy of the Revolution and the Declaration of Independence, which pronounces the verdict of ' guilty ' on King

[1] *Of Civil Government* (Second Essay), Ch. XIV.

George III. But the Constitution qualified, in a sense even repudiated, the legend of the Revolution, and established a balanced system of government the model for which was furnished by the very government which the Revolution had condemned. In reality, therefore, the United States possesses the attributes of monarchy; and it is through the President, the elective king, that it exerts its sovereign will among the family of nations. William H. Seward, Lincoln's Secretary of State, saw all this at a glance and gave cryptic and brilliant expression to it when he said: ' We elect a king for four years, and give him absolute power within certain limits, which after all he can interpret for himself.'[1]

In the United States it is almost a heresy to describe the nation as an empire. The founders so regarded it, as I have shown, and the word continued to be accepted usage through the middle of the nineteenth century, but this has been largely overlooked. The concept of an American empire disappeared with the War between the States, but the consolidation of national power that followed that war meant that it was more than ever an actuality. The learned Dr. Richard Koebner has shown how and for what reasons people in both Britain and America came to deprecate the concept and its purely emotive derivative, ' imperialism '.[2] With the appearance of protest and criticism against the island conquests of 1898 and against the alleged ' big stick ' policies of Theodore Roosevelt, ' imperialism ' became an epithet applied indiscriminately to various nations but to the United States only for the years 1898 to 1912. This period is torn out of context and given a unique frame of reference, leading to the profound historical fallacy that the United States under the influence of Theodore Roosevelt suffered an unfortunate temporary ' aberration ' from its hallowed traditions, from which it subsequently recovered as from a sickness. From this arose the curious belief that only nations with island possessions are empires. The earlier ambition of the United States to expand its continental domain was not, according to one representative historian, imperialism, a truth only in the sense that the word itself was not coined until the 1870s. Then, by way of compounding the confusion, this writer adds: ' In

---

[1] Cited by Edward S. Corwin on the fly-leaf of his book, *The President. Office and Powers, 1787–1957. History and Analysis of Practice and Opinion.* Fourth Revised Edition. N.Y., 1957.

[2] Koebner, op. cit., and also his article, ' The Concept of Economic Imperialism,' in *Economic History Review*, 2nd series, vol. II, no. 1, pp. 1–29.

reality, the extension of American rule over Indian tribes and their lands was imperialism—not recognized as such only because the Indians were so few in number as to be virtually swallowed '.[1]

Here it might be pointed out that American foreign policy has a vocabulary all its own, consciously—even ostentatiously—side-stepping the use of terms that would even hint at aggression or imperial domination, and taking refuge in abstract formulae, stereotyped phrases, and idealistic clichés that really explain nothing. Phrases like ' Monroe Doctrine ', ' no entangling alliances ', ' freedom of the seas ', ' open door ', ' good neighbour policy ', ' Truman doctrine ', ' Eisenhower doctrine ', strew the pages of American history but throw little light on the dynamics of American foreign policy. Parrot-like repetition of these abstractions and other generalities produces an emotional reflex which assumes that American diplomacy is ' different ', purer, morally better than the diplomacy of other powers. There is a strong pharisaical flavour about American diplomacy, easily detected abroad but generally unrecognized at home. No doubt it is a part of the cult of nationalism.

Consider, for instance, the implication behind the well-worn stereotype, ' The United States enforces the Monroe Doctrine '. My dictionary tells me that a doctrine is a teaching—its derivation is the Latin verb, *doceo*, ' I teach '. But actually as American diplomacy manipulates this phrase, the Monroe Doctrine has long since assumed the characteristics of positive law which the United States, the lord of the western hemisphere, applies from time to time as it sees fit. The particular application may or may not be benevolent—that depends on how it is interpreted; but there is no doubt that it is arbitrary. Furthermore, it is an interesting point, I think, that American diplomacy shows a preference for a term that is commonly identified with theological dogma. The Monroe Doctrine has the additional authority of Canon Law behind it. To carry the analogy further, the United States assumes unto itself a function of the mediaeval Papacy: the prerogative of infallibility.

The quotation, ' wheresoever the Roman conquers, he inhabits ', which is incorporated in the title of this first chapter, is from the Stoic philosopher, Seneca. I culled it from the pages of one of the greatest of historians, Edward Gibbon, in the opinion that it applies

[1] Julius W. Pratt, *America's Colonial Experiment. How the United States gained, governed, and in part gave away a Colonial Empire*, N.Y., 1950, p. 4.

with equal truth to the American nation. The idea that America—the ' New World '—would be conquered and inhabited by people of English stock was native to the empire builders of Elizabethan England and bred into the minds of the early immigrants to Virginia and Massachusetts Bay. With the latter, especially with the Puritans who migrated with a sense of grievance against their homeland, it became an article of faith that they were in a new world, a new sphere. Expounded with particular force and clarity by the New England Puritans, who regarded themselves as founders of a new Israel in the North American wilderness, the doctrine of the two spheres became a fixation in the American mind prerequisite to the growth of nationalism. New England, which was ' God's American Israel ' according to its Calvinist divines, assumed from the outset an attitude of political independence toward the mother country. The Great and General Court of Massachusetts—the pretentious title which the legislative assembly of that province bestowed upon itself—audaciously substituted an oath of allegiance to itself in place of the oath to the king.[1]

The notion of a pre-emptive right to the continent was given legal affirmation by the first Colonial charters, which designated the Pacific Ocean, or South Sea as it was then called, as the western boundary of the several colonies. Those who drafted the charters could not have even dreamed of the immense distance from one sea to the other, but as knowledge of the interior began to appear the charters, far from being regarded as ridiculous, were invoked as ' proof ' that the French, who had mastered the vastness of the Mississippi basin, were mere trespassers. To this legal fiction was added the argument that the continent belonged as of right to those who could colonize it. Thus the Virginia planter, Lewis Burwell, in 1751 made a sweeping denial of the right of anyone except the people of the Atlantic seaboard to appropriate the hinterland. To the Board of Trade in London Burwell wrote:

> That, notwithstanding the Grants of the Kings of England, France or Spain, the Property of these uninhabited Parts of the World must be founded upon prior Occupancy according to the Law of Nature; and it is the Seating & Cultivating the soil & not the bare travelling through a Territory that constitutes Right; &

[1] Charles M. Andrews, *The Colonial Period in American History*, 4 vols., New Haven, Conn., 1934–8, I, p. 435.

it will be political & highly for the Interest of the Crown to encourage the Seating the Lands Westward as soon as possible to prevent the French.[1]

Here is perhaps the first invocation of John Locke's law of nature as the basis for territorial claim, and the first linking of natural law to colonization as giving to the Anglo-Americans their claim of superior right to the interior. This concept of the right to colonize, premised upon an assumed ability to implement the right, thus begins to be part of the American mentality in the eighteenth century. John Quincy Adams and James Monroe, employing the same reasoning, gave the doctrine classic expression in 1823; and the Monroe Doctrine became the chosen ideological weapon of the United States in the nineteenth century for warning intruders away from the continent. Manifest destiny, the intriguing phrase utilized by historians to label the expansion of the United States in the nineteenth century, is merely the other side of the coin. It was characteristic of the nineteenth as well as of the eighteenth century, moreover, to assert the right before the actual work of colonization had begun. Burwell in 1751, like Monroe in 1823 and others that were to follow, was speaking of prospects, not of actual accomplishment. Looked at from the standpoint of the sum total of its history, the abstract formulae and principles being disregarded or at least discounted, the United States thus becomes by its very essence an expanding imperial power. It is a creature of the classical Roman-British tradition. It was conceived as an empire; and its evolution from a group of small, disunited English colonies strung out on a long coastline to a world power with commitments on every sea and in every continent, has been a characteristically imperial type of growth.

My reason, then, for invoking the heretical phrase, American Empire, is so that the United States can be studied as a member of the competitive system of national states, with a behaviour pattern characteristic of an ambitious and dynamic national state. This approach gives precedence to foreign affairs over domestic affairs, reversing the customary practice of treating national history from the standpoint of the nation preoccupied with its own internal affairs and only incidentally looking beyond its borders. In other words,

---

[1] Quoted in Lawrence Henry Gipson, *The British Empire before the American Revolution*, 9 vols. pub., Caldwell, Idaho, and N.Y., 1936–56, IV, p. 226.

it is a history of the American national state or, as I prefer, of the American Empire, rather than a history of the American people.

The attitude, predetermined in Elizabethan England, that the ' New World ' belonged exclusively to the English as the people capable of colonizing and exploiting it was germinal in the formation of American ideas of empire. Even in their infancy both Virginia and Massachusetts revealed a conquering spirit, an eagerness to participate or even to assume the initiative, whenever possible, in warfare against their French and Spanish neighbours. The tiny French colonies of Port Royal in Acadia on the Bay of Fundy and of Quebec on the St. Lawrence, though far away, were none the less unwelcome. A raid on Port Royal in 1613 by Samuel Argall, a ship captain in the employ of the Virginia Company, was initiated at Jamestown; and in 1629 the Kirke brothers from London captured and sacked both Quebec and Port Royal. This aggression was fostered by London businessmen, its object being to break the slender French holds in North America and secure control of the St. Lawrence gateway. These first attacks on the French registered a common outlook between English commercial interests and American settlers which was to be of decisive importance in the long contest with France for dominion over North America. On the other hand, taking the view that good relations with France in Europe overrode colonial ambitions, Charles I made peace with that country and repudiated the conquests in the New World. This decision of the King, representative of the agrarian, Tory viewpoint, was the first in a long series of checks which were to restrain English foreign policy from giving blanket support to American ambitions. Only a few years later Governor John Winthrop of Massachusetts attempted an intrigue in the internal affairs of Acadia, apparently with the object of bringing it under the control of its larger Puritan neighbour; and again in 1654 Massachusetts seized the opportunity of open war between England and France to attack the Acadian settlements. The Boston Yankees were already putting the Acadians at a disadvantage in the offshore cod fisheries.[1]

A running war at sea between French and English vessels, with raids and counter-raids on the New England and Acadian

---

[1] Andrews, op. cit., I, p. 319; Gerald S. Graham, *Empire of the North Atlantic. The Maritime Struggle for North America*, Toronto, 1950, p. 65.

coasts, was the rule during the next half century. The object of Massachusetts was permanent conquest; the most that the French could do was to wage defensive warfare in the form of reprisals. Boston again got its opportunity in 1690, when it launched a full scale invasion of Acadia followed the next year by an unsuccessful attempt on Quebec. By this time the New England mind was coming to regard Quebec as an 'American Carthage' which must be destroyed. But the New England provinces were not by themselves strong enough to accomplish their aim, even with the support of New York which had its own reason for wanting to subjugate Canada; and so in 1707 the Americans made their first official appeal to London for help in overthrowing the French. The result was two expeditions in which the British employed naval forces in conjunction with provincial soldiers: one in 1709 for the conquest of Acadia, a second in 1711 for the subjugation of Canada. The first one succeeded but the second was a failure.[1] In the meantime, as far back as 1686, fur traders from New York had driven a wedge into the French hinterland by penetrating as far inland as Michilimackinac on Lake Michigan; and an interest was shown in building a fort on the site of Detroit, calculated to cut in twain the long arc of empire the French were beginning to construct between Quebec and the mouth of the Mississippi.

Whereas the Anglo-Americans, as we have noted, claimed a pre-emptive right to the continent based upon an ultimate movement of population westward from the seaboard, the French, lured into the interior by the great system of rivers and lakes tributary to the St. Lawrence, envisaged a permanent partition of the continent according to the principles of geography. The Mississippi basin was naturally tributary to the St. Lawrence, and the Allegheny Mountains at the eastern edge of the basin constituted a natural barrier to the Anglo-American advance from the seaboard. Just as Cardinal Richelieu conceived of France in Europe as entitled to expand to her natural frontiers—the Rhine, the Alps and the Pyrenees—so the intendant of New France, Jean Talon, thought of a North American empire that would expand south, north and west from the Great Lakes until it reached its natural limits. After La Salle in 1682 had travelled downstream to the mouth of the Mississippi, the process of erecting the arc on a line of forts was begun. Detroit, founded in

[1] Graham, pp. 86–99.

1701 by Captain Cadillac, was the pivot on which turned the French
security system of the interior. It was the gateway to the Wabash
and the Mississippi, and it pointed also to Lake Huron and the great
Northwest. The very next year D'Iberville founded Mobile at the
southern extremity of the arc. D'Iberville had been fighting the
English on land and on sea all the way from Hudson Bay, and he
shared the extreme views of some of his enemies that the continent
was not big enough for both powers.

New England, as we have seen, had repeatedly demanded that
the French be strangled, and the New York fur trading interests at
least as early as 1683 were aroused to the possibilities of hemming
in Quebec from the rear. A Boston merchant, Richard Wharton,
and an Irish governor of New York, Thomas Dongan, had been
among the first to argue in this vein; and Robert Livingston, the
Secretary for Indian affairs in New York, and his son-in-law of
Boston, Samuel Vetch, raised the spectre of encirclement. The
French, wrote Vetch after learning of the building of Detroit and
Mobile, ' have surrounded and hemmed in betwixt them and the
sea, all the English Governments upon the Continent, so that . . . they
may easily in time be able to make the British find use for their
shipping and be forced to transport themselves elsewhere and leave
their improvements to their more powerfull neighbours '.[1] Vetch
helped to promote the abortive attack of 1711 on Quebec as the
most direct method of dealing with encirclement.

But the mother country was not ready for such extreme views,
and at Utrecht in 1713 she agreed to a system of partitioning the
continent that would guarantee a long peace. New England ambitions
were partially appeased by annexing Newfoundland and Acadia
with its ' ancient limits '; the Hudson's Bay Company was assured
of its hold on Rupert's Land in the far north; but the St. Lawrence
and its hinterland south of the Great Lakes were to remain French.
This meant that the French were free to develop their empire to its
natural limits; although as the Canadian historian, Arthur R. M.
Lower, has remarked with pardonable exaggeration, their ' access to
the vast fan-like interior was now dependent upon the rabbit hole
of the St. Lawrence, with the English dogs barking on either side

---

[1] I am indebted for this quotation to Emmett F. O'Neill, *English Fear of French
Encirclement in North America, 1680–1763.* Unpublished dissertation in University
of Michigan Library, 1941.

of the entrance '.[1] This ' rabbit hole ' the French soon set out to safeguard by building the stone fortress of Louisbourg on Cape Breton Island.

Zones of wilderness, ruled over by neutral Indian nations, were intended by this peace system as a security belt in the interior between the two empires. Here appears for the first time the idea of an Indian buffer or barrier state which was to reappear again and again during the next hundred years as Canada's device for protecting herself against the aggressions of the American seaboard. Article XV of the Anglo-French Treaty of Utrecht provides:

> That the Subjects of France inhabiting Canada, and others shall hereafter give no hindrance or molestation to the five Nations or Cantons of Indians subject to the Dominion of Great Britain, nor to the other natives of America who are friends to the same. In like manner, the Subjects of Great Britain shall behave themselves peaceably toward the Americans [Indians] who are subjects or friends to France, and on both sides they shall enjoy full liberty of going or coming on Account of Trade. As also the Natives of those Countrys shall with the same liberty resort as they please to the British or French Colonies, for promoting Trade on one side and the other, without any molestation or hindrance either on the part of the British Subjects or of the French. But it is to be exactly and distinctly settled by Commissarys [commissioners] who are and who ought to be accounted the Subjects & friends of Britain or of France.[2]

Actually more than twenty-five years of formal peace did follow the Treaty of Utrecht. But the neutral zones provided for in Article XV had a way of becoming zones of friction, with a generous supply of frontier ' incidents ' to fan the animosities of a cold war and keep the air alive with sounds of verbal artillery. The French hoped to get the British Government to agree to a fixed boundary along the watershed of the Alleghenies, and the latter at first showed signs of being willing.[3] But local pressures from the colonies, which bore down on the Board of Trade through the governors, the colonial agents, and probably also through London commercial interests

---

[1] Arthur R. M. Lower, *Colony to Nation. A History of Canada*, Toronto, 1946, p. 52.
   [2] Translated from the French text printed in Max Savelle, *The Diplomatic History of the Canadian Boundary, 1749–1763*, New Haven, Conn., 1940, p. 8n.
   [3] Ibid., p. 147.

effectually blocked any agreement over boundaries. South Carolina fretted over the new colony of Louisiana which the French were setting up on the lower Mississippi; Governor Spotswood of Virginia and Governor Keith of Pennsylvania, among others, wrote urgent messages dwelling on the French programme of building forts and of ' debauching ' the Indian nations; and the one way to meet it, so ran this swelling chorus from the colonies, was to initiate a counter-programme of fort building west of the mountains.[1]

Convinced by these warnings, the Board of Trade in 1721 handed the Privy Council a lengthy report which was to serve in due time as the basis for British policy in North America. Accepting the American reports of French encroachments, the Board thought that the British should begin by fortifying the two extremities of the long frontier, especially Nova Scotia. The French population which had been permitted to remain in this province should be displaced as soon as possible by British subjects, and a start made by garrisoning the region with four regiments of soldiers. Since the French were advancing eastward from the Mississippi and making political alliances with the Indians, the British should fortify the passes through the long ridge of mountains. And, the Board added:

> Although these Mountains may serve at present for a very good frontier, we should not propose them for the boundary of your Majesty's Empire in America. On the contrary, it were to be wished that the British Settlements be extended beyond them, and some small forts erected on the great Lakes, in proper places, by permission of the Indian proprietors. . . .[2]

A good example of how the Americans primed the imperial pump in London is to be had in the record of the activities of James Logan, a merchant of Philadelphia and a Quaker but by no means opposed to the use of force. Logan had come to Philadelphia with William Penn in 1699, had amassed a modest fortune in the fur trade, and as Penn's agent acting in close collaboration with the deputy governor he became one of the most influential men of the province. Over glasses of rum shared with his fur traders, he kept himself informed about the French and their efforts to wean the Iroquois who, under

[1] Leonidas Dodson, *Alexander Spotswood, Governor of Colonial Virginia, 1710–1722*, Philadelphia, 1932, pp. 240–9.

[2] E. B. O'Callaghan, ed., *Documents Relating to the Colonial History of the State of New York*, 15 vols., Albany, N.Y., 1851–87, V, pp. 591– 630.

the Treaty of Utrecht, were British subjects. ' Preserve the Iroqouis ' was the burden of his policy; but with shiploads of Scotch-Irish and Palatine Germans arriving at Philadelphia at the rate of two or three a week during the summer seasons, and with the immigrants pressing westward toward the Susquehanna in search of free land, this was not so easy. Far more than the whites, the redmen had grounds for feeling insecure, for theirs was the tragedy of being pushed on either side by inexorable forces bent on exploiting and eventually eliminating them. An Indian at the Albany Congress in 1754 declared:

> We dont know what you Christians, English and French together, intend, we are so hemm'd in by both, that we have hardly a hunting place left. In a little while if we find a bear in a tree there will immediately appear an owner of the land to challenge the property, and hinder us from killing it, which is our livelyhood. We are so perplexed between both that we hardly know what to say or think.[1]

Logan, Vetch of Massachusetts, Governor Spotswood of Virginia, and two agents from South Carolina all had a hand in the Board of Trade's Report of 1721. For Logan the Board reserved special praise for having supplied it with ' the most perfect account ' that it had had of the interior. Ten years later the intrepid merchant, alarmed by the continued progress of the French, wrote a memorial which he sent to his friend Micajah Perry in London. Perry was a well-to-do merchant with an interest in the American trade, especially in Maryland and Virginia tobacco, and had ready access to the Board of Trade. Moreover, he was a Member of Parliament and a friend of the Prime Minister. Logan's memorial reached Sir Robert Walpole's hands direct through Perry in the spring of 1732, and in it he tried an argument that might bring the matter home to the British. He wrote:

> It is manifest that if France could possess itself of those dominions [of Britain in America] and thereby become masters of all their trade, their sugars, tobacco, rice, timber and naval stores, they [sic] would soon be an overmatch in naval strength to the

---

[1] Ibid., VI, p. 813. Frederick B. Tolles, *James Logan and the Culture of Provincial America*, Boston, 1957; Robert L. D. Davidson, *War Comes to Quaker Pennsylvania, 1682–1756*, N.Y., 1957.

rest of Europe, and then be in a position to prescribe laws to the whole.[1]

The French, he continued, ' now surround all the British Dominions on the Main. They have a valley in the interior a thousand miles wide, accessible only from the St. Lawrence and the Mississippi, while the British have merely a coastal strip 300 miles in width '. To these complaints he added facts to illustrate the comparative strength of the French and British dominions and, with one eye on New England whose people, he said, ' are naturally and peculiarly stiff ', he even broached the possibility of a revolution in the colonies. Logan did not favour the complete elimination of the French from the continent, for, he pointed out, their presence in Canada would keep New England on its good behaviour. When it came to influencing the Quaker majority in the local Assembly, his efforts like those of the governors were of no avail; but he had an enthusiastic supporter in Benjamin Franklin, who knew him intimately and who later took pains to copy in his own hand the entire text of the memorial.[2]

Meanwhile the primeval wilderness west of the Appalachians was being transformed into an armed frontier, each side erecting barrier forts against the other, writing diplomatic notes protesting that its opponent was violating the peace treaty, but at the same time building more forts to meet the competition. The New York fur traders had long been a thorn in the side of Quebec: they could sell rum and hardware to the Indians at prices the French could not meet, and they were reaching out ever farther in the direction of the upper Great Lakes. And so, in 1720, Governor Joncaire built a new fort at Niagara in the hope of barring the way. But Governor Burnet of New York countered with a fort and post at Oswego; and though the Five Nations of the Iroquois had been claimed in the peace treaty as British subjects, the New York authorities handled these tribes gingerly and treated them more like a sovereign state. Each Indian tribe west of the mountains came to have its pro-French and its pro-British faction, according to the pressure that one side or the other might bring to bear upon it.

---

[1] Joseph E. Johnson, 'A Quaker Imperialist's View of the British Colonies in America, 1732 ', *Pennsylvania Magazine of History and Biography*, LX, April, 1936, pp. 97–130, which includes the entire text of the memorial.
[2] Ibid.

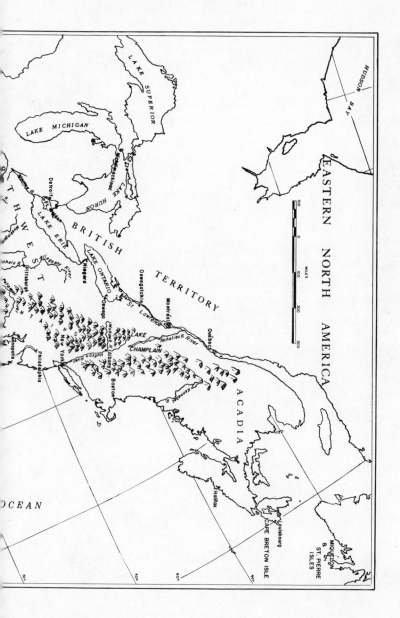

Oswego was the first direct British spearhead aimed at cutting the French interior line to the west, and it was done by New York solely on its own initiative. To the French New York was the nearest and most dangerous neighbour—the most competitive in the fur trade, the most aggressive in currying favour with the Indians, the most able to launch an invasion at the heart of New France. Consequently in 1730 a fort was erected on Lake Champlain to close the road of possible invasion from the Hudson, and from that time on the pace in fort building was stepped up. The Board of Trade, we recall, had mentioned in particular the two extremities of the frontier; and so, bowing to the importunities of the Carolinians who were too weak to assume the lead, the British Government had meanwhile made its first direct move in American defence by erecting Fort King George in 1721 at the mouth of the Altamaha river. The establishment of the colony of Georgia as a military outpost in alliance with the Cherokee Indians followed in 1733. About the same time Pennsylvania and Virginia traders drove a flying wedge into the heart of the Illinois country, setting up a post on the Great Miami river which the French succeeded in dislodging only in 1752. Meanwhile the incorporation by the Crown of the Ohio Company, with a grant of 500,000 acres in the upper Ohio River Valley, sealed an alliance between Virginia landowners and London speculators. Thus the British-American push to the west was a combination of aggressive fur traders, landowners, speculators, and colonial governments, with some active, but for the most part tacit, support from England. To oppose these powerful waves rolling up against them the French relied on military posts garrisoned with professional soldiers and on Indian allies whose fidelity was sorely tried by the tempting goods and prices offered by the traders from the seaboard.[1]

Associated with this general forward movement to the west were the renewed clashes between the New Englanders and the French in the North-east. In New England the moving spirit was William Shirley, an able barrister and politician who had moved in 1731 from London to Boston. Shirley was now governor of Massachusetts,

[1] Francis Parkman, *A Half Century of Conflict*, 2 vols., Boston, Mass., 1894; Clarence W. Alvord, *The Mississippi Valley in British Politics*, 2 vols., Cleveland, O., 1917; Savelle, op. cit.; Gipson, op. cit., IV–V, *Zones of International Friction;* Kenneth P. Bailey, *The Ohio Company of Virginia and the Westward Movement 1748–1792. A Chapter in the History of the Colonial Frontier*, Glendale, Calif., 1939.

having won that coveted post through the friendship of the Duke of Newcastle; and he had the hearty support of the rich merchants of Boston, men of affairs whose interests made them sensitive to every move made by the French. As shippers and suppliers to the Royal Navy, men like Samuel Waldo, Charles Apthorp, Thomas Hancock, Jacob Wendell and William Pepperrell held lucrative contracts from the British Government; and as speculators, they held vast timber-land reserves in Maine. To them Fort Saint Frédéric on Lake Champlain threatened New England from the rear, while Louisbourg on Cape Breton Isle was, in Governor Shirley's words, a dagger pointed at them from the sea. The dagger's blade flashed in 1744 when the French seized the rocky isle of Canso and threatened to overrun all of Nova Scotia. Louisbourg too was a base for raids and forays on Yankee shipping—French privateers were known to get as far south as the Delaware river—but it failed in its major purpose of defending the 'rabbit hole of the St. Lawrence'. This could be done only if France kept a fleet in those waters. With Britain supreme on the Atlantic in 1745, Shirley believed that the time had come to take the offensive. New England business interests rallied around him, and William Pepperrell took command of a motley army of militia which was transported to Cape Breton for an assault on the stone fortress. Shirley meanwhile persuaded the Duke of Newcastle to order Commodore Peter Warren to come up with his fleet from the Leeward Islands and support the attack; and the failure of France to send an opposing fleet left the garrison no choice but to sur-render.[1]

To New England this was a great triumph, and Shirley hoped to follow it up with a blow at Quebec—an army of invasion utilizing the Lake Champlain route, a co-operating British fleet moving up the St. Lawrence. 'The reduction of Canada', he wrote Newcastle from Louisbourg, October 29, 1745, ' seems to be the most effectual means of securing . . . not only Nova Scotia . . . but the whole northern continent as far back as the French settlements on the . . . Mississippi, which are about 2,000 miles distance from Canada. . . . '[2] These

[1] Graham, op. cit., pp. 116–42; J. Bartlet Brebner, *New England's Outpost. Acadia before the Conquest of Canada*, N. Y., 1927, pp. 104–33. I am also indebted to Dr. John A. Schutz of Whittier College, California, for the use of the manuscript of his forthcoming book on *The King's Governor of Massachusetts. His Excellency William Shirley*. Schutz's book is informative on the career of Shirley and on his relations with the Boston merchants.

[2] *Correspondence of William Shirley. Governor of Massachusetts and Military*

plans fell through, however; and at the end of the war the British Government, by returning Louisbourg to the French, demonstrated that it was as yet unprepared to accept the American argument that Canada *delenda est*. Yankee ambitions and Puritan dreams of wiping out the hated ' Papists ' were thwarted again, and the chip on the New England shoulder which had been in plain view from the beginning for the mother country to see was fastened down a little more tightly. That the British Government in 1749 offset Louisbourg by the founding of Halifax, and that New England business got the chief benefits from this new and permanent British naval station seemed to have no effect in softening the grudge which fell on Britain for her failure to satisfy at this time a long-standing Yankee ambition.[1]

All these signs of the Anglo-Americans pushing inward the doors of their empire drove the French to the conclusion by 1749 that a supreme effort was necessary to hold the line at the natural frontier. There followed six years of feverish arming in America, paralleled by a succession of diplomatic attempts at compromise on the part of London and Paris. The British Government talked in terms of returning to the *status quo* of 1713, and each side had its own idea of setting up neutral areas west of the mountains; but neither could convince the other that such arrangements would stick, nor could they agree on what actually was meant by the *status quo* of 1713. The crucial areas were: Acadia, western New York, the Ohio valley, and the coastal plain of the Gulf of Mexico where Spain shared with France in the desire to drive the Americans back to the Atlantic coast. In all four of these areas the French energetically pushed forward their programme of fort building. To their minds, if they lost the interior to the British, whose wealth and power were already gaining on them so rapidly, France's position in Europe would be jeopardized. This conclusion, that if Britain were to be kept from becoming the mistress of Europe she must be checked overseas, was the compelling factor in the French hope of making forts and garrisons stand up against the rising tide of commerce and population. On the British side opinion was divided: a disposition to compromise in such a way

Commander in America, 1731–1760, Charles Henry Lincoln, ed., 2 vols., N.Y., 1912, I, p. 284.

[1] There is sound reason, however, for believing that Halifax was accepted by New England as a satisfactory substitute for Louisbourg, and that no hostile feeling was generated by the return of the latter. See my *Genesis of American Nationalism* (Waltham, Mass., Blaisdell-Ginn, 1970), pp. 41–2, where, as a result of further research, I concluded that historians had erected a legend on the

as to leave the interior to the French, manifested by such men as Sir
Thomas Robinson, the Secretary of State; a more warlike attitude
displayed by Lord Halifax and the Board of Trade, who were committed to the expanding mercantile empire and who therefore lent a
ready ear to the arguments of the Americans.[1]

Most expansive of these arguments were those set forth by
Franklin in a pamphlet written in 1751, which he called *Observations
concerning the Increase of Mankind*. In this and in a second pamphlet
which he put out three years later, Franklin shows himself both a
precursor of T. R. Malthus and a disciple of Machiavelli. Prophesy-
ing that the colonial population would double itself every quarter of
a century, Franklin demanded more living room and admonished the
British that a prince ' that acquires new Territory, if he finds it
vacant, or removes the Natives to give his own people Room'
deserves to be remembered as the father of his nation. Past gains
established the duty that Britain now owed her Colonies:

> What an Accession of Power to the *British* Empire by Sea as
> well as by Land! What Increase of Trade and Navigation! What
> Numbers of Ships and Seamen! We have been here but little
> more than 100 years, and yet the force of our Privateers in the
> late War, united, was greater, both in Men and Guns, than that of
> the whole *British* Navy in Queen *Elizabeth's* Time. How important
> an Affair then to *Britain* is the present Treaty for settling the
> Bounds between her Colonies and the *French*, and how careful
> should she be to secure Room enough, since on the Room depends
> so much the increase of her People.[2]

Then, after the Albany Congress in 1754, Franklin resumed his
attack even more vigorously. Britain should establish two colonies
west of the Alleghenies and south of the Lakes in order to prevent
the ' dreaded juncture of the French settlements in Canada with
those of Louisiana '.
Otherwise:

> They [the French] will both in time of peace and war (as they
> have always done against New England) set the Indians on to

memory of Louisbourg.
　　[1] Savelle, op. cit., pp. 21–78, contains a brilliant summary of the diplomatic
negotiations, 1749–1755.
　　[2] *The Writings of Benjamin Franklin*, Albert Henry Smyth, ed., 10 vols., N.Y.,
1905–7, III, pp. 68–9, 71–2.

harass our frontiers, kill and scalp our people, and drive in the advanced settlers; and so, in preventing our obtaining more subsistence by cultivating of new lands, they discourage our marriages, and keep our people from increasing; thus (if the expression may be allowed) killing thousands of our children before they are born.[1]

Graphically supporting these arguments were two maps of the continent, the first of their kind to be issued in England: that of Lewis Evans, first published in 1749 and re-issued in 1755, and that of John Mitchell, published in the latter year under commission from the Board of Trade. Both Evans and Mitchell knew America first-hand, and their maps challenged the only other map of the continent previously published—that by Delisle of Paris in 1718. Neither Evans nor Mitchell allowed for French claims west of the mountains and south of the lakes.[2]

In the aftermath of war, when the whole of the eastern half of North America from Hudson Strait to the Gulf of Mexico had fallen to the British Empire, and when the seeds of internal discontent and revolution against the mother country sprouted in the Colonies, an ugly legend took hold in America that the colonists had been made the unwilling victims of British ' imperialism '. It is a commonplace to remark that post-war periods are periods of disillusionment, discontent and quarrelling among the victors; and the mutual recriminations that were exchanged across the Atlantic almost as soon as this war was over show that it ran true to form.   Nor is it perhaps too much to say that the American Revolution registered the failure of the Peace of 1763, because it broke up the solidarity of the Empire for which the Great War had been fought. Historical distortions and misrepresentations come easily in an atmosphere thus poisoned. Even Benjamin Franklin distorted the picture of the war only three years after it was over.   Franklin in 1766 actually declared before a committee of the House of Commons that the Americans had had no concern with the territorial disputes over North America, that until a British army was sent they had been ' in perfect peace with both French and Indians ', that the conflict had been ' really a British war ', and that the Americans had unselfishly come to

[1] Ibid., p. 359.
[2] O'Neill, op. cit. On Franklin consult especially Gilbert Chinard, ' Looking Westward ', in Meet Dr. Franklin, Philadelphia, 1943, pp. 135–50, and Gerald Stourzh, op. cit., pp. 33–82.

Britain's assistance.[1] What an astonishingly false statement for a man of Franklin's extraordinary intelligence.

The legend was popularized by revolutionary agitators and propagandists such as Tom Paine, the English Quaker who left his motherland in 1774 with a grudge. With a flourish Paine blamed England for all the past wars into which the Americans had been 'dragged', and promised eternal peace and prosperity as the reward of independence. And somehow or other the succession of wars between 1689 and 1763, in all of which American territorial questions had been major issues, went down in American history books as private wars of the kings of England. Such nomenclature as 'King William's War', 'Queen Anne's War', 'King George's War', and even 'The French and Indian War', does not make for good history. I have never succeeded in tracing the origin of these queer titles, though it seems probable that they belong to the legacy of republicanism and anti-British feeling left by the Revolution. The term 'French and Indian War', as a substitute for which the phrase 'Great War for the Empire' is indeed more meaningful, was actually first introduced in the early national period.[2] All four of these terms survive to this day as living historical stereotypes, although the animus which inspired them has died. Nevertheless, the distortion they represent is as great as would be the case if the two world wars of the twentieth century were stamped respectively 'Woodrow Wilson's War' and 'Franklin Roosevelt's War'.

Yet, to state the antithesis of this legend by charging that the Americans 'dragged' Britain into war would be resorting to the other extreme. British commercial and speculative interests, well represented in the government by the Board of Trade, were thoroughly committed to a war for empire in North America. Certainly they were not prepared to see the French eliminate Britain from that continent, as Newcastle, the Secretary of State, himself declared. And the French insistence that the watershed be made the boundary, with no British trade or settlement to the west of it was regarded in this sense. On the other hand, British counter-proposals

[1] *Writings*, IV, pp. 438–9. See also Lawrence Henry Gipson, 'The American Revolution as an Aftermath of the Great War for the Empire, 1754–1763', *Political Science Quarterly*, LXV, 1950–1, pp. 86–104.

[2] Gipson, *The Great War for the Empire*, VI: *The Years of Defeat, 1754–1757*, N.Y., 1946, pp. 4–19.

rendered in March 1755 were so drastic as to require the French to demolish even their inner line of forts along the Great Lakes and in the Illinois country, thus leaving Canada and Louisiana protected only by a scrap of paper.[1]

Meanwhile by 1754 the French, under the guidance of three very able governors—La Galissonnière, La Jonquière and Duquesne—had so advanced their military positions southward from Lake Erie to the forks of the Ohio that they were ready to make good on their claims to the watershed. Encirclement, which the Board of Trade had apprehended as far back as 1721, now seemed real, especially after the French had repulsed a small force of Virginia militia under the twenty-two-year-old George Washington and driven him east of the mountains. When in October 1754 the British Government learned of Washington's defeat, it decided on sending an expeditionary force to retrieve the Ohio valley. The sending of this expedition in March 1755 meant that Great Britain for the first time was assuming responsibility for the defence of the Colonial frontier. It meant that she viewed the defence of that remote frontier as vital to her own defence as a great power. That is the real significance of General Braddock's tragic campaign in the Virginia wilderness.

In America there was a ' stop-the- French movement ' sponsored by the governors of Massachusetts, New York, Pennsylvania, Virginia, Maryland and South Carolina and supported by the trading, landed and speculative classes in which the names of Benjamin Franklin, the Washingtons, the Lees and many other prominent families headed the list. In the Southern and Middle Colonies, appeals to the people on the ground that the French were close to the passes through the mountains and could, with Indian help, invade and annihilate the coastal settlements met with considerable indifference and opposition, if the lack of response from the elected assemblies is a fair indication. Thus Governor Dinwiddie of Virginia could not carry his legislature with him in getting men and money enough to give Washington a respectable force. And even after the disaster to General Braddock, none of these colonies was prepared to defend itself, much less to take the offensive. Even Virginia and Pennsylvania, the colonies most exposed, were paralysed; while Governor Sharpe of Maryland was reprimanded by his Assembly for garrison-

[1] Savelle, op. cit., pp. 54, 66–77.

ing a small fort which, according to that body, was more useful to its
neighbour than to itself. The elements of indifference, pacifism,
class and religious feeling, and intercolonial jealousy compounded
an anti-imperial, anti-war sentiment which virtually deadened local
action. Success in whipping up a war spirit among the populace
never seems to have penetrated very deeply. There is no ground for
believing that the war was popular, or that anything more than a
small fraction of the colonial public was concerned with western
expansion.[1]

To be sure, the Northern Colonies were more responsive, and
ready to raise men and vote appropriations. Connecticut did particularly well; and Massachusetts, under the steady leadership of its
war governor, Thomas Pownall, displayed an eagerness to take part
in the occupation of old Acadia. At long last, the opportunity to
possess that region and monopolize its fisheries was at hand.[2] But
in the entire seven years of warfare the provincial militia participated
only as auxiliaries to the main armies, and the provincial legislatures
rendered only such aid as they saw fit. Britain took over the war
and fought it through to a triumphant conclusion sending the armies,
planning the campaigns, and furnishing the major portion of the
funds and equipment. Perhaps because she carried so much of the
burden, and because the Americans were never in any real danger of a
French and Indian invasion, the post-war legend that it had been
' Britain's war ' took root the more easily.

We recall that the Board of Trade had urged in 1721 that the
Acadians should be displaced by an English-speaking population.
We recall too the hostility of Massachusetts toward the Acadians,
and the ill-concealed eagerness of men like Governor Shirley to get
rid of them. In the years just before the outbreak of the Great War,
an irridentist movement developed among the Acadians which
furnished a satisfactory pretext for deporting them. Subversive
activities, incited by the fighting priest from Quebec, Père Le Loutre,
who was notorious for organizing Indian raids on the frontier

[1] Gipson, VII, *The Victorious Years, 1758–1760*, pp. 287–328; Max Savelle,
' The Appearance of an American Attitude toward External Affairs, 1750–1775 ',
Amer. Hist. Rev., LII, July 1947, pp. 655–66.

[2] Gipson, *supra;* John A. Schutz, *Thomas Pownall, British Defender of American
Liberty. A Study of Anglo-American Relations in the Eighteenth Century*, Glendale,
Calif., 1951, pp. 125–80.

villages of New England, alarmed the authorities in Halifax who saw, or chose to see, a Trojan horse within their gates. Halifax itself, a British naval base, was an outpost of New England mercantile influence; and since the disappointment of seeing Louisbourg restored to France, Governor Shirley had never lost sight of the possibility of crowding out the Acadians with a colonizing population from New England. In September 1754 the Lieutenant-Governor of Nova Scotia, Charles Lawrence, and three members of his council, all from New England, asked the Board of Trade for authority to deport all Acadians who refused to take an unqualified oath of allegiance. At first only a limited deportation seems to have been planned; but in the months of crisis that followed, the decision was made to execute a mass eviction of the French-speaking population. Between 1755 and 1758 some 6000 to 10,000 Acadians were forcibly removed from their native land, while others fled into the wilderness. This created the necessary vacuum in good farm lands for which the New England leaders had been waiting; and in 1759 Governor Lawrence, confident that his province would prove attractive to the restless farming population of Massachusetts, Rhode Island and Connecticut, proclaimed the country open to speculators and settlers upon terms that, for liberality, could hardly be excelled anywhere. Any group of promoters might obtain possession of one or more townships of 100,000 acres each; and any individual settler might acquire as much as a thousand acres for himself, with fifty additional acres for each member of his family, free of quit rent or other obligation for ten years. An inundation of farming families, chiefly from the Connecticut valley, ensued during the next few years so that Nova Scotia—'New Scotland'—became in fact an extension of New England.[1]

Among the most energetic of the promoters was an Alexander McNutt, a native of Ulster who had gone out to Virginia in 1753 and then on to Boston, where he identified himself with the firm of Apthorp & Hancock, engaged in the shipping and supply business under contract with the authorities at Halifax. McNutt in 1759 obtained an option on lands aggregating 817,500 acres; and in 1765

[1] Gipson, V, op. cit., pp. 167–206; VI, 243–55; John Bartlet Brebner, *The Neutral Yankees of Nova Scotia, A Marginal Colony during the Revolutionary Years*, N.Y., 1937, pp. 24–306.

he was joined by Benjamin Franklin and certain Philadelphia capitalists, who obtained a grant of two more townships. Franklin subsequently secured an allotment of 20,000 acres for himself in the hope of inducing emigrants to go from Pennsylvania. These men overshot the mark, however. McNutt went home to Ulster in search of prospective emigrants, but found his plans blocked by the Board of Trade, while Franklin abandoned his own project in favour of his older speculation in Ohio lands.[1]

The Peace of Paris of 1763 fulfilled the fondest dreams of the American empire builders. The war had been fought, as Lord Shelburne put it, for the security of the British colonies in America, a sentiment with which Benjamin Franklin heartily concurred. But Franklin by no means stopped short with mere security, for he was now dreaming of a world empire. In 1760 he wrote to his friend Lord Kames:

> No one can more sincerely rejoice than I do, on the reduction of Canada; and this not merely as I am a colonist, but as I am a Briton. I have long been of opinion, that the foundations of the future grandeur and stability of the British empire lie in America; and though, like other foundations, they are low and little seen, they are, nevertheless, broad and strong enough to support the greatest political structure human wisdom ever erected. . . . All the country from the St. Lawrence to the Mississippi will in another century be filled with British people. Britain itself will become vastly more populous, by the immense increase of its commerce; the Atlantic sea will be covered with your trading ships; and your naval power, thence continually increasing, will extend your influence round the whole globe, and awe the world! . . .[2]

Post-war difficulties soon set in, however, rendered unavoidable by the profound changes wrought by the war and giving rise to the myth which we have already discussed. Franklin, as we have seen, was among the first to subscribe to the myth, the occasion being his opposition to the Stamp Act. But he and other empire-minded Americans did not really change their objectives. Rather, they were led to think more directly of ' a new Empire, stiled the United States

[1] Gipson, IX, pp. 138–45; Franklin, *Writings*, V, pp. 508–9.
[2] Franklin, *Writings*, IV, p. 4.

of America '. American nationalism, separatist and isolationist by its inheritance, and strengthened by the new position of security achieved through the Great War for the Empire, henceforth began generating forces of defiance and resistance eventuating in a war for independence. Britain, on her part, found herself trying to function under a new, untried, and indeed unworkable concept of Empire solidarity and centralized authority. A Canadian historian, Harold A. Innis, has gone straight to the heart of the problems facing the post-war government of George III. As Professor Innis writes:

> The complexity of an empire including the West Indies and Newfoundland with strong influential groups of lobbyists in England, the colonies including Nova Scotia in possession of a powerful tradition of assemblies, a conquered territory in Quebec, and a charter company in Hudson Bay, imposed too severe a strain on the constitutional resources of Great Britain taxed by the addition of Scotland in 1707 and the corruption of parliament under Walpole and George III.[1]

Nevertheless, in conclusion, it is beyond argument that the entire future of the embryonic American empire rested upon the triumph of 1763.

[1] Quoted without reference in John Bartlet Brebner, *North Atlantic Triangle. The Interplay of Canada, the United States and Great Britain*, New Haven, Conn., 1945, p. 40.

CHAPTER II

INDEPENDENCE AND THE ALLIANCE WITH FRANCE
(1775-1778)

' This Grand Empire now in Embrio '

I TURN now to the War for Independence, more familiarly known as the American Revolution. Here again it is unnecessary for me to quibble over historical terminology. That the American Revolution *was* a revolution—i.e., a fundamental political overturn—is an undeniable historical fact, and historians will—and should—continue so to treat it. But the Revolution was also a very important episode in international history, and with this fact uppermost in mind I shall deal with it as the War for American Independence. What began as a local insurrection within the British Empire against the authority of the central government developed swiftly into one of the most ambitious programmes aiming at the formation of a new national, sovereign state to be found in history. Certainly it is historically defensible to see in the United States of America the first of the truly national states; and with the consummation of the American Revolution the Age of Nationalism is definitely under way.

Now this eight-year war, so characteristic of the eighteenth century in its long duration, was not at any point a mere British-American war. It was, like its several predecessors of that century, a great international war. In the factual sense it was an international war almost from the outset, though the stickler for the historical conventions will probably insist that it did not become so until the formal intervention of France in May 1778. But the French were parties at interest to the American rebellion even before the fighting started, and French co-belligerency—for the French role, by the early months of 1776, was just this—supported with varying degrees of caution by Spain, the Netherlands and Prussia, meant that the War for American Independence was a war for the encirclement of Great Britain. If the Seven Years War had been the Great War for the Empire, this struggle was a war for the disruption of the Empire, the French objective being to force England to return at least part way to her island status of the seventeenth century. Actually as we shall see, the American war aims became for a while even more drastic than those of the French, for American ambitions visualized a new empire rising on the ashes of the old. Circumstances and sober second thought tempered these ambitions before the conflict was over.

In the United States the war generated three movements in addition to independence, all closely inter-connected and aimed at the creation of a new empire. The first was an alliance with France, regarded as indispensable to the winning of the war; the second was a movement to conquer or absorb all of the British Empire's holdings in North America, meaning Canada, Nova Scotia, Cape Breton Isle, Newfoundland and the Floridas; the third was maritime, pointing at the expansion of the merchant marine, the capture of trade outlets in western Europe, and the creation of a navy able to dominate the waters of the western Atlantic.

The movement for an alliance with France grew out of the secret intrigues between French and American agents for the shipment of guns and ammunition from French ports in aid of the American rebels. These intrigues apparently started with the Duc de Choiseul, outraged by the abasement of France in 1763 and the elevation of England; but Choiseul's agents found the Americans, in spite of their century-old enmity toward France, disposed to be receptive. *Angleterre: c'est notre modèle et notre rivale, notre lumière et notre ennemie.*' This sentiment expressed a widely held French view of the time.[1] But Choiseul meant to convert the sentiment into a programme. Sea power, he believed, had won the previous war for Britain; and only sea power could regain for France her independence and her prestige in Europe. In 1764 he sent an experienced naval officer, a M. de Pontleroy, to explore the North American coast, to make a study of economic conditions in the English Colonies, and to draw up plans for capturing the fisheries and the principal ports. The Americans, Pontleroy reported, were 'too rich to be obedient, eager to be the sole masters of their fur trade, and restive to shake off the fetters and restraints on their commerce '.[2]

About that time—just when and how it is impossible to say— certain American and French merchants, notably Willing, Morris & Company of Philadelphia and MM. Penet and Pliarne of Nantes,

[1] Frances Acomb, *Anglophobia in France, 1763–1789. An Essay in the History of Constitutionalism and Nationalism.* Durham, North Carolina, 1950.

[2] As paraphrased by Claude H. Van Tyne, ' French Aid before the Alliance of 1778 ', *Amer. Hist. Rev.*, XXXI, 1925–26, p. 25.

started a profitable business relationship based on the illicit export of tobacco; and it was this relationship, firmly established by 1775, that made possible the extensive purchase of arms and munitions from France. Willing, Morris & Company kept some of this business in their own hands, but before the summer ended they were acting as agents both for the revolutionary government of Pennsylvania and for the Continental Congress. Robert Morris held key positions in both of these bodies; and his firm, having its own agents in France, in the French West Indies, in Virginia, in the Carolinas, and in New England, was indispensable in making the contracts for the exchange of American tobacco, rice, indigo, timber and other produce for French war *matériel*.[1]

Tangible evidence of the existence of a gun-running trade began to accumulate during the summer months of 1775, and it was soon common knowledge in all three countries—in England, in America, and in France. ' We know for certain ', declared Lord Rochford, Secretary of State for the Southern Department, ' the particulars of several cargoes loaded at Bayonne, St. Malo and especially at Bordeaux, from whence a ship was to sail about Sept. 1 with 300 casks of gunpowder and 5,000 muskets complete with bayonets for the account of the Americans'; and on the strength of these reports Lord Stormont, the regular British Ambassador, was returned to his post in Paris.[2]

Captured letters, written by Americans to friends in England, give an impression of the magnitude and importance of this trade. It made armed resistance possible for the Americans. Thus a Samuel Swaine of Philadelphia, writing to an old friend in Manchester, England, under date of February 12, 1776, declared that he had talked with many people from the different Colonies. At the beginning the Americans were everywhere without arms or ammunition. But things were different now, he said. Three thousand stand of arms have arrived in one ship, 1,500 in another, and small quantities were coming in every day. Powder and saltpetre were also being imported in considerable amounts. Another letter, written to Robert Crafton, a merchant of London, by his son in Philadelphia, confirms these

[1] Robert Morris Papers. Correspondence 1776–1777. Accession 1805. National Archives, Washington, D.C. See also Clarence L. Ver Steeg, *Robert Morris. Revolutionary Financier*. Philadelphia, 1954.

[2] Rochford to St. Paul, No. 12, July 27, 1775, and No. 19, Sept. 29, 1775. Public Record Office (P.R.O.). State Papers 78/296.

statements. Parcels of saltpetre, weighing from three to ten tons each, are continually entering the different ports, writes young Crafton. Britain's neighbours, conscious now that she has grown so weak that she cannot control her own subjects, will cheerfully furnish every kind of supply to them underhand. The American coast is so extensive, he adds, that it cannot be guarded; and the price we have published is so high that the matériel will force its way here from all parts of Europe.[1]

Meanwhile, apparently without any connection with, or even knowledge of, the transactions of Willing, Morris & Company, Arthur Lee, the Virginian, had started an intrigue of his own with Caron de Beaumarchais, the French playwright, in London. Lee was a resident of London, having been admitted to the English bar, and he represented the Province of Massachusetts. Beaumarchais was there on a special errand for the Comte de Vergennes, the French Foreign Minister, and shared with Lee the friendship and hospitality of John Wilkes, the notorious English radical. Both Lee and Beaumarchais appear to have acted in the early stages without official authority; but the French Ambassador, the Duc de Guines, was an enthusiastic interventionist, and between him and Beaumarchais France was persuaded to take the first step. A special agent named Achard de Bonvouloir, a former officer in the French navy and now disguised as a merchant from Antwerp, was authorized to go to Philadelphia and take soundings in the Continental Congress.[2]

Meanwhile, in America opinion differed over the wisdom of seeking official French aid. Thomas Jefferson at this time opposed it, since he wanted reunion with the parent country and considered that the price of foreign assistance would be a lasting break. ' I would rather be in dependence on Great Britain, properly limited, than on any nation upon earth . . . ' he declared. ' But I am one of those too who rather than submit to the right of legislating for us assumed by the British parliament . . . would lend my hand to sink the whole island in the ocean '.[3] But Jefferson's fellow Virginian, Patrick

[1] P.R.O., C.O. 5/40. Original Intercepted Letters, Copies of, 1775–1776.
[2] Josephine Fennell Pacheco, *French Secret Agents in America, 1763–1778*. Unpublished dissertation in the University of Chicago Library, 1950; John J. Meng, *Despatches and Instructions of Conrad Alexandre Gérard, 1778–1780*, Baltimore, Md., 1939, p. 45. On Beaumarchais, see Elizabeth S. Kite, *Beaumarchais and the War of American Independence*, 2 vols., Boston, 1918.
[3] To John Randolph, Aug. 25, 1775. *The Papers of Thomas Jefferson*, Julian P. Boyd, ed., 15 vols., Princeton, N.J., 1950–8, I, pp. 241–2.

Henry, during the same month of August, favoured foreign aid. Benjamin Franklin did not at this time take a position, though he hinted that he was not opposed to foreign aid.[1]

The clearest voice in this matter was that of John Adams, who in October 1775 advocated opening diplomatic relations with France.[2] But Adams would hang the connection entirely on trade and let the French make the first move. The profits of a direct trade were so great, he insisted, that French merchants could not resist the temptation. They would send military stores in exchange for tobacco, rice, indigo, furs, etc. It was natural for a Bostonian, familiar with the wealthy American shipping and export businesses, to put his faith in the economic power of the country and to base political independence upon it, as Adams did. To be hasty in sending over ambassadors to Europe would be a mistake, he asserted:

> [Our Ambassador] might possibly, if well skill'd in intrigue, his Pockets well filled with Money and his Person Robust and elegant enough, get introduced to some of the Misses and Courtezans in Keeping of the statesmen in France, but would not that be all? . . . What then can We offer? An Alliance, a Treaty of Commerce? What Security could they have that we should keep it? Would they not reason thus: These People intend to make Use of us to establish an Independency, but the Moment they have done it Britain will make Peace with them, and leave us in the Lurch, and we have more to dread from an Alliance between Britain and the United Colonies as an independent State, than we have now they are under one corrupted administration. . . .

Curiously enough, Arthur Lee had employed this same argument for an opposite purpose: if France refused aid, the Americans might have to submit and then, reunited with Great Britain, they might fall upon the French and Spanish West Indies.[3] Lee's argument—essentially the argument of the separate peace—was to be used again and again as a weapon for clubbing France into an alliance, as the Americans early in 1776 began to swing over in favour of an alliance.

Bonvouloir's mission to Philadelphia, consummated in December, settled this question of which party should assume the initiative. It stimulated the Americans to think beyond foreign aid to the possi-

[1] Franklin to Joseph Priestley, July 7, 1775. *Letters of Members of the Continental Congress*, Edmund C. Burnett, ed., 8 vols., Washington, D.C., 1921–36, I, p. 156. (Hereafter: Burnett).

[2] Adams to James Warren, Oct. 7, 1775. Ibid., pp. 218–20.

[3] Van Tyne, op. cit.

bility of concluding an alliance with the French, and it also led the Comte de Vergennes, to decide in favour of giving aid. But it was to be assistance only, minus any political commitment on the part of France.[1]

From the start the decision in Philadelphia to seek foreign aid was linked with the movement for independence. Thus Franklin, writing to Charles Dumas, a Swiss man of letters living in The Hague, wanted to know whether, if the Americans decided to declare themselves independent, there was any power in Europe (meaning, no doubt, France) willing to enter into an alliance for the sake of commerce.[2] Even Adams, though sure that France would be forced to intervene without any prompting from the Americans, was not adverse to opening negotiations. Her own independence and position as a great power were at stake in this war, he insisted.[3] The Americans should not do more than offer their trade to her. That trade would be a vast resource to her, and redress the balance of naval power in her favour. More hesitant, however, was Carter Braxton, a member of the Virginia delegation in Congress. Independence without an alliance with a naval power was impossible, he said. The war could not go on without foreign trade, and the Americans had no fleet of their own to protect their commerce. To declare independence of Great Britain without first concluding an alliance with France was to court disaster; but to risk an alliance when the relationship was so unequal was just as bad. So Braxton would continue to temporize, hoping for reconciliation with the mother country.[4]

It remained for Richard Henry Lee, the author of the resolution of June 7, 1776, in favour of independence, to tie the two movements firmly together. To Patrick Henry he wrote that all the danger from Great Britain

may be prevented by a timely alliance with proper and willing

[1] Meng, op. cit., pp. 45–52. Bonvouloir thought the Americans had already resolved upon asking for aid, and he was undoubtedly right. The Committee of Secret Correspondence, set up Nov. 29, 1775, had sent Thomas Story to France, Holland and England on a secret mission. Burnett, II, pp. 110–11. In the Franklin Papers, Miscellaneous 1750–1780, Hist. Soc. of Penn., is the copy of a resolution offered by the committee of safety of the Continental Congress, 1775 (no exact date given), to the effect that any vessel bringing gunpowder, good muskets, field pieces and other military stores should be permitted to load provisions to the amount of the value of such stores.

[2] Dec. 19, 1775. Francis Wharton, *Revolutionary Diplomatic Correspondence of the United States*, 6 vols., Washington, D.C., 1889, II, pp. 64–7. (Hereafter: Wharton). [3] Burnett, I, pp. 350–2 n.

[4] Carter Braxton to his uncle, Landon Carter, April 14, 1776. Ibid., pp. 420–1.

powers in Europe. Indeed we are a singular instance in modern times of a people engaged in war with a powerful Nation, without taking steps to secure the friendship or even neutrality, of foreign states—leaving to our enemies the full opportunity of engaging all. . . . But no State in Europe will either Treat or Trade with us so long as we consider ourselves Subjects of G.B. Honor, dignity, and the customs of states forbid them until we take rank as an independent people. The war cannot long be prosecuted without Trade, nor can Taxes be paid until we are enabled to sell our produce, which cannot be the case without the help of foreign ships, whilst our enemy's navy is so superior to ours. . . . Our clearest interest therefore, our very existence as freemen, requires that we take steps now, whilst we may, for the security of America. . . .[1]

And just five days before proposing his famous resolution Lee wrote:

It is not choice . . . but necessity that calls for Independence, as the only means by which foreign Alliances can be obtained and a proper confederation by which internal peace and union may be secured. Now altho' we might safely venture our strength . . . against that of Great Britain only, yet we are certainly unequal to a Contest with her and her Allies, without any assistance from without, and this more especially, as we are incapable of profiting by our exports for want of Naval force.

Lee, it should be added, did not anticipate a need for receiving a French expeditionary force. ' Supplies of Military Stores and Soldiers clothing, Ships of war to cover our Trade & open our Ports, which would be an *external* assistance altogether, could never endanger our freedom by putting it in the power of our Ally to Master us, as has been the case where weak States have admitted powerful Armies for their defenders '.[2]

It would of course be overshooting the mark to say that independence was decided upon in order to persuade France to enter an alliance. Nevertheless, these documents show that the Americans sorely felt their need for an alliance; that indeed they had discussed the prospects for an alliance even before they had seriously considered independence; and that they reached the conclusion that a declaration

[1] *The Letters of Richard Henry Lee*, James Curtis Ballagh, ed., 2 vols., N.Y. 1911, I, pp. 176–8.
[2] To Landon Carter, June 2, 1776. Ibid., p. 198. Italics mine.

of independence from Great Britain was practically the only way by which the alliance could be obtained.

In the meantime, the Committee of Secret Correspondence, after long hesitation, had sent the Connecticut merchant, Silas Deane, to Paris with instructions to seek material assistance on a large scale and to test French opinion on the subject of an alliance.[1] Deane had been associated with Willing, Morris & Company and was a close friend of Robert Morris, with whom he corresponded frequently. Like many other Americans, he speculated in Ohio lands and was bitterly resentful of ' that most execrable Quebec Act ' by the passage of which the Imperial Government signified that it had thrown its support to the hated French Catholics to the north.[2] A member himself of the Continental Congress, he had also been working hard for a permanent union of the Colonies, the only means, as he saw it, of extracting terms from the home country. The alternative, he asserted, was ruin. Deane was in on the gun-running from France in 1775, and he was determined to nullify the Navigation Laws and open up commerce with foreign states. 'A naval force is a favourite object of mine ', he told a friend in October 1775. ' I have a prospect

[1] Wharton, II, pp. 78-80. This committee of five men, one of the numerous committees through which Congress did its work and performed the functions of an executive as well as a legislative body, had been functioning since Nov. 29, 1775. Deane's instructions were dated March 3, 1776.

Thomas Jefferson had remained silent on the issue of an alliance, but on May 17 he admitted there was no alternative. During the debate in Congress on the independence resolution, James Wilson of Pennsylvania, Robert R. Livingston, the two Rutledges, John Dickinson and others pleaded for delay in declaring independence because, among other things, there was little hope for an alliance. ' France & Spain had reason to be jealous of that rising power which would one day certainly strip them of all their American possessions—it was more likely they should form a connection with the British court, who, if they should find themselves unable otherwise to extricate themselves from their difficulties, would agree to a partition of our territories, restoring Canada to France, & the Floridas to Spain, to accomplish for themselves a recovery of these colonies.'

Adams, Lee, Wythe and others took the opposite position: ' that independence alone would convince European powers of the necessity to treat with us; that without it they would not receive our vessels into their ports; that though France & Spain might be jealous of our rising power, they must think it will be much more formidable with the addition of Great Britain and will therefore see it to their interest to prevent a coalition; that the present campaign may be unsuccessful, & therefore we had better propose an alliance while our affairs wear a hopeful aspect; that it is necessary to lose no time in opening a trade for our people, who will want clothes, and will want money too for the paiment of taxes; and that the only misfortune is that we did not enter into alliance with France six months sooner. . . .' *Jefferson Papers*, I, pp. 309-13.

At this time no report had been received from Silas Deane.

[2] Deane to Patrick Henry, Jan. 2, 1775. *The Deane Papers*, I, 1774-7, p. 37. Collections of the New York Hist. Soc. for the Year 1886.

now of carrying that point, having succeeded in getting our Con-
necticutt & the Rhode Island vessels into Continental pay. . . . I am
of your opinion that N. London harbour is well situated for the
rendezvous of an American Navy, and my freind [sic] is it not worth-
while for N. London to labour to obtain the advantages of such a
collection of navigation, spending their money there? '[1]

Deane was only one of a number of agents who, beginning in
March 1776, were sent to France to increase the volume of trade in
arms, powder, saltpetre, field pieces, blankets and soldiers' clothing.
Arrangements were to be made with French merchants to take
tobacco, indigo, rice and other American products in exchange and
to furnish the necessary credit. Agents were also stationed in the
French and Dutch West Indies (Martinique, Cap François in St.
Domingue, Eustatia and Curaçao) for the purpose of expediting
inbound cargoes of arms from Europe and of aiding in the marketing
of outbound cargoes of produce from the United States. There is
a note of urgency in these dispatches and reports, some of which
still lie buried in the unpublished *Papers of the Continental Congress*,
a desire that the arms be sent to American ports direct unless the
safety factor appeared to require that they be routed round through
the West Indies. The first eight months of 1776 were months of
intensive preparation and activity, but the results in the form of
large-scale shipments from France did not come until later.[2]

While the Americans were thus attempting to expand their
purchasing programme in France and get that country involved
politically, the latter had determined to make aid short of war her
national policy *vis-à-vis* the rebels, and to persuade Spain to do likewise. The decision was by no means an easy one, however, for despite
the zeal of the merchants for the American trade and the widespread
resentment against Great Britain—regarded by French conservatives
as a modern Carthage—suspicion of the Americans was far from
absent. Vergennes himself was assailed with doubts, which he aired
unexpectedly in a long conversation with Lord Stormont. Their

[1] Deane to Thomas Mumford of New London, Conn., Oct. 15, 1775. Silas
Deane Papers, Miscellaneous. Manuscripts Room of the N.Y. Pub. Lib.
[2] Morris Papers. Correspondence 1776–1777. Accession 1805. Item No. 37:
Reports of the Marine Committee and Board of Admiralty, 1776–1780 (Instructions
and Letters of the Secret Committee to American Couriers and Agents Abroad).
National Archives, Washington, D.C. See also the Henry Laurens Correspondence
1762–1780 in the Hist. Soc. of Penn. and the Franklin Collection in the Lib. of the
Amer. Phil. Soc., Philadelphia.

real aim was independence, he told the British Ambassador when the latter had first returned to Paris, and if they won it, they

> would immediately set about forming a great marine, and as they have every possible advantage for ship-building [it] would not be long before they had such fleets, as would be an overmatch for the whole naval power of Europe. . . . With this superiority and every advantage of situation they might, when they pleased, conquer both your islands and ours . . . . They would not stop here, but would in process of time advance to the Southern Continent of America and either subdue the inhabitants or carry them along with them, and in the end not leave a foot of that Hemisphere in the possession of any European power.[1]

But by the time Bonvouloir had returned from Philadelphia Vergennes had reached a decision. The temptation to intervene was now too strong. Vergennes put his plans in writing on March 12 and got them approved by the King a month later. When on May 2, 1776, it was decided at Versailles to appropriate one million livres for the support of the American cause, the French were embarked on a programme of lend-lease to the United States. But they did this without waiting for the Americans to declare their independence. John Adams had been right in his estimate of French policy, and Richard Henry Lee wrong. Before Lee had offered his resolution in Congress, France—and Spain too—had become cobelligerents in the warfare against Britain. But American independence was not the French, or the Spanish, goal. Rather it was the waging of a preventive kind of warfare and, as John Adams had put it, ' the bare dismemberment of the British Empire '. Vergennes assumed that there would be another war in any event between Great Britain and the continental powers; once separated from her colonies, she would be at a disadvantage; but, on the other hand, if she were allowed to suppress the American revolt, she would be stronger and more menacing than ever.[2]

Now before proceeding further, we must retrace our steps in order to call attention to another important factor leading to the French alliance. I refer to the failure of the Americans to annex,

[1] As reported by Lord Stormont to Rochford, Oct. 31, 1775. State Papers (S.P.) 78/297. Acomb, op. cit., pp. 51–68, is a discriminating analysis of French attitudes.
[2] Vergennes' policy is discussed at length in Meng, op. cit., pp. 43–90. In terms of comparative purchasing power the livre was equivalent to about 2½ U.S. (1959) dollars.

either peacefully or by force, the Province of Quebec to the north. To the minds of the seaboard Colonies the passage of the Quebec Act by the Imperial Parliament in June 1774 undid the gains of the previous war. The reaction was especially sharp and bitter in Massachusetts, whose delegates got the First Continental Congress to reiterate her charges against Britain of fostering Roman Catholicism and the French way of life. But all the seaboard Colonies were aroused not merely because of religious prejudice, but because the Quebec Act threw the weight of the Imperial Government behind the commercial empire of the St. Lawrence in its struggle for the control of the trans-Allegheny interior.[1] This ' shocking ' alliance between London and Montreal spelled defeat and danger for the seaboard. The fruits of the Seven Years War were being sacrificed, and the terror of being hemmed in by Indians and French from the north and west was easily revived.

Congress tried two methods in its attempts to head off this disaster. First it tried to flatter the French Canadians into sending a delegation to Philadelphia. This approach having failed, the Canadians being neutralists in the quarrel, Congress decided on a military offensive. The number of friends it would have in Canada, so it was told, would be conditioned by the size of its army and its success in expelling the King's troops. We should note at this point that, although the American army was scarcely organized in June 1775, a major effort was put into this offensive which lasted into the summer of the following year. Two American columns converged upon the St. Lawrence during the fall of 1775; one by way of Lake Champlain, the other from Boston via the Kennebec river. The first column captured Montreal, but the combined efforts of the two failed at Quebec. In an effort to save the situation, Congress in March 1776 resorted again to conciliation methods. It sent three commissioners, of whom Benjamin Franklin was one, to invite the Canadians into the American union, even promising them free and undisturbed exercise of the Catholic religion. But it was all to no avail. By June 18, 1776, the last American soldier had left Canada.

High hopes had attended this invasion, and in spite of the scarcity of ammunition and field artillery repeated efforts were made to

---

[1] Murray G. Lawson, ' Canada and the Articles of Confederation ', *Amer. Hist. Rev.*, LVIII, 1952–53, pp. 39–54; Donald G. Creighton, *The Commercial Empire of the St. Lawrence* (Toronto, 1937).

ensure its success. If Quebec could be captured and held, the St. Lawrence could be blocked against a British expedition which was expected in the spring, and the northern approaches to the United States secured. 'If we have the greatest force we have the Canadians our friends ', wrote General Wooster, one of the invading officers, to Washington. ' On the other hand should our Enemies arrive with a superior force to ours, I fear the consequences may be fatal. . . .'[1] But it was not men who were lacking, it was food and ammunition. Reinforcements and heavy cannon were moved northward from Albany in March 1776, but without powder and without provisions. ' We have now 4,000 troops in Canada and not a mouthful of food ', reported Samuel Chase, one of the commissioners, in May.[2] And General Schuyler, whose headquarters were at Albany, wrote Washington: ' We shall lose Canada, which will be attended with many disagreeable consequences '.[3] Schuyler did not know, when he wrote this, that a British fleet carrying General Burgoyne and his army was on its way up the St. Lawrence.

I have found no disagreement among the American leaders on the importance of taking and keeping Canada. John Adams declared that opinion was unanimous on the subject. Robert Morris, the chairman of the committee on finance, wrote General Gates in April that ' Canada must be ours at all events: should it fall into the hands of the enemy they will soon raise a nest of hornets on our backs that will sting us to the quick '.[4] There is no doubt but that the army did all that it could to make the invasion a success. Furthermore, many private letters which have come to light show that the expedition was being followed with great interest and anxiety.[5] And the report of its failure was taken hard. ' The ill successes in Canada had depressed many,' wrote Thomas Jefferson on July 23, ' when we shall hear the last of them I know not '.[6] John Hancock, the wealthy Boston merchant who, as president of the Continental Congress, had been directing the enterprise, was all for making another attempt.

[1] Feb. 25, 1776. The Washington Papers, Division of Manuscripts, Library of Congress.

[2] Samuel Chase to R. H. Lee, May 17, 1776. The Lee Collection, Alderman Library, University of Virginia.

[3] Schuyler to Washington, May 16, 1776, Washington Papers.

[4] Burnett, I, pp. 354–55, 416.

[5] Letterbooks of John Hancock in Papers of the Continental Congress (P. C.C.),National Archives, Washington, D.C. The Washington Papers and the Lee Collection also contain many allusions to Canadian affairs.

[6] *Jefferson Papers*, I, p. 473.

After learning that Burgoyne had reached Quebec, Hancock wrote
urgent letters to General Washington and to the legislatures of New
York, New Jersey, Massachusetts, Connecticut and New Hampshire.
' The present is not a time for delay,' he insisted. ' Everything we
have a right to expect from that quarter depends on expedition.
Without it, we shall inevitably be ruined. . . . Remember, your own
safety & the security of Canada are exactly one & the same thing.
If our enemies are not opposed at a distance, we must engage them
in our Borders '.[1]

The invasion of Canada was a sound piece of strategy. Had it
succeeded—had the Americans been capable of taking and holding
Quebec—they would have possessed the advantage over the British.
In that event, it is unlikely that they would have mustered an interest
in an alliance with France. But the failure in Canada showed unmis-
takably that the Americans were over-extended and ill-equipped.
They were incapable of taking the offensive. On the other hand,
the presence of a large British expeditionary force on the St. Lawrence created alarm and made an alliance with France a necessity.
John Adams, one of those who had been reluctant, makes the
connection clear. ' For my part ', he wrote on the 24th of June,

> I confess my mind is impressed with other objects, the neglect
> of which appears to me to have been the source of all our mis-
> fortunes in Canada and everywhere else. Make the tree good, and
> the fruit will be good. A declaration of independence, confedera-
> tion, and foreign alliances, in season, would have put a stop to that
> embarrassing opposition in Congress, which has occasioned us to
> do the work of the Lord deceitfully in Canada and elsewhere.[2]

In spite, then, of the Canadian setback, the Americans quickly
recovered their self-assurance. The British generals in Canada
failed to follow up their advantage and launch an invasion. British
warships were being withdrawn from the coast and concentrated at
New York, giving ' fine opportunities of getting in powder. We see
the effect already ', wrote Jefferson.[3] Meanwhile Congress, elated
with its boldness in declaring for independence, was busy drawing up
the draft of a treaty to be proposed to France. The military situation
looked bright. Congress had 80,000 men in its pay. Frigates were

being launched and fitted for sea. Privateers and continental armed vessels were distressing British commerce, and armed boats operating in the rivers and bays were annoying British men-of-war. The construction of a navy was now ' a capital object ' with Congress, and its marine committee was ordered to prepare a plan.[1]

Voicing this new spirit of aggression, William Henry Drayton, the Chief Justice of South Carolina, invoked history in his enthusiasm for naval power. Naval actions, he said, have decided the superiority of nations—of Greece over Xerxes, of Rome over Carthage, of England over France.

> If America is to be secure at home and respected abroad, it must be by a naval force. Nature and experience instruct us that a maritime strength is the best defence to an insular situation. Is not the situation of the United States insular with respect to the power of the old world: the quarter from which alone we are to apprehend danger? Have not the maritime states the greatest influence upon the affairs of the universe?[2]

Cheering on this spirit was the news from France. M. Penet wrote from Nantes to Washington personally to tell him that he could be assured of all the arms and supplies he needed.[3] French ports were now open to prizes taken by American privateers, and the governors of the French West Indies had been given orders to furnish the Americans with whatever they wanted, to protect their vessels and even to convoy them through the line of British cruisers.[4] Better yet, a steady stream of supplies was flowing in. During the first week of November 1776 there were thirty French ships moored at Annapolis, Maryland, alone, and ships were arriving regularly at the ports of South Carolina, Maryland and Pennsylvania.[5] A British naval officer, returning to England, reported that between December 1, 1776, and January 27th, 1777, twenty-three sail of French merchantmen entered the single port of Charleston, South Carolina. Philadelphia, he said, had had uninterrupted trade with the French all through the year 1776; and under the pretence of being

---

[1] The Secret Committee to Silas Deane, Aug. 7, 1776. P.C.C., Item No. 37.

[2] William Henry Drayton. Manuscript Copy of his Treatise, ' The Confederation of the United States ', in possession of the Penn. Hist. Soc.

[3] Penet & Co. to Washington, Aug. 3, 1776. Washington Papers.

[4] The Secret Committee to Bingham, Sept. 21, 1776, P.C.C., Item No. 37. Jefferson to Edmund Pendleton, Aug. 26, 1776. *Jefferson Papers*, I, p. 505.

[5] Stephen Stewart to Willing, Morris & Co., Nov. 3, 1776; Willing, Morris & Co. to Bingham, Nov. 8 and Dec. 6, 1776. Robert Morris Papers.

en route to their island of Miquelon near the fisheries, French vessels put into American ports laden with ammunition and soldiers' clothing.[1]

But perhaps the best news of all was that France herself was preparing for war. Fleets were fitting out at Brest and Toulon, ammunition and other stores were being bought up by the French court, and Spain too was arming. Silas Deane, arrived in France by June 1776 and posing as a merchant from Bermuda, set about energetically making friends with French businessmen and bankers and devising schemes for securing alliances with France, Spain and Prussia. A shrewd and knowledgeable observer of the European scene, Deane was certain the continental powers would soon go to war, and his mission, he believed, was to get them all involved on the American side as soon as possible. France, of course, was the most likely prospect, and the surest avenue of approach to her was to play upon the acquisitive spirit of her merchants. Nothing could be so effectual as to get into their debt for supplies and employ persons of family and influence in the American service. Eventually the debt could be redeemed through the sale of Western lands, which would be in great demand after the war. King Frederick of Prussia, Deane reported, was ambitious to become a maritime power, and once he was finished with the partition of Poland, he would turn his attention to overseas commerce. What more natural than to show him the advantages of trade with America? As for Spain, Deane wrote Morris, ' if you will give commissions to seize Portuguese ships, you may depend ' on her friendship and alliance. ' I urge you to do this. Much may be got, nothing can be lost, by it. Increase, at all events, your navy '.[2]

Through his connections in Paris, Deane saw Vergennes and immediately began plying that cautious statesman with arguments

[1] *A Letter to the English Nation, on the Present War with America.* By an OFFICER returned from that Service, London, 1777, pp. 12–13. (Rare book in possession of the Henry E. Huntington Library, San Marino, Calif.). This book is a daring condemnation of the British Government for its misconduct of the war, and represents the view of the Opposition Whigs. ' Our navy ', comments this officer, ' would not have observed much delicacy with them, if the commanders of our ships had not been *privately* instructed to be extremely cautious in their conduct towards the French; and it is owing to the unpardonable timidity of Administration, that France has dared to assist America, and that a little despicable island [Miquelon], rendered inaccessible half the year by ice, should pretend to more commerce, in the depth of winter, than the first trading port in Europe '.

[2] Silas Deane to Robert Morris, June 23, 1776; to the Secret Committee, Aug. 18; to Morris, Sept. 17. *Deane Papers*, I, pp. 141–42, 195–218, 247.

for an alliance and especially for naval help in the form of a convoy. Supplies shipped in French bottoms and convoyed by French warships would enable the Americans to take the offensive and win the war. Speed was important, Vergennes was told, for there was a danger that the British Government would, after the winter meeting of Parliament, ' come under the management of a Great Genius, a Man of Liberal and extensive Views '. With Chatham again at the helm, peace with the Colonies would follow and France would again be confronted by her indomitable foe.

Deane possessed a masterly comprehension of the French mentality, and knew how to play upon French fears and jealousies, but he overdid it. This contest, he advised Vergennes, is one of the most important ever to engage the attention of Europe. The issue? Should Great Britain be allowed to make herself absolute in North America over territory as large as all Europe, abounding in every necessary resource for the support of the human race? Should she have all these advantages, which would make her so formidable to all the maritime powers of Europe? This was the critical, the ' extremely Critical Period ' for France. If she acted now, she could advance her own ' Interest and happiness ' and at once put it beyond the power of Great Britain ' to disturb her repose on the Continent or insult her on the Ocean '. But if she held back, the Colonies would negotiate with Britain, and together they would turn their whole force upon France.[1]

So carried away was the American emissary with these thoughts that in November he submitted to the French Foreign Office a draft treaty providing for a perpetual union of France, Spain and America. Under this agreement Britain would be deprived of all her possessions in North America and the West Indies, which would be distributed among the three allies. 'Nor shall France, Spain or the United States ever hereafter admit British Shipps into any of their Ports in America, North or South, or the Islands adjacent, nor shall this Article ever be altered or dispensed with but only by and with the consent of each of the Three Contracting Parties '.[2] This amazing proposition to encircle Great Britain with a ring of permanent foes and strip her of her own independence encountered only silence at Versailles. It

[1] Memoirs to French Foreign Office, Aug. 22 and Sept. 24, 1776. Ibid., pp. 223-27, 252-85.
[2] Deane to Gérard, Nov. 23, 1776. Ibid., pp. 361-4.

could not have failed to reawaken in the mind of Vergennes his former fears of American ambitions. ' France of all the Kingdoms in Europe ', pleaded Deane, ' is their most natural ally. Nor is it possible, while each pursues its own most obvious Interest, to find an instance in which they can interfere with or rival each other; on the contrary, they are as naturally situated to increase and promote each other's true Interest and happiness as any Two Countries on the Globe . . . . ' But no echoing sentiment came back from the Court of Louis XVI.

Deane's ideas and aspirations were shared in the main, however, by the rebel leaders in Philadelphia. They too were confident that France would soon be in the war, and that they would be the beneficiaries. Wrote Robert Morris to John Jay:

> It appears clear to me that we may very soon involve all Europe in a War by managing properly the apparent forwardness of the Court of France; it's a horrid consideration that our own Safety should call on us to involve other nations in the Calamities of War. Can this be morally right or have Morality and Policy nothing to do with each other? Perhaps it may not be good Policy to investigate the Question at this time.[1]

And Richard Henry Lee to Washington:

> The train is now so laid that we have the fairest prospect of being soon supplied, & copiously too, with military stores of all kinds, and with soldiers' clothing. . . . The French court has given us so many unequivocal proofs of their friendship that I can entertain no doubt of their full exertions in our favour, and as little, that a war between them and G.B. is not far distant.[2]

Even General Howe's victory in occupying New York could not dampen this optimism. If the French would send twenty ships of the line, argued the Secret Committee, they could easily master the British in American waters, and then the Americans could manage the British army. ' If France will but join us in time there is no danger but America will soon be established an Independent Empire, and France drawing from her the principal part of those sources of wealth & power that formerly flowed into Great Britain will immediately become the greatest power in Europe. . . .'[3] By September 24

[1] Sept. 23, 1776. Burnett, II, p. 197 n.
[2] Oct. 26, 1776. Washington Papers.
[3] Secret Committee to Deane, Oct. 1, 1776. *Deane Papers*, I, pp. 294–300.

Congress had come to an agreement on the proposed treaty, and had appointed Franklin and Jefferson special commissioners along with Silas Deane to negotiate with Versailles. The commissioners were to solicit the French Court for immediate delivery of twenty or thirty thousand muskets and bayonets, and a large supply of ammunition and brass field pieces to be sent under convoy from France. The commissioners were also empowered to try to draw Spain into the war.[1] There was even a veiled threat in the instructions. European ministers were to be reminded of their need for American products, and to be warned that American friendship had political value. If France, Spain or Portugal should close its ports to American vessels at the behest of Great Britain, they should bear in mind that ' injuries now done us will not be easily effaced ', especially since those countries all have colonies in America.[2]

A month later Congress was emboldened to ask for a loan of eight ships of the line to break the British blockade, and hinted that it would like to see in addition the French and Spaniards send a large fleet at their own expense. And in December a further instruction was dispatched to the commissioners to ask for a loan of two million pounds sterling to help stabilize the American dollar, and pressure was to be exerted to induce the French to delay their entry no longer.[3] Now was ' the favourable moment for establishing the Glory Strength and commercial Greatness ' of France ' by the Ruin of her ancient Rival. A decided part now taken by the Court of Versailles and a vigorous Engagement in the War in Union with North America would with Ease sacrifice the fleet and Army of Great Britain at this time chiefly collected about New York '. The British West Indian islands were now defenceless, and could easily be reduced. On the other hand, if France ignored the opportunity, she might later lose her own islands to the British in alliance with the Americans.[4]

Clearly Congress and its committee of secret correspondence (soon to become the committee for foreign affairs) were in a headlong rush to get France and Spain into the war. There was no lack of energy displayed; whether there were reflection and perspective was another matter. The United States would collaborate with France to exclude Britain and all other nations from the cod fishery. France

[1] *Journals of the Continental Congress*, V, pp. 813-7.
[2] Wharton, II, pp. 157-61.
[3] Ibid., pp. 176-7; *Journals*, VI, pp. 1035-7; P.C.C. Item 79, vol. 1.
[4] Burnett, II, 182; *Journals*, VI, pp. 1054-8.

might annex half of the island of Newfoundland, the United States to take the other half along with Nova Scotia and the island of Cape Breton. In case this offer was not tempting enough, His Christian Majesty was to be promised support in conquering the British West Indies. The United States would furnish six frigates mounting not less than twenty-four guns each and provisions to the value of $2,000,000, and 'would render any other assistance which may be in their power as become good allies'. As for Spain, the commissioners might promise her help in subjugating the Floridas and, if agreeable, an American declaration of war against Portugal.[1] Nor did the Americans intend to confine their attentions to France and Spain. Holland, that 'treasury of Europe', that 'republic of mammon', as Silas Deane described her, was to be wooed for the credit that she could furnish. Vienna, Prussia and Tuscany were to be approached. Even the sceptical John Adams was growing jubilant:

Our accounts from Europe are that great Preparations are making for War and that every Thing tends to that Object, but when or where, or how Hostilities will commence is yet unknown. France and Spain will act in concert and with perfect Amity, neither will take any Step without the other.[2]

But a few weeks later Adams had a sober second thought. 'I must confess', he wrote to his friend James Warren,

that I am at a loss to determine whether it is good Policy in Us to wish for a War between France and Britain, unless We could be sure that no other Powers would engage in it: But if France engages Spain will, and then all Europe will arrange themselves on one side and the other and what Consequences to Us might be involved in it I don't know. . . .

It is a cowardly Spirit in our Countrymen, which makes them pant with so much longing Expectation, after a French War. I have very often been ashamed to hear so many Whigs groaning and Sighing with Despondency, and whining out their Fears that We must be subdued unless France should step in. . . .[3]

Meanwhile the three American commissioners (Arthur Lee in place of Thomas Jefferson as the second commissioner), had interviewed Vergennes and made formal application for the eight

[1] *Journals*, VI, pp. 1055. Deane had repeatedly urged an American attack on Portugal.
[2] Adams to James Warren, March 31, 1777. Burnett, II, pp. 313.
[3] May 3, 1777. Ibid., p. 354.

capital ships, the twenty or thirty thousand muskets, and the other equipment which Congress had instructed them to get. The response of the French was to refuse an alliance for the time being, to reject the request for the eight ships, but otherwise to increase their assistance. The commissioners made an excellent bargain with the Farmers-General for the exchange of tobacco for munitions; and they secured an interest-free loan of two million livres, in support of the Continental currency.[1] Within a month three vessels, heavily laden with military stores, had left Nantes and Le Havre for America.[2] The safe arrival of two of them (the third was captured) is believed to have been of decisive importance in equipping the army which faced General Burgoyne at Saratoga the following October. But in other respects the Americans continued to plead for French naval assistance: the British had again blockaded Delaware and Chesapeake Bays, and they were having trouble in exporting their produce.[3]

Through the spring months of 1777 the commissioners energetically concentrated on getting more European allies, especially Spain and Prussia: the former because of her fleet which, combined with the French, would ' pinion ' Great Britain for ever; the latter, because of the desire for a northern port as a base for raids on British commerce. As many of the trade routes as possible should be attacked: the Baltic, the Greenland whale fishery, the Hudson's Bay, the Indian Ocean, above all the West Indian trade. Congress should send over frigates, laden with tobacco for Nantes or Bordeaux; then let them be refitted so that they could carry the war into the enemy's waters. For the ' importance of having a considerable naval force is too obvious to need our saying more than that we conceive no apparent difficulty or obstruction to deter us from pushing it forward to the utmost of our power '.[4] But though American and French privateering operations made serious inroads on British commerce and sent insurance rates skyrocketing, both the commissioners in Paris and the committee of foreign affairs in Philadelphia recognized that French or Spanish intervention held the key to victory. In October the commissioners reported they were running a deficit of eight millions of livres in their purchases, while great stores of tobacco,

---

[1] Wharton, II, pp. 248–51. The rate of exchange in May 1777, was six Spanish dollars per $100 in American paper money. Ibid., p. 324.
[2] Ibid., p. 261.
[3] Ibid., pp. 273–5.
[4] Ibid., pp. 325–7.

naval stores, rice, indigo and other products were piling up in America unable to break through the blockade. 'A war in Europe', pleaded the committee on foreign affairs, 'would greatly and immediately change the scene'. It would draw British attention away from North American shores.[1]

All this time Vergennes had been carefully building up his European, especially his Spanish, fences. The French Foreign Minister had a healthy fear lest Great Britain come to a settlement with the Americans, even recognizing their independence. The arrival of Benjamin Franklin had somewhat reassured him in this respect, at least to the extent that the Americans would not make peace short of independence. Franklin's mission made a deep impression in both France and England, and he forthwith assumed seniority over Deane in the negotiations with the French Court.[2] 'Their hearts are universally for us', he reported in January 1777, 'and the Cry is strong for immediate war with Britain. Indeed everything tends that way, but the Country has its reasons for postponing it a little longer. . . . Their preparations will keep the English fleet at bay, coop up more seamen, and leave us more sea room to prey upon their commerce, and a freer coast to bring in our prizes— and also the supplies we shall be able to send you'.[3] This proved to be an accurate estimate of what the French were prepared to do throughout the ensuing year.

Evidently Vergennes had taken the measure of British policy correctly. The North ministry, well informed though it was of French and Spanish machinations, harboured the illusion that it could avoid war with the continental powers while having its hands full with the distant American rebellion. Lord George Germain put its hopes into words in a memorandum which he drew up on March 18, 1777. It was important to discourage France from interfering in the war, he wrote, and the way to do it was to wage a decisive campaign in America and break the communications between the Americans and the European nations. The latter object could be

---

[1] Ibid., pp. 404–6, 438–41.

[2] Deane in the meantime had run afoul of the jealousy of Arthur Lee and his quarrelsome brother William. Through their elder brother, Richard Henry, the Lees formed a powerful clique in Congress against him and subsequently forced him to return to Philadelphia to answer charges of corruption. Ironically, Deane returned to Europe in 1780 and went over to the English side. He became a resident of London in 1783 and lived on charity.

[3] Letters of the Joint Commissioners. P.C.C., Item No. 85.

accomplished by capturing the American ports and establishing a chain of cruisers off the coast between St. Augustine and Halifax.[1] Germain's ideas may have been sound in theory, but they were impracticable. The British navy was expected to cope with a multitude of problems in this war which were beyond its strength. It was hopelessly spread out, engaging in transport and convoy duty, trying to blockade the American coast (which it actually did from time to time) while coping with a horde of privateers, maintaining an adequate fleet in the Caribbean and protecting the trade route from the West Indies, and all the while keeping a force in European waters. It was an impossible task, as Lord Amherst, the retired commander-in-chief of the British army in the previous war, declared, but given the policy of fighting the Americans, there was no alternative.

Within the British Government there were important differences of opinion regarding strategy and the conduct of the war that were never resolved. Germain and the King insisted upon concentrating British power against the Americans, relying upon the army and treating the navy as of only secondary importance. Lord Barrington, the Secretary at War, advocated confining hostilities to naval operations off the North American coast, thus concentrating on an offshore blockade; but his opinions never got a hearing. Lord Amherst would do neither of these but, on the contrary, would concentrate all of Britain's force against her continental rivals and take no direct action against the rebels. This was the view taken by Chatham and the other brilliant leaders of the Parliamentary opposition, but it was not the one which the King and the party in power were disposed to follow. The ministry hoped to make a generous peace with the Americans, recognizing their grievances but withholding a grant of independence. It acted on the theory that it could keep the war confined to the farther side of the ocean and bring it to a close before the French and Spanish could act. Chatham attacked this theory in a powerful speech delivered in the Lords on May 30, 1777, depicting ' the gathering storm ' already bursting around Britain. If you conquer, he declared, ' you conquer under the cannon of France; under a masked battery then ready to open '.[2]

The Americans, it will be remembered, played on French fears of Chatham's return to power and of a reunited British Empire.

[1] Lord George Germain Papers. The William L. Clements Library, Ann Arbor, Mich.   [2] *Parl. Hist.*, XIX, p. 316.

With them nothing less than the full participation of France in the war was essential. In Paris Benjamin Franklin became an editor of an interventionist journal, *Les Affaires de L'Angleterre et de L'Amérique*, and devoted his journalistic talents to the cause. The *beaumonde* and the bourgeoisie, lured by the easy prospects for wealth and national glory at Britain's expense, were convinced interventionists.[1] Vergennes belonged in this camp too, but until December 1777 he was restrained partly, though not wholly, by Spanish objections. Nevertheless, the ' masked battery ' was not at any time during this year 1777, kept hidden, though the British Government, hoping for victory, was determined not to see it. French policy had been pointed at war for almost two years, not only through aid to the Americans but also through extensive rearmament. By this time France had rebuilt and expanded her navy which, she now had reason to believe, was superior to the British. It is evident that she could not much longer postpone a decision for war, and the news of Burgoyne's surrender at Saratoga brought the issue to a head.

Sometime in December (just when will probably never be known) the French Foreign Office entered into serious negotiations with Franklin for the treaty which the Americans had long desired. The story of these negotiations will probably always remain a secret. Few records of the conversations and no texts of treaty drafts have come to light. Even after the two treaties had been signed, February 6, 1778, the French continued for upwards of a month to deny their existence. The British Ambassador, Lord Stormont, knew of the negotiations, however; and as early as January 2 it was commonly believed in England that a treaty had been concluded.[2] The ministry of Lord North, however, made no effective use of its knowledge. It made no show of strength against the French; it made no adequate peace offer to the Americans; and, finally, it allowed a French squadron under the Comte D'Estaing to escape from the Mediterranean and cross the Atlantic.

Since we are unable to reconstruct the day-by-day negotiation of the Franco-American alliance, we are obliged to admit an unfortunate gap in this story. The Americans had been consistent suppliants for an alliance, yet the fact that the actual period of negotiation extended through at least six weeks suggests that there must have

[1] Acomb, op. cit., p. 87.
[2] Weymouth to Stormont, No. 1, S.P. 78/306, P.R.O.

been some very close bargaining. One document that I have found leads me to believe that Vergennes was most reluctant to recognize the United States as a sovereign state. At one point, it appears, the negotiation almost broke down on this issue.[1] The American commissioners won the argument, however, as the definitive treaty contains an explicit acknowledgment by France of the ' liberty, sovereignty, and Independence absolute, and unlimited' of the United States.[2]

The significance of this concession becomes clear when we recall that Vergennes had not aimed his policy at American independence. On the other hand, the alliance was to endure ' forever '. This is an extraordinary word to insert in a war-time alliance, and so it should engage our attention for a moment. No scholar has been able to show how it got into the text of the treaty, or even to identify the person who first proposed it. Of one thing we may be sure: the several negotiators, American as well as French, were too experienced and too sophisticated not to grasp the significance of the word. Vergennes, we know, hoped to bind the United States ' forever ' to the French system. Certainly he had no reason for objecting to the word. But neither, I think, did the Americans. They too had been thinking in terms of a long-range union with France and Spain based on a programme of plundering the British Empire and dividing up the spoils. This had been the constant theme of Silas Deane, nor is there anything to show that Benjamin Franklin differed. Like the French merchants with whom they had been trading so successfully, the Americans were fascinated by the vision of lucrative markets that this new relationship would afford.

It is sometimes argued that, had Britain at this time offered independence, the Americans would have rejected the French alliance. Thus the New York conservative, John Jay, declared before he had seen the French treaty: ' If Britain would acknowledge our independence, and enter into a liberal alliance with us, I should prefer a connection with her to a league with any power on earth '.[3]

---

[1] In the Lee Collection at the University of Virginia there is this note of the commissioners addressed to Conrad Alexandre Gérard, the French under-secretary for foreign affairs: ' Paris. Jan. 27, 1778: We have concluded to make no farther Propositions for the present treaty, We only wish the word *Sovereignty* may be inserted in the two places proposed, if not thought absolutely improper. . . .'

[2] Text of the treaty in Hunter Miller, *Treaties and Other International Acts of the United States of America*, 8 vols., Washington, D.C., 1931–48, II, pp. 35–41.

[3] Wharton, II, pp. 565–6.

An Anglo-American 'foederal alliance' was, to be sure, what a minority in Parliament also desired. But, assuming that a straightforward offer of independence could have come from Whitehall in order to head off the French treaty, the best that it could have accomplished, I think, would have been to arouse doubts and possibly cause delay. Actually Congress took but two days, May 2—4, 1778, to ratify the treaty. Some of this haste, no doubt, was due to relief and joy that at last the United States had a strong ally. But the French treaty did more than offer mere relief. It also fired ambitions. As I study the letters of some of the members of the Continental Congress, I cannot avoid the conclusion that great things were expected to come out of this alliance. Thus the committee of foreign affairs held that Nova Scotia and Canada would be forced to join the United States.[1] (The treaty gave the Americans a free hand to conquer and annex these Colonies and the Bermudas.) William Ellery of Rhode Island contemplated 'divesting Britain of every foot upon this Continent'.[2] The French alliance, in other words, whetted the American appetite for conquest and power. It inspired John Adams to prepare a new discourse on his favourite doctrine of national interest; and in this discourse, penned for the edification of his cousin Samuel, Adams candidly expounds his philosophy of international statecraft. France, he asserted, completely reversing his pre-war attitude, is 'the natural ally' of the United States.

The reasons are plain. As long as Great Britain shall have Canada, Nova Scotia, and the Floridas, or any of them, so long will Great Britain be the enemy of the United States, let her disguise it as much as she will.

It is not much to the honor of human nature, but the fact is certain that neighboring nations are never friends in reality. In the times of the most perfect peace between them their hearts and their passions are hostile, and this will certainly be the case forever between the thirteen United States and the English colonies. France and England, as neighbors and rivals, never have been and never will be friends. The hatred and jealousy between the nations are eternal and ineradicable. As we therefore, on the one hand, have the surest ground to expect the jealousy and hatred of Great Britain, so on the other we have the strongest reasons to depend upon the friendship and alliance of France, and no reason in the world to expect her enmity or jealousy, as she has given up

[1] Burnett, III, pp. 236–37.   [2] Ibid., p. 269.

every pretension to any spot of ground on the continent. The United States, therefore, will be for ages the natural bulwark of France against the hostile designs of England against her, and France is the natural defense of the United States against the rapacious spirit of Great Britain against them. France is a nation so vastly eminent, having been for so many centuries what they call the dominant power of Europe, being incomparably the most powerful at land, that united in a close alliance with our States, and enjoying the benefit of our trade, there is not the smallest reason to doubt but both will be a sufficient curb upon the naval power of Great Britain.

This connection, therefore, will forever secure a respect for our States in Spain, Portugal, and Holland, too, who will always choose to be upon friendly terms with powers who have numerous cruisers at sea, and indeed in all the rest of Europe. I presume, therefore, that sound policy as well as good faith will induce us never to renounce our alliance with France, even although it should continue us for some time in war. The French are as sensible of the benefits of this alliance to them as we are, and they are determined as much as we to cultivate it.[1]

And so I close this chapter with a bit of humour taken from the *Connecticut Courant* of June 2, 1778. Under a London date line the *Courant* published the following story:

We hear that a *divorce* of a very extraordinary nature, between *John Bull* and his wife *Americana*, is shortly to take place, which will astonish all Europe. The cause of quarrel originated one morning over their *tea*, which would have been instantly made up, but for the roguery of Mr. Bull's servants, who had an *interest* in keeping them at variance. Now it has spread so wide, that a *reconciliation is thought impracticable;* as every meeting, instead of mediating, ends in hostilities. The consequences of this divorce will be, that *John Bull* will have nothing to live upon but the *little farm* he had before marriage; whilst his wife will be in the *sole* possession of the *great estate she brought him;* and if she marries *Nick Frog* (as there is a great probability she will) God knows whether they may not strip John Bull of his paternal inheritance, and turn him out into the street. So true it is what the poet sings:

' Heaven has no rage like love to hatred turn'd
   Nor Hell a greater fury than a woman scorn'd.'

[1] Wharton, II, pp. 667–8.

CHAPTER III

THE FRENCH ALLIANCE: MARRIAGE AND DIVORCE
(1778–1800)

' This Nascent Empire '

THE French Alliance was the instrument through which the American revolutionaries expected to win their war for independence and realize their commercial and territorial objectives. Well-meaning, though ineffective British peace proposals, based not upon independence but upon the *status quo ante*, were brushed aside. The evacuation of Philadelphia by Lieutenant-General Sir Henry Clinton and the subsequent arrival of the French squadron from Toulon were hailed as signs of imminent victory. But the signs were wrong: Admiral Lord Howe retained command of American waters, and the French retired to the West Indies, where their interests were uppermost.[1]

In the meantime, Burgoyne having been defeated and the route to Canada once more open, plans were revived for another attempt on that country. Influenced by the young Marquis de Lafayette, who at the ripe age of eighteen was a major-general in Washington's army, Congress in February 1778 endorsed a scheme to mount a full scale invasion. Lafayette and other French military adventurers who had been streaming across the Atlantic during the last twelvemonth would ' explain ' to the French Canadians how important it was for their own best interests to open their arms to the United States.[2] This plan was suspended as too hazardous and premature, but hopes soared again with the news of the French alliance. Wrote George Mason of Virginia to Richard Henry Lee:

. . . We are apt to wish for peace, I confess I am, altho I am clearly of opinion that war is the present interest of these United States;

[1] Capt. W. M. James, R.N., *The British Navy in Adversity. A Study of the War of American Independence*, London, 1926, Chs. 6–7. A. T. Mahan, *The Major Operations of the Navies in the War of American Independence*, London, 1913, Ch. 4. Mahan calls Howe's defence of New York against the French ' an achievement unsurpassed in the annals of naval defensive warfare '.

[2] *Journals*, IX, pp. 985–7, 999–1000. Murray G. Lawson, ' Canada and the Articles of Confederation ', *Amer. Hist. Rev.*, LVIII, 1952–3, pp. 39–54. Louis Gottschalk, *Lafayette Joins the American Army*, Chicago, 1937, Ch. 17.

the union is yet incomplete, & will be so, until the inhabitants of all the territory from Cape Breton to the Mississippi are included in it; while G. Britain possesses Canada & west Florida, she will be continually setting the Indians upon us, & while she holds the harbours of Augustine & Hallifax, especially the latter, we shall not be able to protect our trade or coasts from her depredations; at least for many years to come; the possession of these two places wou'd save us more than half a million a year, and we should then quickly have a Fleet for the common protection of our coasts; for without some strongholds in America, or naval magazines in our neighbourhood, G. Britain could never or seldom keep a squadron here. . . .[1]

Lafayette again came forth with a plan whereby he would lead an American army of invasion from the Hudson, to be met at Quebec by a French expeditionary force of four or five thousand men, four ships of the line and four frigates; and Congress, eagerly falling in with the idea, sent the young marquis back to France to get the co-operation of his king. But Lafayette's dream of a brilliant campaign that would duplicate the triumph of the British General Wolfe in 1758, and that would thrust this young Frenchman to the fore as the hero of the American Revolution, evaporated when he got back to his own country. It did not fit in with Vergennes' policy, as we shall see. Nevertheless, Congress continued into the new year 1779 to pass resolutions in favour of the ' liberation ' and annexation of Canada.[2]

Quite naturally the Americans were not at first disposed to be critical of the French alliance. Washington congratulated Congress with ' heart felt joy ', and noted with satisfaction that a war in Europe was ' inevitable and of speedy consequence '. To his brother he wrote, with an unaccustomed enthusiasm, that France had made the treaty ' in the most generous manner, and to our utmost wish. This is great, 'tis glorious news, and must put the Independency of America out of all manner of dispute '.[3] John Adams said of it that it

[1] July 21, 1778. Lee Coll. Mason concludes this letter with an expression of regret over the death of Lord Chatham, ' a wise & a good man; yet it is certainly a favourable event to America; there was nothing I dreaded so much as his taking the helm, & nothing I more heartily wish than the continuance of the present ministry. After his most Christian Majesty & happiness & prosperity to the French Nation my next toast will be ' long life to the present British Ministry ' in the first bottle of good claret I get, & I expect some by the first ships from France '.

[2] Lawson, op. cit., pp. 49–50; Gottschalk, op. cit.

[3] Washington to Henry Laurens, May 1, 1778; to General Heath, May 13; and to his brother, May 31. Washington Papers.

' is a rock upon which we may safely build '.[1] And Arthur Lee renewed his pleas to the Spaniards as friendly neighbours to join with the French in crushing British naval power.[2] But between Lafayette's soaring personal ambitions, Vergennes' skilful threading of his way through the wilderness of conflicting national interests, and factional and sectional jealousies in Congress, the Americans began to have doubts. Vergennes had no intention of letting the control of French policy slip into the hands of the Americans, nor of giving them a choice of going on with the war or making peace with Great Britain. So he sent his under-secretary, Conrad Alexandre Gérard, who had negotiated the alliance, to Philadelphia. Although the treaty had given the United States the freedom to conquer all the remaining British dominions in North America, it contained no commitment on the part of France to go beyond guaranteeing the ' independence ' of the United States. There was no pledge of French help, and no foundation for the enthusiastic hopes for all-out aid. The immediate French interest was to keep the Americans from making a separate peace and to bind them into a permanent union with France. Furthermore, it became Gérard's mission to discourage conquests by the Americans; and so he gradually let it be known in Philadelphia that France did not favour the subjugation of Nova Scotia or Canada, that she considered Spain had a prior claim to the Floridas and the Mississippi, and that the Americans should not expect to go west of the Alleghenies. Apparently the Virginia-New England coalition in Congress, which had been the loudest in its demands for Canada and Nova Scotia, seized upon the youthful Lafayette as a medium for trying to alter the course of French policy.[3]

But in Paris Franklin, who had probably already discounted French willingness to help in the subjugation of Canada, began experimenting with another approach. Franklin had always kept up his old friendships in England, notably with David Hartley and Dr. Richard Price. He even maintained a banking account with a London firm, and drew on it too from time to time while he was in Paris. His writing paper was furnished him by a London stationer.[4]

---

[1] To James Warren, Aug. 4, 1778. Wharton, II, pp. 657–77.
[2] A. Lee to Gardoqui, Paris, Aug. 27, 1778. Ibid., pp. 694–6.
[3] Meng, op. cit., pp. 91–122.
[4] Franklin Coll. in the Lib. of the Amer. Phil. Soc. The name of the London banking firm was Brown, Collinson & Tritton. Franklin's stationer was W. Woodmason.

Hartley had been consistently opposed to the war, and was among the most outspoken of the English Whigs. In the preceding April he had offered a motion in Parliament in favour of recognizing the United States and had proposed five bases for peace, including the repeal of the Quebec Act.[1] Franklin wrote Hartley on October 26, 1778, to suggest how England might appease the United States. No treaty could now be concluded without France but, looking to the future, England might do more than she was compelled to: she could

> cede all that remains in North America, and thus conciliate and strengthen a young power which she wishes to have a future and serviceable friend. I do not think England would be a loser by such a cession. She may hold her remaining possessions there, but not without a vast expense; and they would be occasions of constant jealousies, frequent quarrels, and renewed wars. The United States, continually growing stronger, will have them at last; and by the generous conduct above hinted at all the intermediate loss of blood and treasure might be spared, and solid lasting peace promoted. . . .[2]

Such an argument, humorous now in retrospect but put forth seriously then, was designed, I think, to be a trial balloon. It seems like a shrewd suggestion as to how Britain, having committed the folly of allowing America to throw herself into the arms of France, might encourage the Americans to think of getting a divorce. And with ' Nick Frog ' opposed to his wife's aggrandizing herself, her old husband might win her back with a sudden show of generosity. Franklin was hinting how the desired result might be brought about, though he told Hartley that a change in government in England would first be necessary. His diplomatic manoeuvre led to an earnest plea from Hartley to declare a truce for a period of five to seven years, to be regarded as a cooling off period while a peace commission settled the terms. Hartley also reasoned that France, in her own interest, would be glad to release the United States from the alliance; and he got Lord North's consent on condition that the Franco-American alliance first be dissolved. But Hartley overlooked the main purpose of French policy and, moreover, his peace feeler contained no terms—it did not even embody a proposal made by

---

[1] *Parl. Reg.*, IX, pp. 124 ff.
[2] Wharton, II, pp. 810–12.

Edmund Burke in Parliament that British troops be withdrawn from America, a move that would constitute a tacit recognition of independence. And so Franklin rejected the overture with a virtuous reference to the obligation of gratitude and justice that America owed to France.[1] Seriously, however, he put a high value on the French alliance; the French were now carrying the main financial burden of the war; their immense naval preparations, in conjunction with the Spaniards, were keeping British troops and ships at home; and eventually, he thought, the French might even collaborate in the reduction of Halifax and Quebec.[2]

But during the next two years American economic extremities grew worse, while the quest for more French aid and for new allies went on. Mounting inflation, war weariness, sectionalism and factionalism in Congress, speculation and private trading by individual members, mob violence and threats of mutiny in the army all pointed at disaster. Aroused by the exorbitant New England demands for Nova Scotia and the fisheries, the North Carolina delegation recommended withdrawal from the war and suggested to South Carolina that she do likewise.[3] In June 1779 Congress drafted a letter to its ' Great, Faithful, and Beloved Friend and Ally ' complaining of the irregular and scanty flow of supplies and pleading for more help in arms, ammunition and clothing.[4] Congress also wanted a subsidy from Spain, and pledged anew provisions and naval stores if the Spaniards decided on attacking the Floridas. It was not yet ready, however, to yield its claims to the Mississippi.[5]

In August the Chevalier de la Luzerne arrived to replace Gérard at Philadelphia. Disembarking at Boston, la Luzerne was immediately importuned for naval aid in defence of New England shipping and for support in launching an invasion of Canada and Nova Scotia.

---

[1] Ibid., III, pp. 36–7, 127–31, 154–6. Franklin never gave Hartley any encouragement, and dismissed his overture in a letter of May 4, 1779.

[2] Franklin to the Committee of Foreign Affairs, May 26, 1779. Ibid., pp. 186–94.

[3] Burnett, Letters, IV, pp. 238–40, 307 n., 332, 345–6, and other entries. In a long dispatch of May 14, 1779, to Vergennes Gérard discussed at some length the internal weaknesses of the United States and the need for subsidies. The indignation against New England, he thought, would lead to the dissolution of the union once the common danger was over. ' . . . il paroit que neuf et peutêtre dix Etats refuseront de continuer la guerre pour cet avantage accessoire en faveur de la nouvelle Angleterre, lequel ne leur offre aucune réciprocité d'intérêt. . . .' Meng., op. cit., p. 640.

[4] *Journals*, XIV, pp. 737–8.

[5] Ibid., pp. 938, 1046.

En route to Philadelphia, he stopped at West Point for a conference with Washington and repeated to the commander-in-chief what he had told the Boston businessmen: that the French would like to see the United States support Spain in the Floridas, and that ' his Christian majesty had a sincere and disinterested desire to see Canada and Nova Scotia annexed to the American Confederacy, and would be disposed to promote a plan for this purpose '.[1] But the French envoy made no concrete proposals, and since his remark was contrary to Vergennes' consistent policy, we can only conclude that it was meant as a pleasantry designed to keep the Americans from getting too discouraged. The one thing the French feared was that their ally would quit fighting and make a separate peace with Great Britain. On his part, General Washington appears to have taken la Luzerne seriously, especially when Lafayette returned from France full of enthusiasm and faith that Versailles would soon send a fleet and an army. Washington ordered Benedict Arnold to prepare with the greatest secrecy a proclamation addressed to the Canadians; and he requested two other officers to prepare invasion plans. But the prerequisite for a successful campaign against either Quebec or Halifax was the establishment of French naval superiority in the North Atlantic, and since this did not develop, the conclusion was reached in July 1780 that the proposed campaign was impracticable.[2]

Meanwhile throughout 1779 France had ignored American appeals for help and, having coaxed Spain into an alliance with herself (but not with the United States), she prepared to oust the British from European waters. A combined French and Spanish fleet manoeuvred in the Channel during the summer months with the intention of covering the landing of 40,000 French troops at Gosport or on the Isle of Wight. Sickness and faulty planning for the provisioning of this invasion army led the French to call off the expedition in October. Nevertheless, this was the time when England felt the full force of ' the gathering storm ' which Lord Chatham had predicted in Parliament two years before.[3] Her predicament inspired John Adams, now back in Massachusetts, to gloat over her impending

[1] Wharton, III, pp. 318–22.

[2] Washington to Duane, May 14, 1780; Washington to Arnold, June 4, 1780; St. Clair to Washington, July 7, 1780; Wayne to Washington, July 10, 1780. Washington Papers.

[3] *The Papers of Lord Sandwich*, 4 vols., London, Naval Records Society, III, pp. 164–71.

ruin and to reflect on the possibilities of unlimited benefits which the United States might secure through the alliance with France, now the first power in Europe. Britain ' resembles the melancholy spectacle of a great wide-spreading tree that has been girdled at the root. . . . If peace should unhappily be made, leaving Canada, Nova Scotia, or the Floridas, or any of them, in her hands, jealousies and controversies will be perpetually arising '. And ' if the King of Prussia could be induced to take us by the hand, his great influence in the United [Dutch] Provinces might contribute greatly to conciliate their friendship for us '. Loans of money would be forthcoming, and new horizons of commercial wealth be opened.[1]

This unstinted praise of France, the ' natural ally ', and denunciation of England, the ' natural enemy ', may be attributed in part to Adams's war fever, though his anxiety for French and Spanish fleet support in American waters is plainly visible in his several dispatches. Natural allies, he advised the French, are nations which have the same interests; natural enemies are those which have opposite interests. And of all the circumstances which go to make up ' interests ', commerce is the most important. In England, France and America had a natural and habitual enemy, *ergo* ' the more completely she is exhausted, humbled, and abased before the peace the securer we shall be for ever after '.[2]

Two elements stand out boldly and consistently in the writings of this calculating but intemperate New England Yankee: his extreme chauvinism and quickness to press an advantage whenever in the ' national interest ', and his avid dream of a dazzling commercial empire that lay just over the horizon. Actually Adams, like Arthur Lee, aroused the dislike of the French Foreign Minister, who wearied of his frequent importunities. On July 29, 1780, Vergennes curtly declined further intercourse and announced that thereafter he would deal only with Franklin.[3] Off Adams went to Amsterdam in quest of a loan from the Dutch, whose ' councils ', he

[1] J. Adams to the President of Congress, Aug. 4, 1779. Wharton, III, 278–86. This communication is a sweeping survey of the European scene, with an attempt to evaluate the relative benefits that the United States might expect to derive from future contacts with the Continental states.

[2] J. Adams to Genet, May 17, 1780; to the President of Congress, May 20, 1780. Ibid., pp. 685–95. Adams also wrote that there was ' a new power rising in the west ', which had effected a revolution in the political system and a variation in the balance of power in Europe.

[3] Vergennes to J. Adams, Wharton, IV, pp. 16–17.

subsequently reported, ' are the most inscrutable of any I ever saw '.[1] He did not get his loan.

Meanwhile la Luzerne in Philadelphia had been tantalizing Congress with hints of a powerful Franco-Spanish naval diversion and of renewed supplies of arms and ammunition for the American armies. But what would the Americans do in return? How effective an army would they put in the field? And especially, would they submit to reconciling their territorial claims with those of Spain, yielding the Floridas and the trans-Allegheny West (including the exclusive navigation of the Mississippi) to the Spaniards? Congress replied, reaffirming its loyalty to the alliance and promising an army of 25,000 provided the French furnished the necessary clothing, tents, arms and warlike stores.[2] Two French squadrons sailed from Brest for American waters during the spring months of 1780, the second one bearing an expeditionary force of five thousand men under Count Rochambeau. We do not know why Rochambeau's force was sent—the Americans had never asked for a French army, and they must have been taken by surprise. But perhaps Vergennes took this as a means of letting them know that France regarded the war as hers. Rochambeau disembarked at Newport, Rhode Island, which was regarded as second only to New York in strategic value. But the French warships sailed away for the West Indies, making no effort to expel the British from the American coast.[3]

This must have been a sore disappointment to the Americans: they had been living in the expectation that the French would join in operations against New York and Halifax. Indeed Washington had been planning his spring campaign with this in mind.[4] But equally disappointing was the French failure to bring the much needed arms and stores, while the internal economy was deteriorating to the point of collapse. Dollar bills were ' not fit to make the tail of a paper kite ', and in November Congress sent instructions to Franklin to ask

[1] J. Adams to the President of Congress, Aug. 9, 1780, April 6, 1781. Ibid., pp. 29–32, 351–52.

[2] La Luzerne to Congress, Jan. 25, 1780; Report of the Committee to answer the communications from la Luzerne, debated and agreed to, Jan. 31, 1780. *Journals*, XVI, pp. 87–8, 106–09, 111–16.

[3] A British squadron reached New York to strengthen the forces already there almost at the same time that the French reached Newport.

[4] Washington to Heath, May 15, 1780; to Duane, May 14, 1780; to La luzerne, May 14, 1780; to the committee of co-operation, June 19, 1780. To the latter he complained of his embarrassment because he did not know the French plans. Washington Papers.

France for a loan of at least 25,000,000 livres *in specie*. Even that, they confessed, was inadequate, and they went on to express the hope that His Christian Majesty would support their applications for loans from Spain and Holland.[1]

All the evidence leads to the conclusion that the American cause was by the close of the year 1780 on the brink of disaster, and that only succour from France could save it. Whatever good intentions the Spaniards might have entertained, they evaporated with the news of the loss of Charleston to the British. ' The effect of it ', wrote John Jay from Madrid, ' was as visible the next day as that of a hard night's frost on young leaves '.[2] Not a single nail would drive. In consequence Congress resolved upon the final plunge in the hope of getting Spanish aid: it sent word to Jay to give up the American claim to the lower Mississippi.[3]

Pressure upon Vergennes to send help now became heavy. He was told that the situation was extremely critical, that a separate peace might be necessary, and that if the British were suffered to recover America

> such an opportunity of effectual separation as the present may not occur again in the course of ages; and . . . the possession of those fertile and extensive regions and that vast seacoast will afford them so broad a basis for future greatness . . . as will enable them to become the terror of Europe . . . .[4]

At first Vergennes refused. France was now herself in dire straits. For their part the Dutch had absolutely refused to grant any credits. But after a month's deliberations the French changed their minds and undertook to make one more effort.[5] His Christian Majesty made an outright grant of 6,000,000 livres; 4,000,000 in gold to be shipped to the United States to rescue the vanishing dollar, 2,000,000 to finance additional purchases in France. Another 4,000,000 livres was allocated to redeem unpaid bills for past purchases. Moreover, the King agreed to underwrite a Dutch loan of an additional 10,000,000, and in case the Dutch still refused, to make the loan

---

[1] *Journals*, XVIII, pp. 1068, 1080–5, 1101–04.
[2] Jay to the President of Congress, Nov. 6, 1780. Wharton, IV, pp. 112–50.
[3] Feb. 15, 1781. Ibid., p. 257. The purpose was simply to remove ' every reasonable obstacle ' to an alliance. But no specific condition was put on this important concession.
[4] Franklin to Vergennes, Feb. 13, 1781. Ibid., pp. 254–5.
[5] Vergennes to la Luzerne, Feb. 14, 1781; the King of France to Congress, March 10, 1781. Ibid., pp. 256, 277.

himself. Thus to save the sinking ship the French risked 20,000,000 livres at the expense of their already perilously unbalanced economy. But this was not all. If the war was to be won, the French must secure naval supremacy in American waters. Louis XVI decided to take this final chance, and so he promised to issue orders to the fleet to co-operate with the American armies.[1] Word that the French at last meant business had a noticeable effect upon American morale; and by September large stocks of arms and stores were reaching American ports.[2] These stocks, plus the timely arrival of Admiral de Grasse off the capes of Virginia, led to the successful Yorktown campaign and the end of the fighting.

Now it should be evident that a basic incompatibility existed between the two allies. The Americans entertained imperial ambitions for their newly-founded sovereign state. They wanted: Nova Scotia and at least an equal share in the Newfoundland fishery, regarded by the New England merchants as indispensable to their economy; preferably all of Canada, but at least a northern boundary that would confine that colony to the lower St. Lawrence Valley and place the north shore of Lake Ontario inside the United States; a western boundary at the Mississippi and free navigation of that river to the sea; a southern boundary between Georgia and the Floridas.[3] France, it was believed, would respond favourably to these plans and see them as advantageous to herself: they would ensure the ' perpetual union ' between the two countries contemplated by the alliance. But Vergennes never accepted this thesis of a union of equals. If ' the rising new republic ' became exclusive mistress in North America, the tables would be turned and she would ' make a very hard law ' for the other nations. Only if the United States were hedged in on both land and sea and kept as a loosely united seaboard confederacy, could French interest be served properly.

Vergennes' instrument for thwarting the Americans was the *pacte de famille* with Spain, whose aspirations for regaining her ascendancy in the Gulf of Mexico exactly fitted in with his intentions. La Luzerne urged upon Congress the desirability of an alliance with Spain upon terms prescribed by His Catholic Majesty. The United

---

[1] Vergennes to John Laurens, May 16, 1781. Ibid., pp. 418–19.

[2] The changed situation is reflected in the sundry letters written between May and September 1781 that appear in Burnett, VI.

[3] Draft of Instructions to Franklin, Oct. 21, 1778; Report of a Committee on Nova Scotia, April 7, 1779. P.C.C. Reports of Committees, No. 25, vol. I.

States, insisted the latter, must agree to an 'invariable' western boundary at the Alleghenies. All the territory beyond the Proclamation line of 1763 was British and, like the Floridas, was open to conquest at the hands of Spain. The Americans had no just claims to any of these territories nor, of course, to the use of the Mississippi.[1] Apprised of these harsh conditions and of French endorsement of them, Congress in its extremities in 1781 bowed to the extent of offering to relinquish American claims to the navigation of the lower Mississippi. But, in spite of the many wartime protestations of loyalty to France, the alliance was in reality a marriage of convenience. After Yorktown the Americans at least began to want a divorce.

It was the tragedy of British foreign policy during this war that it failed to show the foresight, the boldness and the imagination necessary to prevent the American-French union. To the minority in opposition the Government's persistence in prosecuting a distant civil war in the teeth of mounting perils in Europe had seemed, from the outset, mad and suicidal. 'There is no man', gloomily declared Lord Rockingham early in December 1776, no man 'who has access to his Majesty, who has Integrity & Magnanimity of Mind sufficient to enable him to go & say to his Majesty—the Measures & the Policy of the Measures toward America are erroneous, the Adherence to them is Destruction'.[2] Yet even among the Whig Opposition, at all times more alive to the perils of 'the gathering storm' than the ministers of the Crown appeared to be, a simple grant of independence did not seem the right course of action. In the Lords the young Duke of Richmond and in the Commons the ex-governor of Massachusetts, Thomas Pownall, were almost alone in this respect. To such enlightened intellects as Chatham, Shelburne, Charles James Fox, for instance, the matter appeared much more complex and uncertain in its outcome than this. Like Burke, Fox would not go past withdrawal of the troops—he would not concede formal independence. The bills for reconciliation drawn up by Lord North and enacted into law by Parliament in March 1778 represented the limit of concession.

There is a striking parallel between the British position on this

[1] Communication of the Minister to the Committee relating to Spain, Feb. 2, 1780. Ibid.
[2] Holograph letter in the Rockingham Coll., Sheffield City Libraries, written probably to Sir George Savile. Quoted by permission of Earl Fitzwilliam and the Trustees of the Wentworth Woodhouse Estates.

question of American independence and the American position under Lincoln toward the seceding Southern States in the war of 1861-65. Like Lincoln and the war party in the North, Chatham and Shelburne were unionists to whom the American proposition of independence was repugnant because it meant the disintegration of the Empire. Shelburne, addressing the Lords on December 7, 1778, brings this point out very effectively. He would not have two sovereignties, he said, one in Great Britain, the other in America. He would have a union in which the constitutional prerogatives of the Crown, the claims of Parliament, and the liberties, properties and lives of all the subjects of the Empire would be equally secured.[1] President Lincoln propounded a similar point of view in 1862 when he asserted that his paramount object was to ' save the union '; and, for the remainder of his life, Lincoln, while prosecuting the war, hoped and worked for reconciliation. But the basic conditions under which Britain fought her war for the preservation of the Empire were altogether unlike those under which the United States laboured in 1861-65. To the Lincoln Government foreign intervention was no serious problem, and the United States was left unhampered in devoting its energies to suppressing the Southern rebellion.

Like the Americans and the French, the British believed during the war that American independence would spell the end of Britain herself as an independent country. Britain's own self-preservation was at stake. The most thoughtful of the speakers in Parliament voiced this fear not once, but many times. The most lucid expression of this attitude that I have encountered comes from a speech by Lord Cardiff on October 31, 1776. Since the Colonies had first been established, Cardiff declared, the state of Europe had undergone an almost total change.

> Great states are our rivals for power and greatness. The wealth and additional strength which we have hitherto derived from our colonies, have enabled us to retain our consequence and superiority in the grand European system. What then would be the probable effect, merely on consideration of self-preservation, but that, stripped of so ample a support, we should dwindle so as, in the first instance, to lose our importance in that system and in the

[1] *Parl. Reg.*, 14th Parl., 5 sess., XIV, 127-8.

end to become a province of the first ambitious power, who might think proper to attack us?[1]

This is an anxiety from which Lincoln was spared in his war. Lord Shelburne stressed it, however, in his speech for reconciliation. Without a reunion with the Colonies, he argued, Britain could not exist as an independent state with respect to the other powers of Europe. Deprived of America, she would sink to the level of a petty state, at best no stronger than the Netherlands. Shelburne and North agreed on one point: that American independence would spell the end of Great Britain. Shelburne still held to this position as late as February 4, 1782. But five months later he publicly admitted he had changed his mind. He was now ready to acknowledge independence, though he still feared it would have disastrous results. He thought the sun of England would set, but he was determined to improve the twilight and prepare for the time when the sun would rise again. The best way to do this was to prevent France from dictating the peace terms.[2]

What happened during the ensuing peace negotiations must be very briefly told. The Americans continued to pay lip service to the principle of no separate peace, but in fact they did negotiate separately with the British. Franklin made a private overture to this effect in March 1782; and in Richard Oswald, an elderly and genial Scottish merchant who had had extensive pre-war business connections with the Americans, Shelburne found an envoy much to the taste of Franklin and his fellow commissioners, John Adams and John Jay. Oswald's weakness was his desire to meet the wishes of the Americans, but Shelburne did not allow him to go far in exercising his own discretion. For the negotiation with Vergennes, on the other hand, Shelburne employed a professional diplomat, Alleyne Fitzherbert. The surprising factor here is the passivity of the French Foreign Minister, his non-interference in the bilateral talks between Oswald and the American commissioners. This procedure was surely contrary to the spirit and the intent of the Franco-American alliance, under which France proposed to treat the United States as a junior partner who would look to her to make the ultimate decisions. The alternative which Vergennes had to consider, however, was a continuation of the war; and since the British were now prepared to

[1] Ibid., 3 sess., VII, p. 6.
[2] Ibid., 15th Parl., 2 sess., VIII, pp. 103, 366ff.

concede that which they had never before been ready to offer—namely, independence—Vergennes really had no choice. If he went on with the war, which France was in no shape to do, he would find himself left in the lurch. The Americans had too much at stake in the British offer to allow themselves to be governed blindly by French wishes. Actually in these peace negotiations of 1782 they were tasting for the first time the fruits of independence—the power to bargain freely without supervision at the hands of a third party. Apparently Vergennes had never really thought through his policy, since in 1782 he was forced to concur in that which he had always dreaded. Perhaps he counted too much on Britain ' never ' recognizing American independence.

Of the four major parties at interest—Great Britain, France, Spain, the United States—Britain occupied the strongest position. It was within her power to define the terms and conditions of American independence; and Lord Shelburne, who was now the king's first minister, proceeded to do so with consummate skill. The Spanish failure to recover Gibraltar and Admiral Rodney's recapture of the control of the Caribbean Sea were, of course, valuable cards in his hand. Shelburne told Oswald, even before he admitted it publicly, that ' if America is Independent, She must be so of the whole world. No Secret, tacit, or ostensible Connection with France '.[1] Franklin was to be informed that the price of refusing to break the connection was renewed and vigorous prosecution of the war. Neither the Americans nor the French could afford this eventuality, and the Americans did not want the connection anyway.

During the negotiations Franklin revived the familiar American argument that if Britain wanted durable peace, she should hand over Nova Scotia and Canada, but Shelburne waved this aside. Instead he offered a handsome compromise: readmission of the Americans to the use of the Newfoundland fisheries and—his trump card—outright cession of the trans-Allegheny hinterland south of the Great Lakes. Thus the United States was not to be a coastal confederacy, which was the declared objective of the Bourbon powers, but a country with a hinterland extending to the Mississippi. The Spaniard was subsequently given back the Floridas, including the lower portion

[1] Memoranda of general instructions, in Lord Shelburne's handwriting, given to Oswald in conversation, April 25, 1782. The Shelburne MSS. of the Wm. L. Clements Library.

of the Mississippi River, which meant that he flanked the United States on the south and west; and Britain flanked the new country on the north and east. Halifax safeguarded her naval interest in the North Atlantic; Montreal protected her interest in the St. Lawrence waterway. Added to these safeguards was a guarantee to the vested Canadian right of trade and travel throughout the American interior. That there was a reciprocal American right on the Canadian side of the boundary meant little in terms of the actual conditions existing at the time.

Shelburne ardently hoped to induce the United States to enter a federal alliance or union with Britain, thus restoring the old ties and creating a clean break with France. This concept had been a favourite with the English Whigs, and had been discussed in Parliament from time to time during the war. With the United States accorded the treaty grant of independence, the proposed federal alliance contained the following stipulations: an unreserved system of naturalization as between the two countries; a customs union; and a defensive alliance for the protection of each other's territories in North America, the British to defend the United States by sea, the republic to furnish a quota of recruits and supplies for the British navy by way of compensation.[1] To the Americans the proposition meant a partial return to colonial status, and so it is not surprising that they rejected it. We have very scanty documentation on the American side on this matter of a federal alliance. Obviously they were not interested in it, and both Franklin and Adams seized upon the opportunity to remind Lord Shelburne, through Oswald, that the United States was still under treaty obligations to France.[2] With this single disappointment, however, Lord Shelburne scored a great victory. British diplomacy in 1782 was once more at its best for, to reverse a trite saying of our own time, Britain may have lost the war, but she won the peace. She virtually broke up the Franco-American alliance—her prime object—and in so doing, she put the United States again within the range of her influence.[3]

[1] Shelburne to Oswald, July 27, 1782. Ibid.

[2] J. Adams to Jay, Oct. 17, 1785. W. R. Manning, ed., *Diplomatic Correspondence of the United States: Canadian Relations, 1784–1860*, 4 vols., Washington, D.C., 1940–5, I, pp. 321–2. (Hereafter: Manning).

[3] It is, of course, no part of the plan of this book to describe the peace negotiations in detail. Professor Vincent T. Harlow, *The Founding of the Second British Empire 1763–1793*, London, 1952, I, pp. 223–447, has done this admirably. Although my own research for this chapter was done independently of Professor

Of necessity the remaining portion of this chapter must be in the nature of an epilogue. The Americans got a formal acknowledgment of their independence and a liberal cession of territory in 1783, but not for some years were they in a position to take advantage of their victory. The war leaders—the men on whose words and actions I have based these lectures—were moved by the idea of forming a nation state, an empire. But the thirteen united states, joined together in a loose confederacy, did not justify this idea; and the opportunity to act upon it was deferred until 1789, when substantially the same leaders recaptured control and began operations under a central government.[1] ' However unimportant America may be considered at present, . . .', Washington had written three years previously, ' there will assuredly come a day, when this country will have some weight in the scale of Empires. . . . Altho' I pretend to no peculiar information respecting commercial affairs, nor any foresight into the scenes of futurity; yet as the member of an infant empire . . . I cannot help turning my attention sometimes to this subject. . . .'[2]

Washington's words seem modest when compared with the writings of Jedidiah Morse, the Congregational minister of Boston who published his book *American Geography* in 1789 and justified it on the ground that now that the United States ' have risen into Empire ', its citizens should not rely upon Europeans for knowledge of its geography. Proceeding in this book, we learn that ' it is well known that empire has been travelling from east to west. Probably her last and broadest seat will be America . . . the largest empire that ever existed. . . . We cannot but anticipate the period, as not far distant, when the AMERICAN EMPIRE will comprehend millions of souls, west of the Mississippi. . . . Europe begins to look forward with anxiety to her West India Islands, which are the natural legacy of this continent, and will doubtless be claimed as such when America

Harlow and before reading his book, I find that my interpretation tallies closely with his. The older work by Samuel Flagg Bemis on *The Diplomacy of the American Revolution*, N.Y., 1935, deserves recognition for its scholarship, but cannot escape the charge of a nationalist bias.

[1] Merrill Jenson *The New Nation. A History of the United States during the Confederation, 1781-1789*, N.Y., 1954, best describes the party struggle between the nationalists and the federalists during this period, terminating in the adoption of the Constitution which meant victory for the former. Unfortunately, however, Jensen is oblivious to the external affairs of the country.

[2] *The Writings of George Washington from the Original Manuscript Sources, 1745-1799*, 39 vols., Washington, D.C., 1931-44, J. C. Fitzpatrick, ed., XXVIII, pp. 518-20.

shall have arrived at an age which will enable her to maintain her right '.[1]

While Morse was conjuring up future populations as the basis for empire, Alexander Hamilton in *The Federalist* was appealing to the ' adventurous spirit' of commerce and arguing for a federal navy which could turn the scales in the West Indies. Our position there is naturally a most commanding one, and can be put into effect by a few ships of the line, he declared.

By a steady adherence to the Union, we may hope, erelong, to become the arbiter of Europe in America, and to be able to incline the balance of European competitions in this part of the world as our interest may dictate.[2]

When the new American Federal Government headed by George Washington assumed power in 1789, the international political position of the United States was not noticeably better than in 1783. Its ' independence ' was still in doubt. But its economic position had grown markedly stronger. During the interim the country's foreign trade had regained its pre-war volume, thanks in part to the connections re-established with the British merchants and financiers, particularly the banking firm of Baring, & Company. Sir Francis Baring, a member of the Rockingham group and a war-time adviser of Lord Shelburne, had quickly restored his pre-war relationships with Robert Morris and other American merchants, who just as quickly forgot their erstwhile associations with the merchants of France. Through their outlets on the Continent, principally Hope & Company of Amsterdam, the Barings had marketing facilities to offer with which the French merchants could not compete.[3] With its strongest pillar thus knocked out, the ' perpetual ' alliance with France fell away during the 1780s abandoned by the very men who had sought it so eagerly for the promised riches they had imagined it would bring them.[4]

---

[1] *The American Geography; or a View of the Present Situation of the United States of America*, Elizabethtown, N.J., 1789, preface, p. 469, and app. note I.

[2] *The Federalist* (Lodge edition), no. XI, pp. 60–7.

[3] Ralph W. Hidy, *The House of Baring in American Trade and Finance. English Merchant Bankers at Work, 1763–1861*, Cambridge, Mass., 1949, pp. 12–23.

[4] Alexander De Conde, *Entangling Alliance. Politics and Diplomacy under George Washington*, Durham, N. C., 1958, starts out on the dubious, unsupported premise that in 1789 ' the French alliance was the cornerstone of American foreign policy ', and that ' the pro-French orientation of the United States was logical '. It is difficult to see why Professor De Conde should think so. The mere fact that an alliance between two countries is legally in effect does not make it actually so. Mr.

Meanwhile the future of the trans-Allegheny hinterland, juridically a part of the United States, remained in suspense and was fated to be so for some years to come. This country had been Canada's hinterland too; and its cession in far away Paris to the United States, abolishing at one stroke the grant made to Canada by the Quebec Act of 1774, caused consternation in Montreal. The cession entailed the transfer to the United States, ' with all convenient speed ', of a number of garrisoned posts extending from Lake Champlain along the south shores of the Great Lakes to Michilimackinac, which commanded the three upper lakes of Michigan, Huron and Superior. Remarkably little seems to be known about the history and usefulness of these several posts. Niagara had once been an important centre for the fur trade, but by 1784 this had all but vanished. Detroit was strategically the most valuable for, as its founder, Captain Cadillac, had foreseen, it was on the main route to the Wabash and the lower Ohio. This was, we recall, the ' life line ' of the old French empire. Around all of these posts, even the smaller ones like Sandusky on Lake Erie, had been built associations between the Canadian fur merchants and the Indian tribes. There was a natural alliance here, rooted in history, and the Indians had stood by the British against the encroachments of the Americans. The profits of the fur trade as such were by this time open to question, and the merchants do not seem to have feared that their business would be threatened for some years to come. Furthermore, the new fur empire of the Canadian Northwest, pioneered by the ' pedlars ' of Montreal, was beginning to overhaul the old trade south of the Lakes. The fur merchants did protest the loss of the territory to the United States; and, failing in that, they pleaded for a delay in the surrender of the posts so as to afford time to adjust their affairs. Actually this problem of the posts required very skilful management because, if the evacuation was suddenly carried out, it involved the spectacle of the British deserting their Indian friends. The fur merchants feared the consequences and

De Conde's resort to such emotive expressions as ' pro-British ' and ' pro-French ', not to mention other questionable features of his book, suggests that he has simply revived the arguments of the political enemies of the Washington administration. Using the techniques of ' objective ' scholarship, Mr. De Conde has nevertheless produced a partisan tract lamenting the disintegration of the alliance at the hands of Washington, or rather of Hamilton, who was the ' brain ' of the administration. But the alliance was already moribund before this administration started.

A much more discerning, and better supported book is Bradford Perkins, *The First Rapprochement. England and the United States, 1795–1805*, Philadelphia, 1955.

told Governor Haldimand so, but the governor was of the same mind. His reports to London leave us in no doubt of his anxiety for the Indians, should they learn the bitter truth.

A visit in June 1783 by Joseph Brant and John the Mohawk, the two most influential of the chiefs, confirmed the governor in his fears. He dared not tell the Indians what he himself had learned as fact and what they had heard as rumour, namely, that their country had been turned over to the Americans, their traditional enemies, without consulting them and without making provision for them. In November he dispatched a warning of the perils of another Indian uprising. ' The Indians entertain no idea . . . that the King either has ceded or had a right to cede their territories or hunting ground ' to the United States but, he thought, a general war could be averted ' by allowing the posts in the upper country to remain as they are for some time '. As a permanent policy he recommended that the country ' should be considered entirely as belonging to the Indians, and that the subjects neither of Great Britain nor of the American States should be allowed to settle within them, but that the subjects of each should have liberty to trade where they please '. This proposal was a reversion to the system contemplated under the Treaty of Utrecht, and it met with favour in London. Lord Sydney, the Secretary of State, wrote to reassure Haldimand that no certain time had been fixed for evacuation and that his advice had been heeded.[1]

The Americans, on the other hand, took the treaty proviso ' with all convenient speed ' literally; and when they found the occupation of the ceded territory unexpectedly difficult, they poured out their wrath on the British for keeping the posts. Thus Lieutenant-Colonel Harmar, who was stationed at Fort McIntosh, thirty miles down the Ohio from Pittsburgh, and engaged in negotiating treaties with the Indians, complained that he could do nothing until the posts on the Lakes had been taken over. ' Villainous emissaries have been

---

[1] On the fur merchants and their fears see especially D. G. Creighton, *The Commercial Empire of the St. Lawrence, 1760–1850*, Toronto and New Haven, 1937, pp. 90–5. The excerpts from the correspondence between Governor Haldimand and Lord Sydney come from A. L. Burt, *The United States, Great Britain and British North America*, New Haven and Toronto, 1940, pp. 87–95. See also Arthur R. M. Lower, *Colony to Nation*, Toronto, 1946, pp. 127–43. An appreciation of Canadian history is indispensable to an understanding of this and many other problems in Anglo-American relations, but unfortunately Canada still remains a *terra incognita* to the vast majority of American and British historians.

continually sallying from thence, poisoning the minds of the Savages & depreciating the character of the Americans ', he reported. ' One Treaty held at Detroit would give Dignity & Consequence to the United States and answer every purpose. . . . Elsewhere it would be of little or no effect '. But, knowing that he lacked the necessary force, Harmar refrained from provoking the Indians. Two years later, in 1787, he reported his determination to advance as far as the Wabash river and occupy the fort at Vincennes, where ' there are a number of British traders, who are the real cause I believe of all the Indian disturbances '. Subsequently he reported from Vincennes, but failed to mention the ' British traders '.[1] Whether these accusations were sound or whether they were grossly exaggerated, supplying later historians with an easy rationale, is a question not capable of being answered because to this day the facts are not really known.

While Harmar was thus being thwarted on the Ohio, John Jay, the Secretary for Foreign Affairs in Philadelphia, decided on invoking French aid under the terms of the alliance. Would France exert pressure on London to surrender the posts? Under Article 11 of the Treaty each party guaranteed the possessions of the other in America. It was a good test of the peace-time value of this instrument, but nothing came of it. Thomas Jefferson, who was now the American minister in Paris, put the question to Vergennes, but perhaps not unexpectedly discovered that the French Foreign Minister was indifferent. While admitting liability under the Treaty, Vergennes threw a doubt on what precisely the limits were. ' I told him ', Jefferson reported, ' there was no question what our boundaries were, that the English themselves admitted they were clear beyond all question. I feared however to press this any further *lest a reciprocal question should be put to me*, & therefore diverted the conversation to another object '.[2] Obviously Jefferson did not want to get involved in a guarantee of the French West Indies.

The post-war indifference of the American merchants toward France, therefore, seems to have been matched by French indiffer-

---

[1] Harmar to Col. F. Johnston, June 21, 1785; to Maj.-Gen. Knox, July 1, 1785, and July 13, 1786, July 7 and Aug. 7, 1787. Harmar Papers. Wm. L. Clements Library.

[2] Jefferson to Jay, March 12 and May 23, 1786. *Jefferson Papers*, IX, pp. 326, 369. Even though they abandoned any thought of asking France for help, however, Jefferson and even Jay hoped and expected to retain her goodwill. She was at this time regarded as America's only friend. See Jay to Jefferson, July 14, 1786; Jefferson to Jay, Sept. 26 and Nov. 12, 1786; Jefferson to Madison, May 30, 1787. Ibid., X, pp. 135, 406, 520; XI, pp. 92–7.

ence toward helping the United States establish its independence. The French were cool toward the American movement to establish 'a more perfect union', and they planned to block any effort the Americans might make to loosen the Spanish hold on the Mississippi. French statesmanship in the 1780s appreciated the veto power that Spain, in barring the use of the river, possessed over the United States making good its claims to its hinterland. Observing all this and apparently spurred on by the eagerness of Frenchmen living in America, Eleonore F. Moustier, the minister accredited to the new government, dispatched to Paris in 1789 an exhaustive report on the Mississippi valley—its economics, its geography, and its politics. Moustier pressed upon his government the splendid opportunities it now had for recovering its empire in North America. But this time the French empire would be based on New Orleans, the bustling little city on the lower Mississippi, rather than on Quebec. Linked with St. Domingue and the French West Indies, and furnishing the latter with provisions, the Mississippi valley would be far better for France than was ever the St. Lawrence. Moreover, Moustier argued and with good reason, once these prospects were held out to the pioneers who had settled in Kentucky and Tennessee, the latter would go over to France. Their future depended on New Orleans, and the United States could do nothing for them. As for the Spanish, who were then in possession of this French town, the minister was confident they would be glad to make an accommodation. As she had made abundantly clear during the war, Spain regarded the Americans as her principal enemies—her only interest in them had been in depriving them of British support. And if the French could interpose themselves between the United States and the Spanish Empire south of the Floridas, Spain would be more than pleased.[1]

M. Moustier wrote with both knowledge and prescience. Separatist movements were already under way in the American West, and at least three of the leaders of these movements had made overtures to the Spanish governor in New Orleans. Moustier's report was received in Paris too late for the distracted Bourbon monarchy even to give it a thought; but out of it came a shrewd scheme hatched by

---

[1] Moustier's report, covering more than 300 pages, is given a brief summary in Arthur Burr Darling, *Our Rising Empire, 1763–1803*, New Haven, Conn., 1940, p. 120. For a lengthier treatment of the exceedingly involved story of the American trans-Allegheny West for the years 1783–1803 the reader is referred to this book and also to my *American Diplomacy in Action*, Stanford, Calif., 1947, pp. 57–73 and 707–14.

the leaders of Republican France to revive the alliance and make it an instrument for the attainment of French ambitions. Edmond Charles, Citizen Genet, an engaging and zealous young revolutionary Republican, came to America in 1793 with plans for stimulating popular sentiment in a crusade for ' Liberty ' and for enlisting the aid of the Government, if possible, in war against Britain and Spain. France would be permitted to raise American volunteers for expeditions against New Orleans and the Spanish South-west; the United States could attack Canada and the Spanish Floridas, and its seafaring interests reap the benefit of privateering operations against British commerce. These schemes undoubtedly had their appeal: applause greeted Genet from the moment that he landed at Charleston; public personages like the governor of South Carolina and the mayor of Philadelphia came out openly on his side; ' democratic clubs ' sprang up, chanted the slogans of the French Revolution, and passed resolutions demanding that the Washington administration honour the alliance; Genet's plentiful supply of commissions and letters of marque appealed to the cupidity of American shipmasters and sailors who yearned to go a-privateering; and Dr. James O'Fallon and his friend, George Rogers Clark, heroes of the Revolutionary War in the West, made known their eagerness to enlist under the French banner for an attack on New Orleans.

The one fly in this ointment was the Washington administration, particularly the President and the Secretary of the Treasury, Alexander Hamilton, who saw only trouble in such embroilment. Courageously the Chief Executive proclaimed strict neutrality in the war between France and Britain and, moreover, took steps to enforce the proclamation even though no statutory provision had been made. Loud cries greeted the proclamation, its conservative supporters were denounced as ' monarchy men ', and the government had a difficult time in carrying out its purpose. Eventually, however, Citizen Genet accepted his defeat and public passions subsided for the time being. But when John Jay returned from England in 1795 with a working agreement with that country, the malignant attacks started all over again. Jay's treaty provided for the transfer of the occupied posts in the Northwest, to be completed by June 1, 1796, but in the eyes of the Republican enemies of the administration it compromised the extreme position on ' freedom of the seas ' which the latter insisted on taking.

Between the Neutrality Proclamation and the Jay treaty the French alliance received a death blow. The treaty was ratified, but the ideological warfare between ' republicans ' and ' monarchists ' kept up, with the French minister openly intriguing against the government and hoping for the triumph of the ' pro-French ' party at the coming elections. Aware of this, the President somewhat spoiled it by delivering a ' farewell address ', which has since become a classic, and by making pointed references in the address to ' the insidious wiles of foreign influence ' and to the folly of harbouring ' inveterate antipathies against particular nations and passionate attachments for others '. The conservatives won the elections of 1796, but the French continued to hope and scheme for a turn of the tide in their favour. General Victor Collot, a capable military engineer who possessed a familiarity with the habits and speech of American frontiersmen, journeyed down the Ohio from Pittsburgh to St. Louis in 1796, making sketches, assembling information relative to a possible invasion by way of New Orleans, and sounding out secessionist sentiment among the inhabitants.[1] French corsairs, under orders from the Directory, waged war on American shipping on the Atlantic; and French propaganda, under the direction of Talleyrand, engaged in subversive activity designed to make of the United States a tool in the war against Britain. But by these moves France over-reached herself, stimulated the building of a navy in the United States, caused the Government to look again in the direction of England for possible help, and aroused a militant nationalism reflected in the slogan ' Millions for defence but not a cent for tribute '. Patient diplomacy on the part of the Adams administration brought this ' quasi-war ' to an end in 1800.

The French alliance, eagerly solicited by the Americans during the War for Independence and readily accepted as a permanent relationship, led first to a separation between the two parties, an estrangement in 1793, and then a final decree of divorce in 1800 sweetened by a formula written into the treaty of that year. Contrariwise, a British-American *rapprochement* started with the treaty of

---

[1] George W. Kyte, 'A Spy on the Western Waters: the Military Intelligence Mission of General Collot in 1796', *M.V.H.R.*, XXXIV pp. 427–42. De Conde, op. cit., contains illustrative material relating to French intrigues and popular agitation in the United States. This author admits the purposes of French diplomacy (pp. 446–7), yet thinks that the populace, under the influence of anti-British propaganda, was fitted to choose more wisely than Washington and Hamilton (pp. 503–10).

1783 and gathered strength during the 1790s, as the Washington administration demonstrated its competence and its will to be independent. Lord Shelburne had put his finger on the essential factor in British-American relations: ' If America is Independent ', he had said, ' She must be so of the whole world. No Secret, tacit, or ostensible connection with France '. It remained for President Washington to convert this idea into practical American statecraft when, in 1793, he refused to be sucked into a new world war under cover of the still existing alliance with France. Washington's policy of neutrality was, as he himself expounded it in his Farewell Address of 1796, a policy of national independence; and this policy fitted into the requirements of British foreign policy.

CHAPTER IV

THE BIRTH OF THE AMERICAN LEVIATHAN, 1789–1823

' *The Finger of Nature* '

THE War of American Independence was conceived and fought under the spell of an imperial idea, an idea inherited from the remote past of the seventeenth century. It was the idea that the continent of North America belonged, as of right, to the people of the thirteen colonies of the Atlantic seaboard. Jedediah Morse, the Boston minister who was determined to teach his countrymen the facts of geography, reminded them of this. Said Morse:

> Judging upon probable grounds, the Mississippi was never designed as the western boundary of the American empire. The God [Law] of nature never intended that some of the best part of his earth should be inhabited by the subjects of a monarch 4,000 miles from them. And may we not venture to predict that, when the rights of mankind shall be more fully known, and the knowledge of them is fast increasing both in Europe and America, the power of European potentates will be confined to Europe, and their present American dominance become like the United States, free, sovereign, and independent empires.[1]

Surely Morse is here speaking in the classic tones of American isolationism—the lofty relegation of crowned potentates to Europe, the reservation of America for sovereign, independent republics. Slightly modified in language, this dogma was to be made the official government text in 1823.

In the meantime, while Morse was writing his *Geography*, Thomas Jefferson was trying to think up practical methods for accomplishing this object. As a Spanish diplomat, Señor Yrujo, was to write of him, Jefferson was ' all his life a man of letters, very speculative and a lover of glory '.[2] When he was in Paris as the first American minister, he secretly procured a copy of a map of South America which a Spanish cartographer had drawn but which the Spanish Government

---

[1] Morse, op. cit., p. 469.

[2] Yrujo to Cevallos, Washington, Dec. 2, 1802. *Before Lewis and Clark. Documents illustrating the History of the Missouri, 1785–1804*, A. P. Nasatir, ed., 2 vols., St. Louis, 1952, p. 714.

had tried to suppress; and intelligence respecting a secret survey that Spain had made of the Panama Isthmus for a possible canal greatly excited him. The latter, he exclaimed, was ' a vast desideratum for reason political and philosophical'. Jefferson's reputation for intrigue must have preceded him to France, for both a Brazilian and a Mexican revolutionist sought his aid in promoting subversive activities in their respective countries. To each of them Jefferson gave guarded answers, but in reporting the incidents to John Jay he wrote:

> I trouble Congress with these details, because, however distant we may be both in condition and dispositions, from taking an active part in any commotions in that country, nature has placed it too near us to make its movements altogether indifferent to our interests or to our curiosity.[1]

The Pacific Northwest, however, was strategically too important to risk its loss to some other nation, particularly if that nation had a reputation for colonizing successes. A report that ' a very large sum of money ' had been subscribed in England ' for exploring the country from the Mississippi to California ' excited Jefferson just as he was about to leave for France in 1783. The Missouri river had long been regarded as the future route across the continent. But probably at that time Jefferson had his mind on the Nor' Westers, the pedlars of Montreal, who were energetically pushing their fur empire westward from Lake Superior. In Paris Jefferson's suspicions fell on French shoulders. Learning of preparations at L'Orient for an exploring expedition to the Pacific under Captain La Pérouse, he feared a French design to plant a colony on the west coast of America. How readily he could magnify the slightest rumour, how morbid his jealousy on anything, no matter how remote or how unlikely, relating to the American continents! To set his own mind at rest, Jefferson asked Captain Paul Jones to go to L'Orient to spy on La Pérouse.[2]

A year later, by the time the latter had reached Brazil and was reported bound for Tahiti and the California coast, Jefferson got an unexpected opportunity through the exploring spirit of John Ledyard, a youthful Yankee sailor who had been a corporal of marines under Captain James Cook. Ledyard had witnessed the ready market in China for the sea otter skins that Cook's men brought from the

---

[1] Jefferson to Jay, Marseilles, May 4, 1787, *Jefferson Papers*, XI, pp. 338–43. See also X, pp. 212–17 and XII, p. 178n.

[2] Ibid., Aug. 14, 1785, VIII, p. 373.

Pacific Northwest, and he came to Paris in the hope of raising capital for a trading venture. But Jefferson preferred exploration to the fur trade, and he outlined an amazing route for Ledyard to follow. The young mariner was to ' go by land to Kamchatka, cross in some of the Russian vessels to Nootka Sound [on the west coast of Vancouver Island], fall down into the latitude of the Missouri, and penetrate to and through that to the United States '. Faithfully Ledyard set out, and the Russians let him through unmolested until he was within two hundred miles of Kamchatka. Orders from the Empress caught up with him, and he was arrested and taken back in a closed carriage to the Polish border. Evidently the Russians objected to a Yankee using their route as a means of finding an alternative route to the Pacific for a potential rival. ' Thus failed ', recorded Jefferson, ' the first attempt to explore the western part of our northern continent '.[1]

Back in the United States, Jefferson revived his original thought of an exploring expedition up the Missouri river. To the American Philosophical Society in Phildaelphia he appealed for money; and a proposed transcontinental expedition under Meriwether Lewis seems to have been linked in his mind with knowledge of contemporary French plots for taking New Orleans away from the Spaniards. The French botanist, André Michaux, was to carry messages and money to George Rogers Clark in Kentucky. Clark was an unemployed hero of the American Revolution, and was ready to raise a band of American frontiersmen under the French banner for an attack on New Orleans. Michaux was to accompany Lewis on an exploring party up the Missouri, but the project fell through because it required collaboration with France and the re-activation of the alliance of 1778, to which the Washington administration was opposed.[2]

Jefferson finally realized his dream in the celebrated Lewis and Clark expedition of 1804–06, but the expedition was twenty years behind its schedule according to his way of thinking. Furthermore, the Canadian Nor' Westers had long since beat him to it in being the first explorers to cross the continent, and by this time the North

---

[1] Jefferson, ' Memoir of Meriwether Lewis ', in *History of the Lewis and Clark Expedition*, 4 vols., Elliott Coues, ed., N.Y., 1893, I, pp. xviii–xix. There is also Ledyard correspondence in the *Papers*, X, pp. 220–2, 315–6, 548–9; and XI, pp. 216–8, 637–9.

[2] See my article ' International Rivalries in the Pacific Northwest ', *Ore. Hist. Quart.*, XLVI, 1945, pp. 185–218.

West Company was laying out a line of trading posts extending from Fort William on Lake Superior to the Columbia river. From this thin line was to grow eventually the Dominion of Canada, a very solid obstruction to the American ambition to take over the whole continent.

Now it will be recalled that the Americans in 1782 had been blocked in the south and west by the Spaniards, who re-entered the Floridas and the town of New Orleans and shut off the lower Mississippi to traffic from upstream. At first Jefferson felt he could be complacent on this, for the natural course of events would work in favour of the United States. In 1786 he declared, for example:

> Our confederacy must be viewed as the nest, from which all America, North and South, is to be peopled. We should take care too, not to think it for the interest of that great continent to press too soon on the Spaniards. Those countries cannot be in better hands. My fear is that they are too feeble to hold them till our population can be sufficiently advanced to gain it from them piece by piece. The navigation of the Mississippi we must have. This is all we are as yet ready to receive.[1]

But, on the other hand, Spain showed signs of a determination to keep the Mississippi closed; and her control of this river gave her the whip hand over the American settlements west of the mountains. Not long before the Constitutional Convention opened at Philadelphia, a crisis was precipitated as a result of some negotiations which John Jay had been carrying on in New York with the Spanish envoy, Don Diego de Gardoqui. Gardoqui dangled the tempting bait of an open Spanish market before the eyes of American merchants, provided the government would agree to a fixed boundary giving Spain all the country south of the Yazoo river and would waive its claim to the right of navigation of the Mississippi. Miscalculating the political effects of such a treaty and discounting Spanish chances over the long run for holding the Southwest, Jay went ahead with his negotiation. The Southern States reacted violently, and a wave of separatist agitation broke out in the West. Over in Paris Jefferson protested that abandonment of the Mississippi was tantamount to separating the two parts of the country. It would mean relinquishing five-eighths of the national territory, upon the coloniz-

---

[1] To Archibald Stewart, Jan. 25, 1786. *Papers*, IX, p. 218.

ation of which everything depended. The sale of Western lands would pay off the national debt; otherwise the United States would be burdened with debt forever. And, in view of the temper of the settlers, he continued, 'we must suppose their *separation possible* at every moment '. If they can be retained, they will be ' a precious part of our strength '. ' But this affair of *the Missisipi* by shewing that *Congress is capable* of hesitating on a question which proposes a *clear sacrifice* of the *western* to the *maritime states* will with difficulty be obliterated. . . .[1]

This was a clear statement of the importance of the hinterland, but at the moment Jefferson felt gloomy. A proposal that he go personally from Paris to Madrid in the hope of retrieving the ground lost in New York he regarded as ' desperate ', though he thought wistfully of asking France for help. But a better idea occurred to him: once Spain got entangled in a war in Europe, she would be unable to keep her position in America. In the meantime the United States should keep quiet and prepare for eventualities.[2]

Jay's negotiation with Gardoqui fell through, but the Spanish envoy left the country, confident on his part that the United States could not last long. A conspiracy hatched in Kentucky to unite with the governor of New Orleans if the latter would allow the Westerners port privileges strengthened this belief. Besides, there were the four large Indian tribes in the Southwest, who could be depended upon to oppose the Americans. The new Federal Government of George Washington dared not attack them; but in 1790 it concluded a trade treaty with Alexander McGillivray, a Scotch half-breed who had made himself the leading chief of the Southwest. The administration did not reveal a secret article in this treaty by which it promised to commission McGillivray a brigadier-general in the United States army with a salary of $1,200 a year and to make appropriate payments to the other chiefs. But McGillivray gave in return only an implied pledge of friendship, and he continued to look south to Pensacola for arms and equipment that would aid him in building a strong Indian confederation capable of resisting the Americans. Panton, Leslie & Company, a Scottish trading house which had started business in Pensacola while West Florida was a

[1] To Madison, May 30 and June 20, 1787. Ibid., XI, pp. 92–97, 480–4. The italics are Jefferson's, as is also the misspelling. At this time there were no western states.

[2] To John Brown, May 28, 1788. Ibid., XIII, 211–2.

British colony and which Spain had wisely permitted to remain, was helpful in this respect.[1]

In 1795 the Spaniards themselves, however, sounded the retreat when, under fear of a British-American combination against them, they conceded the right to use the port of New Orleans for trading purposes. Jay's treaty of the preceding year was regarded in Madrid, as in Paris, as an Anglo-American alliance against the Continental powers. The treaty was not an alliance, but it certainly was a *rapprochement* which strengthened the hand of the United States against its former wartime allies and associates. Jay's treaty ranks second in importance to the federal Constitution as a basic document in American independence.[2] On Britain's part it was a reward for Washington's strict neutrality policy of the year before, which had worked in her favour, a reiteration of Lord Shelburne's statement that the United States must be rendered independent of the whole world. It is easy to see why Washington discoursed so vigorously against foreign alliances in his Farewell Address. He had long since soured on the French alliance—he himself had been the particular object of French intrigue; and both France and Spain had exerted their utmost influence to frustrate their erstwhile associate and keep it a weak coastal buffer.

This handicap appeared at an end by 1796. With the posts on the Great Lakes secured and with New Orleans now an open port, there seemed reason no longer to question the durability of the American national state. Ordinances enacted by the old Continental Congress had provided for surveying and selling to settlers the vast lands now owned by the central Government, and for erecting new Territories with governments on the model of the British colonial system, which would in due course be elevated to the rank of states and admitted on equal terms to the Union. New Orleans itself grew

---

[1] Arthur P. Whitaker, *The Spanish Frontier, 1783-1795; the Westward Movement and the Spanish Retreat in the Mississippi Valley*, Boston, 1927. But the secret article in the treaty of 1790 was published for the first time by Hunter Miller in his *Treaties*, II, p. 344.

[2] ' The first proof that independent America was important enough to secure any concessions from a major power ', as well put by Bradford Perkins in his book, *The First Rapprochement*, p. 5. But Jay's treaty is celebrated for the wordy war waged against it by the political enemies of the administration and by many American historians ever since. Cf., for example, De Conde, op. cit. The opposition press began denouncing Jay and his treaty even before the contents of the treaty were known. Was this pre-judgment the source for an historical legend about the treaty which so many have accepted?

to a population of eight thousand, supported by the American trade. It was a distributing centre for West Florida, the West Indies, and American and European ports. Barrels of flour brought down the river on flatboats constituted its chief export in exchange for imports of merchandise and Mexican silver dollars.

But Spain herself benefited hardly at all from this business—it was controlled by French Creoles, Americans and other nationalities —and the Spanish authorities, once so hopeful of holding back the American tide, ruefully confessed that they could get neither honour nor profit from governing the province. France was now their best hope—she had the desire to take back Louisiana and the presumed ability to keep it—and to her they turned. In 1800 Spain concluded with Bonaparte, the First Consul, a secret agreement re-ceding to France the province of Louisiana ' with the same extent that it now has in the hands of Spain and that it had when France possessed it, and such as it ought to be according to the treaties subsequently concluded between Spain and other states '. The confusing language of the document begs the historical controversy between France and Spain, never resolved, over West Florida, a strategic section of coast flanking New Orleans and the Mississippi on the east.[1]

Moustier's ideas which, we remember, had found a place in the French mind, were about to receive a trial under the leadership of Bonaparte, and were seconded by the influential Creole colony in Paris. France would repossess her old colony on the Mississippi, now grown prosperous, and push up the river. All the west bank was hers under the treaty, and the east bank too was mortgaged. So the American Union might shrink back to the mountains after all and resume its old colonial status. At least that was the fear. Bonaparte's secret was too good to be kept for long—it became public knowledge in June 1801—but in any event the Americans had had plenty of grounds for scepticism ever since Genet's intrigues. Timothy Pickering, the Federalist Secretary of State under John Adams, anticipated the French move as early as 1797, the year when Collot returned from his trip down the Ohio. Pickering thought the French would take the Floridas and Louisiana, and would then foment an irredentist agitation in Canada. To Rufus King, the American minister in London, he confessed his fear that France meant ' to

[1] See Arthur P. Whitaker, *The Mississippi Question, 1795–1803*; *a Study in Trade, Politics, and Diplomacy*, N.Y. and London, 1934.

renew the ancient plan of her monarchs of *circumscribing* and encircling what now constitute the Atlantic States '; and he told King to throw such obstacles as he could in the way of this ambition. King got a sympathetic, but non-committal audience from Lord Grenville, and later, when Bonaparte's secret leaked out, from Lord Hawkesbury. Grenville volunteered a free hand to the United States to attack New Orleans, and Hawkesbury agreed that a French advance up the valley ' would be realizing the plan to prevent the accomplishment of which the Seven Years War took place '. But neither one offered British intervention, which was what King was hinting at.

Between them, King and Robert R. Livingston, the American minister in Paris, they took it upon themselves to apply for British help. ' I have not failed to shew in the strongest light to the minister of Britain ', Livingston reported, ' the danger that will result to them from the extension of the French possessions in Mexico, and the probable loss of Canada if they are suffered to possess it '. In other circumstances the two diplomats might have exposed themselves to a severe reprimand from Jefferson and Madison, who were now in power in Washington; but by March 1802 the President and his Secretary of State had awakened to the practical issues confronting them. Without waiting to sound out the British, Jefferson, in a private communication intended to be seen by official French eyes, brandished the threat of an alliance with Great Britain. ' The day that France takes possession of N. Orleans fixes her sentence which is to restrain her forever within her low water mark. It seals the union of two nations who in conjunction can maintain exclusive possession of the ocean. From that moment we must marry ourselves to the British fleet and nation '. For good measure the President, in another context, tossed out the idea of ' the exclusive appropriation of both continents of America as a consequence. . . . But this little event, of France's possessing herself of Louisiana, which is thrown in as nothing, as a mere make-weight, in the general settlement of accounts, this speck which now appears as an almost invisible point in the horizon, is the embryo of a tornado which will burst on the countries on both sides of the Atlantic and involve in its effects their highest destinies '.

Bonaparte did not frighten as easily as Jefferson hoped: he was having his own troubles in Santo Domingo, but nevertheless went on with his plans for a military occupation of New Orleans in 1803.

Again, however, fate was against him: a hard winter freeze prevented the expedition from sailing. In the meantime the Spanish intendant in New Orleans arbitrarily revoked the right to trade, to which the Western Americans responded with fresh cries of outrage and appeals to the government to come and save them. Edward Thornton, the British minister in Washington, thought that Britain should capitalize the crisis by proffering her services, thereby binding the United States firmly to her side, but Hawkesbury and Addington remained aloof. To pacify the Westerners and discourage them from irresponsibly attacking New Orleans themselves, Jefferson dispatched James Monroe to Paris to ' assist ' Livingston. The appointment was only a political gesture, but Monroe did have orders to ' cross the Channel ' if the French still refused concessions.

Actually the Americans had very little bargaining power of their own, and their actions showed that they knew it. Their chief hope was the probability of another Anglo-French war, in which Jefferson intended as a last resort to participate. He was rescued from this dilemma by some quick work on the part of Napoleon and his advisers who, seeing the futility of trying to hold on to Louisiana, turned an otherwise certain defeat into a brilliant diplomatic victory by offering the whole country to the United States just as France had received it from Spain, in return for $15,000,000. The momentous transaction was completed with great rapidity and the treaty signed on the 30th of April, 1803. By this stroke of lightning Napoleon put the United States back in the French camp. ' This accession of territory ', he told his finance minister, Barbé-Marbois, ' affirms forever the power of the United States, and I have just given England a maritime rival that sooner or later will lay low her pride '.

Still, there is high comedy in this affair of Louisiana. The American Government had not the wherewithal to buy fifteen million dollars' worth of gold francs which Napoleon could use. Moreover, the treaty had to be ratified by the Senate and the payment authorized by the House of Representatives, which meant many months of delay and the raising of ominous controversial questions relating to the Constitution. The treaty provided, not for a cash transaction, but for the delivery of six per cent stock, or bonds. These, however, were unwelcome to Napoleon, who needed francs with which to finance his war. French banks were unprepared to buy the bonds, but Baring & Company of London and Hope &

Company of Amsterdam, accustomed to dealing in American securities, offered to take the risk at a liberal discount. Alexander Baring received permission from the British Treasury to transfer specie from London to Paris; and after more than a year had elapsed since the signing of the treaty, the French Treasury began to receive payment. The war between Britain and France had in the meantime been resumed.[1]

Jefferson, the Reverend J. Morse, and their contemporaries put their trust in the *colonizing* capacity of the United States, in the ultimate triumph of an emigrating population in filling up the continent, and apparently even the *continents*. For Jefferson's dreams seem to have put no bounds to the spread of the American population. The United States was ' the nest, from which all America, North and South ' was to be peopled. And to James Monroe in 1801 he confided his opinion that

> However our present interests may restrain us within our limits, it is impossible not to look forward to distant times, when our rapid multiplication will expand it beyond those limits, & cover the whole northern if not the southern continent, with people speaking the same language, governed in similar forms, and by similar laws. . . .[2]

In other words, he pictured the United States as the homeland for teeming millions who would emigrate and reproduce their kind in all parts of North and South America, displacing not merely the indigenous redmen but also the Latin populations to the south. The continent (or the continents) was destined to be American in blood, in language and habits, and in political ideology. Nature

[1] The diplomatic correspondence concerning Louisiana, from which I have quoted, is printed in Manning, op. cit., I, pp. 101–2, 111–2, 525, 529, 531–2, 547–8, 552, 560–1; in Dumas Malone, ed., *Correspondence between Thomas Jefferson and Pierre Samuel Du Pont de Nemours, 1798–1817*, Boston, 1930, pp. 46 ff.; and in *The Original Letters of Robert R. Livingston, 1801–1803*, La. Hist. Soc., New Orleans, 1953, *passim.* See also: E. Wilson Lyon, *Louisiana in French Diplomacy*, Norman, Okla., 1934; Perkins, op. cit., pp. 159–71; and Hidy, op. cit., pp. 33–4. Authorities differ on the value in gold francs that Napoleon actually received. His agreement with the United States included a deduction of $3,750,000 in satisfaction of past claims of American nationals against France. Dollar bonds actually issued by the U.S. aggregated $11,250,000, which the bankers discounted at 78½.

[2] *The Writings of Thomas Jefferson*, Paul Leicester Ford, ed., 10 vols., N.Y., 1892–9, VIII, p. 105. The context of this excerpt is a question of how to dispose of certain Negro criminals in the State of Virginia. Jefferson considered, but rejected, the notion of establishing a penal colony, his reason being that some day the U.S. might annex the country where the colony was located and would not want these undesirables in its midst.

intended the two Americas to be the beneficiaries of American republicanism, and the achievement was to be the fruit of free and voluntary colonization.

But this concept of an indefinitely expanding American population was one thing, while Jefferson's concept of an expanding American Republic was another. The latter was to be the parent state, the mother country whose territorial domain should take in the boundaries of the British Empire in North America as it had been in 1763: i.e., a western boundary at, or somewhat to the west of, the Mississippi, a northern boundary that would include the Canadian provinces, and a southern boundary that would embrace the Floridas. Jefferson also wanted to include Cuba in his American Leviathan, his reason probably arising from the strategic connection between the island and the mainland. Cuba, he declared, would be ' ours in the first moment of the first war '. It was a marked island, just as the Floridas were marked, for conquest or for some other form of annexation.

The Canadian provinces were the borderlands to the north, to be absorbed and integrated into the American Union. We must bear in mind how persistently, and for what purposes, these provinces were sought after during the War for Independence. For three decades following this war there was a steady flow of emigrants from the United States, attracted by liberal land grants on the part of the colonial governments of Upper and Lower Canada. Then too, Canada was a safer place in which to live than was the American West, where the Indian peril was ever present. On the eve of the War of 1812 eight out of every twelve persons in Upper Canada were of American origin, and two thirds of the elected members of the provincial legislature had been born in the United States. To outward appearances Canada was on the highroad to Americanization, and so Thomas Jefferson joined with the War Hawks in 1812 in the belief that the conquest of the British provinces this time would be ' a mere matter of marching '. The American General Hull crossed the river from Detroit and proclaimed ' liberation '. But the Canadians proved disappointing, and the sundry raids and depredations on their soil during the ensuing two years had an effect opposite to what was intended. A nascent Canadian nationalism began to stir. And so for the second time an estoppel was placed on the northward thrust of the American Republic.[1]

[1] For an interesting and concise account of the military operations of this war

The Spanish Floridas, however, were quite a different story. They were a zone of international friction, where outside of the coastal towns the Indian tribes were the real rulers. Marauding Seminoles sallied forth at will across the border, to scalp and enrage the American families in the bottom lands of Georgia. Jefferson in 1803 regarded the Mississippi river and the coastal region to the east at least as far as the Bay of Mobile as his first requirement; but, though Mobile had been originally a French post, the Spaniards had habitually looked upon it as a trespass on their domain. They safeguarded themselves on this in the secret treaty of 1800, hence Jefferson found his wants only partially satisfied. Naturally he assumed that the French were right, but when the Spaniards demurred, he made a move to seize Mobile by force, taking the precaution, however, to secure advance authorization from Congress. Moreover, he considered pinching off the remainder of the Spanish Floridas to the east, using as an excuse the failure of Spain to indemnify American shipowners for damages done them by French and British privateers operating in Spanish territorial waters. To carry out an aggression against Spain, however, the President felt the need for the approval of Great Britain, and in 1805 he again bethought himself of negotiating a treaty of alliance with that country; but in that same year the British tightened the controls on the lucrative American carrying trade between France and her West Indian colonies, and Jefferson embarked on a programme of reprisals.

The Floridas became American territory ' piece by piece ' in the literal sense of the phrase. First came the Baton Rouge district, a pocket of territory north and east of New Orleans infiltrated by settlers. A bloodless insurrection, stimulated from the American side of the border, occurred there in 1810, followed shortly by annexation. Then came two more ' pieces ' during the war years 1812–13 through steps which in our time would certainly be described as measures of ' protective occupation '. These pieces included the bay and surrounding territory of Mobile, and were taken as safeguards against hostile measures presumed to be intended by the British. An inspired revolt on the east coast north of St. Augustine was executed clumsily, and it fell through. And so, at the end of the War

consult A. L. Burt, op. cit., pp. 317–44. Arthur R. M. Lower, *Canadians in the Making. A Social History of Canada*, Toronto, 1958, pp. 173–86, discusses the war as a stimulant to Canadian nationalism. Mr. Lower, himself quite a nationalist, calls the war a ' constructive conflict '.

of 1812, Spain was left in the ridiculous position of holding on to a fragment of territory isolated by many miles from her remaining coastal holdings to the west of the Mississippi. A temporary American occupation of Pensacola in 1818, incited by a Seminole raid which originated on Spanish soil, was the handwriting-on-the-wall for East Florida and led to the liquidation of Spanish sovereignty by a treaty one year later.[1]

There is a legend well entrenched in American history and repeated *ad nauseam* in the school texts that the United States ' purchased ' the Floridas for the sum of $5,000,000. Actually there was no purchase, and no money changed hands. The treaty of 1819, in so far as it affected the Floridas, was a face-saving device for both countries. It enabled His Catholic Majesty to cover his obvious weakness, and it gave the American Goverment the opportunity to relegate its past aggressions to oblivion. What the treaty does say is this:

> His Catholic Majesty *cedes* to the United States, in full property and sovereignty, *all the territories which belong to him*, situated to the Eastward of the Mississippi, known by the name of East and West Florida. . . .

*　　　*　　　*　　　*

> The United States, *exonerating Spain from all demands in future, on account of the claims of their Citizens*, to which the renunciations herein contained extend, and considering them entirely cancelled, *undertake to make satisfaction for the same*, *to an amount not exceeding Five Millions of Dollars. To ascertain the full amount and validity of those claims, a Commission*, to consist of three Commissioners, Citizens of the United States, shall be appointed by the President . . . ; which Commission *shall meet* at the City of Washington, *and within the space of three years*, from the time of their first meeting, *shall receive, examine and decide upon the amount and validity of all the claims included* within the descriptions above mentioned. . . .[2]

The cryptic phrase in the first paragraph disposes of the embarrassing question raised, but not answered, ever since 1803: what *were* the territories belonging to the King of Spain? The second paragraph

---

[1] I. J. Cox, *The West Florida Controversy, 1798–1813; a Study in American Diplomacy*, Baltimore, 1918; R. K. Willys, ' The East Florida Revolution of 1812–1814 ', *Hisp. Amer. Hist. Rev.*, IX, 1929, pp. 415–45.

[2] Miller, *Treaties*, III, p. 4. Italics mine.

is a waiver of claims on the part of the United States Government lodged against the Government of His Catholic Majesty in behalf of private citizens for *alleged* damage done them by the Spanish Government. There is no relation between the two paragraphs, and there is only a general undertaking on the part of the United States that it will itself decide the validity of the claims and pay them accordingly.

By the acquisition of the Floridas the United States rounded out its coastal frontier. The same treaty provided for a new boundary on the west, one that gave cartographical form to the chunk of territory known as the Louisiana Purchase, which Jefferson had obtained from Napoleon. The Louisiana Purchase was, in spite of the temporary disappointment over Mobile, a diplomatic windfall which had long-range effects, central to which was the fact that after 1803 the United States was in undisputed possession of the heartland of the continent. This gave it a position of independence *vis-à-vis* the European powers so strong that the United States was almost ready to jump on to the same stage with them. Certainly thereafter it was moving away from the company of the small powers. Napoleon in 1803 put a capstone on Vergennes' original policy; he gave the United States a freedom of action calculated to benefit France in her new war with Britain. That was his own shrewd diagnosis, we remember. Jefferson's hands were untied for a stronger policy against British domination of the Atlantic; and, despite the temptation to bargain for British support against Spain, he soon seized the opportunity to hammer away on his theories of freedom of the seas. But one cannot imagine the cautious president, skilled in timing his acts, risking a war for neutral rights unless he had first secured his rear. This was the lesson of the Louisiana Purchase: the United States no longer needed allies.

In the War of 1812—not incorrectly called the Second War for American Independence—the Americans made no headway against the British on the Atlantic or on the St. Lawrence. But with respect to the interior it was a different story. The British relinquished all connection with the Indian tribes south of the Great Lakes, and then followed this concession with a new boundary convention (1818) extending the artificial division between the United States and British North America from the point where it stopped in 1783 at the Lake of the Woods along the 49th parallel to the Rocky Mountains. This

British move in coming to terms with the United States in 1818 compelled the Spaniards to do likewise with respect to their interests in the south and southwest.

Considering that Spain was having her troubles in Mexico and South America during these years, she did pretty well *on paper* in holding the United States to a line that limited the Louisiana Purchase territory on the west. Drawing upon French sources, Jefferson had maintained that the country he had procured extended westward to the Rio Grande, and this became the standard American argument. But Spain, in exchange for a *quid pro quo* of which we shall take due note, managed to hold the line at the Sabine river, thus for the time being saving her two provinces of Texas and New Mexico. Even so, by these two treaties with Britain and Spain respectively, the whole of the Mississippi valley as well as the Floridas passed under American control, giving to the United States an impregnable position to be used in the course of time for further advances.

John Quincy Adams was the master mind behind this new partition of the continent, and the *quid pro quo* which he exacted from Spain had to do with the Pacific Northwest. Stemming from the voyages of Spanish explorers along the Pacific coast, Spanish claims of dominion in North America included California and the coast indefinitely to the north. The occasional appearance of a Spanish warship in these waters kept alive these claims. In 1789, for instance, Spain had a head-on clash with Britain in an ill-fated attempt to exclude British trading vessels. Much was happening during these years to make of the Pacific Northwest a region of intense international rivalries. One need but mention the voyages of the two great British explorers, Cook and Vancouver, the planting of Russian trading posts on the shores of Alaska, the scramble for the sea otter trade over which the Boston Yankees obtained almost a monopoly, the triumph of the Canadian Nor'Westers in linking the basin of the Columbia river with Montreal, and the belated entry of American fur trading interests from St. Louis under the lead of the German immigrant, John Jacob Astor. By 1819 the Spanish interest was no better than a legal shadow; but Adams, bent on pushing out the Russians and the British, left no stone unturned in his determination to gain the upper hand. Spain in 1819 resigned all her claims to the coast and territory north of the 42nd parallel—the present northern boundary of the State of California—in favour of the United States.

Jefferson, we recall, had been sensitive to the potentialities of this region as far back as 1783. His extraordinary assignment to John Ledyard justifies the praise given him many years later that he was 'the first to propose the North American road to India and the introduction of Asiatic trade on that road '. And Jefferson and Adams both looked upon Oregon—the name given to this region of the Pacific Northwest—as the American window on the Pacific, the corridor across the continent which would give the United States the advantage of a direct route to the great trade marts of Asia.

But there was a profound difference between Jefferson and Adams on the question of the political future of the Northwest. To Jefferson the Northwest would be *colonized* by Americans, but not annexed to the parent country. When in 1813 John Jacob Astor set up his trading post of Astoria at the mouth of the Columbia, Jefferson wrote to congratulate him. ' I view it ', he said, ' as the germ of a great, free, and independent empire on that side of our continent, and that liberty and self-government, spreading from that as well as this side, will insure their complete establishment over the whole '.[1] In other words, there was to be a new republic planted in the far northwest, an affiliate of the mother country that would expand in concentric circles and help to safeguard the cause of republicanism in the New World against the systems of government that dominated the Old.

What could be more natural than that Jefferson, a child of colonial Virginia, should have been moved by the old British colonial concept of separate communities migrating westward and breaking off from the parent state? Jefferson's imaginary Pacific Northwest Republic would develop and stand to the United States, its mother country, as Virginia, the ' Old Dominion ' of Charles II, had originally stood to England. And just as the Atlantic was too wide and too formidable a barrier between England and her colonies, so was the great American desert a bar to the expansion of the American Republic. Better that Oregon be independent in its own right, and so carry out the ideological mission of the United States. Perhaps too Jefferson, a classical scholar, unconsciously assimilated the ideas and

---

[1] Nov. 9, 1813. *Writings*, H. A. Washington, ed., N.Y., 1854, 9 vols., VI, p. 248. Astor must have felt flattered to be told that his name would go down with that of Columbus and Raleigh as the father and founder of such an empire.

practices of the ancient Greeks, whose colonists retained only the cultural memories of the mother cities.

Not merely remoteness, but physiographic barriers more difficult than the Atlantic separated the Far West from the United States and gave support to Jefferson's ideas. Expeditions which ventured, during the first three decades of the nineteenth century, across the treeless plains to the Rockies and beyond into the alkali basin of Great Salt Lake reported on these barriers; and until the mid-century the maps of the United States labelled the region as ' the Great American Desert '. The best way to reach the Pacific coast was the one pioneered by the Yankee traders of the 1780s—the sea route around Cape Horn; and the most that was expected of the trans-continental route was that it could be utilized by caravans of traders. Nature would dictate the western boundary of the United States, as Thomas Hart Benton declared in the Senate in 1825:

Westward . . . the ridge of the Rocky Mountains may be named without offence, as presenting a convenient, natural and ever-lasting boundary. Along the back of this ridge, the Western limit of the republic should be drawn, and the statue of the fabled god, Terminus, should be raised upon its highest peak, never to be thrown down. In planting the seed of the new power on the coast of the Pacific ocean, it should be well understood that when strong enough to take care of itself, the new Government should separate from the mother Empire as the child separates from the parent at the age of manhood.[1]

But this belief in the probability of an independent Pacific Republic sometime in the future did not weaken the desire to incorporate the whole continental area and make sure of the trade route. Senator Benton shared a widely held opinion that the government should build a military post on either the Columbia or the Strait of Juan de Fuca. The Columbia and Missouri rivers would form a channel of communication between the Pacific and the Mississippi. As Professor Frederick Merk says:

Along this channel would flow the commerce to and from the Orient. Furs from the Oregon Country would flow to China. In return teas, silks, and spices would move to St. Louis. St. Louis would become the Venice of the New World. A modern Tyre would rise at the mouth of the Columbia.[2]

[1] Quoted by Frederick Merk, *Albert Gallatin and the Oregon Problem*, Cambridge Mass., 1950, p. 13.
[2] Ibid., pp. 15–16. Quoted by permission of Harvard University Press.

Speaking of maps and the influence they exert in planting ideas, the maps of the United States published by John Melish of Philadelphia illustrate very nicely the territorial ambitions of the United States. Melish was the official cartographer for the government, and it is by no means unlikely that the boundaries he drew were officially inspired. In 1816, two years before the Anglo-American Convention delimiting the northern boundary at the 49th parallel, Melish published a map which identified the Louisiana Purchase Territory inside a green border extending from the Rio Grande in the southwest to the 52nd parallel in the north. More interesting still is the fact that the whole of the Pacific coast from the 52nd parallel southward to include San Francisco Bay was inside the green border. In 1820 Melish published another edition. This time he corrected his northern border to conform with the treaty, but he kept the Pacific coast (including San Francisco) inside his green border. Under the Convention of 1818, we recall, the Pacific Northwest was left as an open country, the rivalry being too strong to enable the governments to agree on dividing the region between them. Both the British and the Americans wanted the Columbia river, but the Americans wanted as much of the territory to the north of the Columbia as they could get. Adams made a motion to extend the boundary along the 49th parallel to the sea, but the British rejected this because they too were looking at the harbours and ocean frontage that suggested a trade route to China. So the treaty boundary stopped at the Rocky Mountains. But this did not deter Melish from showing Oregon between the 42nd and 49th parallels in solid green colour, thus giving the impression that this country already belonged to the United States. The British, it should be added, were also not backward in taking liberties with maps. The 1818 edition of the Arrowsmith map, published in London, shows New Albion (the historic name given to the Northwest by Sir Francis Drake) as extending along the Pacific coast from Alaska to San Francisco. The data for this map were furnished by Simon Mc-Gillivray, the London agent for the North West Company.[1]

John Quincy Adams made the treaties of 1818 and 1819, but he did not take them seriously. ' The world ', said he in the latter

[1] Original copies of the Melish and Arrowsmith maps are on deposit in the Huntington Library. See also Merk, ' The Ghost River Caledonia in the Oregon Negotiation of 1818 ', *Amer. Hist. Rev.*, LV, 1949–50, pp. 530–51.

year, ' shall be familiarized with the idea of considering our proper dominion to be the continent of North America '. And unlike Jefferson, Adams acted on the assumption that the boundaries of the United States would be stretched accordingly and the entire continent come under a single flag. Adams's great pre-occupation was the Pacific Northwest, where, as I have pointed out, the keenest competition existed. The Russians were an interested party along the coast, but Adams aimed his main shafts at the British in order to warn them away from planting a colony. He asserted:

It is not imaginable that in the present condition of the world, *any* European Nation should entertain the project of settling a *Colony* on the Northwest Coast of America—That the United States should form establishments there with views of absolute territorial right, and inland communication is not only to be expected, but is pointed out by the finger of Nature, and has been for years a subject of serious deliberation in Congress. . . .[1]

Then Adams, who was addressing himself to George Canning through the American minister, Richard Rush, went on to assert that the claims he had got from Spain supported his contention that no other nation might colonize in North America. Great Britain and other nations had only rights of trade. These assertions were made during the summer of 1823, more than six months before Monroe's celebrated doctrine. Moreover, Canning was forewarned that the United States would suit the action to the word by establishing a territorial (i.e., a colonial) government on the banks of the Columbia, a move which could be regarded as a flagrant breach of the treaty. Sure enough, the very next year the Monroe administration, through Representative Floyd of Virginia, prompted a measure in Congress authorizing the establishment of a military post at the mouth of the Columbia and of a territorial (colonial) government that would exercise jurisdiction over the *whole* of the Pacific Northwest, *with no restriction of northern boundary*.[2] The Floyd bill, which passed both houses with large majorities, reminds us of the technique employed by Jefferson in 1804 with reference to the Floridas. Jefferson's Mobile Act gave him Congressional backing whenever he decided the time was ripe to move in on the Spaniard; and Madison, Jeffer-

[1] Adams to Rush, July 22, 1823, Manning, op. cit., II, p. 58.
[2] Merk, *Albert Gallatin*, p. 7. Samuel Flagg Bemis, *John Quincy Adams and the Foundations of American Foreign Policy*, N.Y., 1949, pp. 482–536. The latter book is a mirror of the tense personality and the absolute sense of rectitude so characteristic of J. Q. Adams.

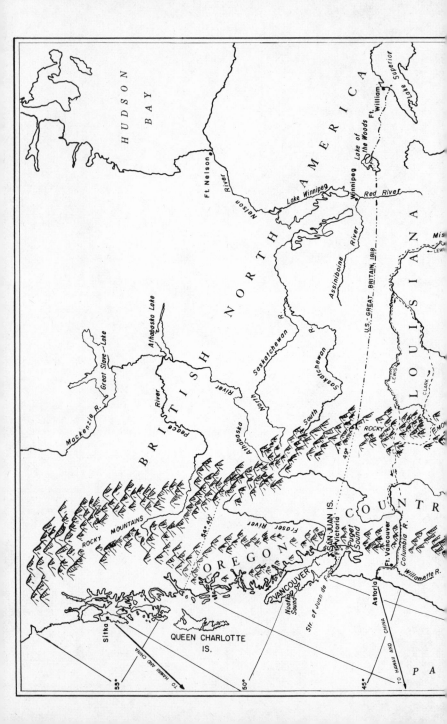

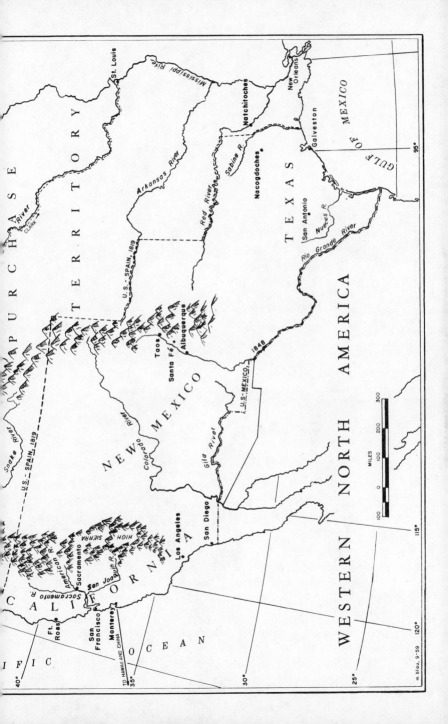

son's successor, chose the right moment in 1812. Monroe and Adams, however, for reasons not too difficult to comprehend, decided on keeping their Congressional stick in the cupboard.

Soon after Monroe had unburdened himself of his famous doctrine, Adams returned to the attack on the diplomatic front in an attempt to bargain the British out of that portion of the Pacific Northwest which was best fitted for settlement. In December 1823, Rush submitted to Canning a proposition for a three-power division of the country. The United States, he reiterated, had an absolute claim to all the territory as far north as the sixtieth parallel; Spain's colonial rights had extended that far, and the United States now possessed these rights. But the American Government would be willing to pledge itself to make no settlements north of the fifty-first, provided Britain would limit herself to a strip of country between the fifty-first and the fifty-fifth, Russia to have all the land beyond the latter line. A partition of Oregon in this manner would give the United States a boundary on a line with the northern extremity of Vancouver Island, with a monopoly over the good harbours and river valleys to the south. Adams chose the fifty-first on the ground that the Columbia river, which was American (so Adams said) by prior right of discovery, traced its source from a point on that line; but it could hardly have escaped his attention that the country north of that line was worthless from the standpoint of colonization. Moreover—and this was probably the important consideration in Adams's mind—Britain's window on the Pacific would be too far north to enable her ever to compete for the trade of Asia.[1]

It is hardly surprising that Canning rejected such an inequitable division. Instead he turned to the Hudson's Bay Company, which had taken over the interests of the Nor' Westers, and urged upon it the wisdom of energetic operations in the region of the Columbia, and the Bay Company found the right man for the job in George Simpson, a young Scot whom it placed in charge of its entire field service from Hudson Bay to the Pacific. Simpson's activities during the ensuing twenty years constitute an epic in the history of the Northwest.[2]   Meanwhile Canning issued a flat denial of Adams's

[1] Richard W. Van Alstyne, ' New Viewpoints in the Relations of Canada and the United States ', *Can. Hist. Rev.*, XXV, 1944, pp. 109–30. Documents in Manning, op. cit.

[2] Frederick Merk, *Fur Trade and Empire*; *Sir George Simpson's Journal*, Cambridge, Mass., 1931.

claims, and told Rush to report that Britain would regard ' as alike open (standing upon the question of right) to her future settlements or colonization, any part of the North American continent . . . on the eastern coast, northern coast, or elsewhere, heretofore undiscovered and unsettled by other powers. . . .[1] Neither Canning nor Adams nor anyone else in Britain or America at the time seems to have had the slightest conception of the potentialities of the small, sparsely populated, and economically retarded Canadian colonies on the banks of the St. Lawrence. But it was those colonies which were to be the ultimate check upon the continentalist ambitions of the United States. Canada has been *the other* colonizing power in North America.

Now in conclusion I am tempted into offering a brief commentary upon the Monroe Doctrine. It is a subject that can hardly be omitted because, taken in context with the diplomacy of the preceding forty years, the Monroe Doctrine is a birthday announcement in behalf of the American Leviathan State. Partly under the prompting of his Secretary of State, President James Monroe assumed certain sweeping positions that have since been recognized as contrary to fact. Those positions were all couched in negative language. They were prohibitions laid on European powers, stating categorically what the latter could not do: (1) they could not colonize the American *continents*; (2) they could not extend their political systems to ' this hemisphere ', an imaginary geographical area which Monroe discreetly refrained from defining; and (3) they could not intervene to put down revolutions that had occurred or that might occur in ' this hemisphere '.

The Monroe Doctrine lowered—or purported to lower—a hypothetical curtain over the American continents, a curtain to stop the passage of political influence and the planting of colonies though not to stop the flow of commerce or of cultural and social intercourse. Its dogmas—all phrased, let us repeat, as ' Thou shalt nots '—were

---

[1] Rush to Adams, Jan. 19, 1824, Manning, op. cit., II, p. 399. The orthodox view, accepted by many historians, is that Adams and Monroe were aiming their words at Russia rather than at Britain. This interpretation probably arises from a disposition to accept literally the words of Monroe's message, which, it is true, refer only to Russia. But presidential messages and other state papers intended for public consumption are not necessarily to be taken at their face value.

For a penetrating criticism of the orthodox interpretation see Merk, *Albert Gallatin*, pp. 26–29. See also Edward H. Tatum, *The United States and Europe, 1815–1823. A Study in Background of the Monroe Doctrine*, Berkeley, Calif., 1936, and Van Alstyne, ' New Viewpoints ', op. cit.

assimilated into the catechism of American nationalism. The Monroe Doctrine is a set of neat formulas expressive of the inherited national opposition and resentment toward Europe. But it is not these negatives that really count; it is the hidden positives to the effect that the United States shall be the only colonizing power and the sole directing power in both North and South America. This is imperialism preached in the grand manner, for the only restrictions placed upon the directing power are those which it imposes upon itself. The Monroe Doctrine is really an official declaration fencing in the ' western hemisphere ' as a United States sphere of influence.[1]

That these things were beyond the strength of the United States in 1823 does not gainsay the point. Adams made no headway against Britain in his notions of pre-emptive right over North America. And it is one of the great ironies of history that, while he was trying to aggrandize the United States in the Northwest at her expense, he was gambling on her protection against the intervention of the continental powers in Latin America. Had she chosen to join France, he himself confessed that the United States would be helpless. But Adams considered the gamble a safe one, and he was right. It would be difficult to find a cooler head than his in the play of international politics. The Monroe Doctrine did not gain anything tangible for the United States; it even brought a rebuff, though Adams managed to conceal the fact. What he and Monroe wanted to say, and they did say, was that the United States was now a great power and as such it would determine the destinies of the ' western hemisphere '. Their assertion was not strictly true, yet it was true enough to justify itself. It was a first-rate expression of the statecraft of a rising imperial republic.

[1] Arthur P. Whitaker, *The United States and the Independence of Latin America, 1800-1830*, Baltimore, 1940, is a careful, documented study of the Latin American phase of the Monroe Doctrine.

CHAPTER V

MANIFEST DESTINY AND EMPIRE, 1820–1870

' No Seat of Empire so Magnificent as This '

SIR JOHN R. SEELEY'S celebrated aphorism of some seventy-five years ago that the British Empire was built during a state of absence of mind applies equally well—and equally ill—to the American empire. In fact, a comparison between the two reveals remarkable similarities. Both empires were the creatures of natural forces—of emigration and colonization, of commerce and religion, and of the desire to extend political influence. But in neither case was expansion unintentional, unplanned or ' absent-minded '. Each empire followed a strategic pattern, and the history of each shows the influence of much conscious planning and direction. The concept of an American empire and the main outlines of its future growth were complete by 1800. Nor is it to be assumed that, while the expansion of England in the nineteenth century lay overseas, the expansion of the United States during the same century was strictly continental and the result of a simple emigrating movement westward by land. Actually American expansion, like British, was global. As a coastal country of the eighteenth century, the United States looked seaward as well as landward, and the paths of its growing empire in the nineteenth century stretched out to sea as well as across the continent. The United States was a commercial and seafaring state, as well as an agrarian state; and its mercantile and seafaring population was busily active in extending and developing long-distance sea routes even while the physical handicaps to transcontinental migration remained unsolved. In the next chapter we shall view the rising American empire in the Pacific Ocean, an empire that was correlative in point of time to the expanding empire on the continent. The present chapter will concentrate upon the continental growth of the United States.

There is a highly conventionalized picture of the United States advancing in a single direction westward, the frontier being pushed back mile by mile from east to west until 1890, when it is said to have been extinguished. But this picture of ' the westward movement ' as a methodical advance from coast to coast is fictitious—a simplified version of the famous frontier hypothesis of Frederick Jackson Turner, who romanticized the American West as the mother of political democracy.[1] From the Mississippi heartland there was an advance south-westward into Texas; there was an advance north-westward into the Columbia river country, then another due west to California; and finally a fourth prong northward by way of the Red River in the direction of the Canadian prairies. Jefferson and Adams, it will be remembered, coveted control of the two corners of the continent—Texas in the southwest, Oregon in the northwest. With these areas under American domination, the remaining portions of the continent could be absorbed at leisure.

We recall how Adams in 1823–24 tried to press home his advantage against the British in the Northwest: he wanted them to hand over all the habitable portion of that country. In the treaty of 1819 with Spain he had consented to the Sabine as the boundary in the southwest, reluctantly as for himself but much to the disgust and violent opposition of such men as Henry Clay and Thomas Hart Benton. Benton denounced what he called the ' mutilation ' of the Mississippi valley, while Clay declared that Adams had actually given away United States territory. Both men, of course, were reflecting Jefferson's notion that the Rio Grande was the boundary of the Louisiana Purchase territory. Jefferson got his idea from the French, but it could not have escaped him or his successors that this boundary would put several key Mexican posts, notably San Antonio, Albuquerque and Santa Fé inside the United States. Adams and Monroe managed to evade the Mexican request to mark the boundary according to the treaty; and no sooner was Adams president in 1824 than he began putting pressure on Mexico in the hope of persuading her to rectify the frontier. Any of the Texan rivers west of the Sabine —the Brazos, the Colorado, the Nueces—was preferable to the Sabine, though the Rio Grande was the one desired. Mexico could have a million dollars for this rectification, if she wished, but having inherited Spanish fears of American ambitions, she turned all the

---

[1] The Turner thesis, which for many years exerted a spell-binding influence over American historical writing, has been the subject of trenchant criticism in recent times. In so far as it adumbrates the American frontier as unique, it is an expression of parochial nationalism. For an example of good criticism of this thesis see Paul F. Sharp, ' Three Frontiers: Some Comparative Studies of Canadian, American, and Australian Settlement ', *Pac. Hist. Rev.*, XXIV, 1955, pp. 369–78.

offers down. At last in 1828 the treaty boundary was marked, but this event seemed only to excite the American feeling that it should be moved to the Rio Grande. Senator Benton again asserted that ' the laws of God and nature ' had intended this river for the United States, and that the nation had been ' despoiled ' of its rightful inheritance; and Andrew Jackson, the new President, was willing to raise the original bid to five millions.

Linked with this programme of buying strategic real estate went an effort on the part of Adams's representative in Mexico City, Joel R. Poinsett, to establish an ascendancy over the Mexicans and extend American political influence in Latin America.[1] Poinsett's diplomacy constituted the first act in the long ideological battle to wean Latin America from Europe. But his successor at the Mexico City legation, Colonel Anthony Butler, had his sights set on more immediate objectives. Having a personal stake in Texan lands, Butler proposed to secure the prize by giving ' presents ' to the right people in Mexico or by taking a chattel mortgage on Texas, to be ' fore-closed ' when the expected Mexican default occurred. Jackson rejected the second proposal, but turned a blind eye to any success that Butler might have in using ' influence ' on Mexican politicians. Butler learned better from experience, however, and after his career as a diplomat was over ruefully confessed his ignorance.[2]

Meanwhile the Mexicans, in the hope of erecting a buffer community on the waste lands of Texas that would keep the United States at a distance, accepted an offer from Moses Austin, a Connecticut Yankee, to bring in settlers. Austin's son Stephen took over shortly after his father's death, and was given a free hand and the authority to distribute land without charge, the only restrictions being that the settlers were to take the oath of allegiance to Mexico and that Roman Catholicism was to be the religion of the colony. The Mexicans appear to have hoped that the new colony would draw upon the Louisiana French and Spanish and thus constitute a true Latin barrier against American encroachment, but they did not make this a condition. Actually the people who responded to this unusual opportunity to acquire free lands, at a time when public land in the United States had to be purchased, were Protestant American families

---

[1] J. Fred Rippy, *Rivalry of the United States and Great Britain over Latin America (1808–1830)*, Baltimore, 1929, pp. 254–302.

[2] Eugene C. Barker, *Mexico and the United States, 1821–1825*, Dallas, Tex., 1928, pp. 32–47.

who made the easy trip across the plains from Missouri or by boat from New Orleans to Galveston.

There was no conspiracy here, or even an interest on the part of Austin and the other *empresarios*, to whom the Mexicans made liberal grants, in wrenching the country away from Mexico. But the Mexicans grew dismayed over the steady flow of American immigrants, which in their minds was linked with the known ambitions of the American Government, and in 1830 they made a futile gesture at closing the door to further immigration. Even so, had they been foreseeing in meeting the wishes of the Texans for political autonomy, they might have staved off a revolution; but an invasion and massacre by the dictator, Santa Anna, aroused armed resistance which finished in 1836 with an independent Texan republic. During the war the Texans appealed widely and successfully throughout the United States for men and funds, promising land in return for services; and this started a fresh flow of immigration that boosted the Texan population to a hundred thousand by 1845, more than three times the reputed number at the time of the revolution.

Texas in its early stage is a good illustration of the Jeffersonian pattern of expansion. It was a colony of Americans, planted on vacant though alien soil, that emerged into a free and independent republic. Nor should its subsequent annexation to the United States in 1845 be regarded as an easily accomplished fact. Texas applied for admission to the American Union in 1837, but the application did not get past the executive branch of the government and it did not meet with a spontaneous desire for annexation on the part of the American public. On the contrary, the issue aroused bitter opposition from the New England abolitionists, who began to see annexation as a conspiracy of slave holders. John Quincy Adams, once so determined to get Texas, now reversed himself. John Tyler of Virginia, a President who needed an issue on which to campaign for re-election, deliberately injected annexation into American politics in 1843, and the question immediately became hotly controversial. When John C. Calhoun, the Secretary of State, signed a treaty with Texas and let it be known that annexation was desirable as a protection for slavery, the Northern states took alarm and the treaty was smothered in the Senate. Mr. Fox, the British minister, judged that sectional divisions were now so great that annexation would create an irresistible impulse throughout the North to attempt an invasion of Canada and the other British provinces as a means of redressing the balance between the slave and the free states.[1] The pro-annexationists, some of whom like Senator Robert J. Walker of Mississippi had speculated heavily in Texas real estate, managed to influence public opinion in both North and South to the point where, on March 1, 1845, sufficient votes were mustered in Congress to authorize admission to the Union. There was a small margin of votes in each house in favour of annexation: in the House of Representatives, 22; in the Senate, only two.

As for Texas itself, many of the leaders developed ambitions of their own and showed little interest in annexation. The Lone Star Republic kept up a running war with Mexico, claiming the Rio Grande as its boundary and seeking to annex the neighbouring province of New Mexico. The latter had the advantage of a rich trade that used the Santa Fé trail leading westward from the American river port of St. Louis. Furs from the Rocky Mountains and precious metals from the mines of Mexico passed over this trail going east in exchange for merchandise imported from Europe going west. By capturing the town of Santa Fé and connecting it by a road with the Texan port of Galveston, the Texans could divert this trade for their own advantage and make themselves the dominant power in the interior of the continent. They could then hope to expand westward and subjugate California, thus acquiring a frontage on two oceans, and their success would attract settlers from the United States and from Europe. There were even dreams of inducing the Southern states to secede from the Union. Between 1841 and 1843 Texas made three attempts on Santa Fé, but each one met with failure. Nevertheless, President Sam Houston still professed to believe that, once Texas got the necessary population, she could control all the country between the Columbia river and the Gulf of Mexico. Said he in his farewell message in December 1844: ' If we remain an independent nation, our territory will be extensive—unlimited. The Pacific alone will bound the mighty march of our race and our empire '.[2]

Pro-annexationists in the United States used the threat of Texas conquering California, including San Francisco Bay, to work up fears among the New England merchants who coveted California

[1] Fox to Aberdeen, March 8, 1843. F. O. 5/391. I am indebted for this note to Professor John S. Galbraith of the University of California.
[2] Quoted in W. C. Binkley, *The Expansionist Movement in Texas, 1836–1850*, Berkeley, Calif., 1925, p. 121.

for themselves. But in spite of their tall talk, the Texans were not very sure of their own ability to maintain their independence. They needed outside support, and the choice lay between Great Britain and the United States. A treaty with the former required concessions in the matter of slavery, which the Texans were not prepared to make. Furthermore, the British showed no desire to support Texan territorial ambitions. Even so, when Captain Charles Elliott, the British chargé d'affaires, at last secured *de jure* recognition from Mexico in a treaty which he brought back to Texas in May 1845, the new president, Anson Jones, favoured its acceptance and the independence that it promised rather than annexation to the United States. In the meantime the American Government had been sending agents into the country to secure popular support for annexation. Just how these emissaries operated is none too clear. They did, however, give the Texans the idea that the American Government under Polk would underwrite their claims to the Rio Grande, and this may have clinched the matter. In July 1845, a popularly elected convention voted Texas into the American Union.[1]

Texan nationalist ambitions for conquest on the Pacific coast apparently jarred the hard-headed merchant princes of the Eastern seaboard. At best these folk were tolerantly indifferent toward Texas, whether independent or incorporated as a state. But any activity or rumour of activity that involved the Pacific coast, particularly San Francisco Bay and the coast to the south, touched them to the quick. Let me emphasize at this point that the American drive for possession of the Pacific coast did not originate in the interior and that, until the approach of the years of climax, the push of emigrants westward was hardly felt on the farther side of the Cascades and the Sierra. Into Oregon the overland trek of farming families from the Middle West did not commence until 1838. It took a depression and a fall in farm values in the United States to get an emigration movement started, and even after that Texas continued to attract many more thousands of settlers than Oregon. Not only was Texas relatively near and easy of access and Oregon difficult and remote, but speculators and jobbers selling scrip for Texan lands furnished an artificial stimulus altogether lacking in Oregon. The year 1844 witnessed an outburst of speculation in Texan lands, and the population of that state reached 100,000

[1] For an extended list of references on the annexation of Texas see the bibliography in my *Amer. Dipl. in Action*, Stanford, 1947, pp. 797-8.

at the time of annexation. By comparison Oregon had only 7,000 Americans, all of whom lived south of the Columbia in the narrow valleys of the Willamette and Walla Walla. As for California, the arduous overland journey across the desert and over the dangerous passes of the High Sierra was reserved for hardy mountain men, explorers and trappers. It was not until 1841 that the first small emigrant party managed to make its way by land to California.

The truth is that the Pacific coast belonged to the commercial empire that the United States was already building in that ocean. With Yankee merchants off the Columbia in the 1790s, their ships roaming the entire coast from Mazatlán in Mexico to Sitka in Alaska in search of the sea otter, the demand for control of its ports and harbours came from the seaboard towns and cities of New England, New York, Pennsylvania and Maryland. The ruthless hunt for sea otter so thinned out the herds by the 1820s as to affect the profits of the business; but interest shifted to the hide trade of California during that decade, and for another twenty years the New England merchant aristocracy flourished on the sale of California hides, bought from the Spanish missions and rancheros, to the boot and shoe manufacturers of Massachusetts. Thus the Boston house of Bryant & Sturgis, which pioneered in the sea otter trade and opened a business in Macao, the Portuguese concession in China, began in the 'twenties to shift its interests away from furs to hides. In 1829 it established itself in Santa Barbara, moving northward a few years later to Monterey. Three of the men who were later prominent in stirring popular interest in California were employed by this firm: Alfred Robinson, who published a widely read book on California in 1845, T. O. Larkin, who came to Monterey in 1832 and later was appointed the first United States consul, and Richard Henry Dana, whose fascinating account of the voyage round the Horn and of the hide trade survives as literature to this day.

These interests were so strong as to develop a sense of ownership over the Pacific coast long in advance of the event. We remember the haughty attitude assumed by John Quincy Adams in 1819 and the deliberate inclusion of the Pacific coast in United States territory as pictured on the maps of John Melish. In 1829 the Navy Department, proposing to make an examination of harbours on the Pacific coast, made the slip, perhaps intentional, of describing them as already *belonging* to the United States. And in 1838, in handing the explorer, Lieutenant Charles Wilkes, his instructions, the Secretary of the Navy again called attention to ' the territory of the United States on the seaboard '.

British and French interest in the Pacific coast was stimulated at this time by travellers, explorers and naval officers, all of whom disliked what they saw of American encroachment and pondered how it might be checked. Their fears at the prospect of seeing San Francisco slip under American control because of the effect it would have upon the trade of the Pacific was echoed in the British and French press. A British naval officer when he entered San Francisco Bay in 1845 stormed ' D—n it! is there nothing but Yankees here?' And *The Times* (London) commented sourly, after watching the annexation of Texas, that Americans conquer provinces ' as the cuckoo steals a nest '. The *Journal des Debats* (Paris) perhaps unconsciously reiterated an idea already thrown out by de Tocqueville regarding the distant future. It said:

> Between the autocracy of Russia on the East, and the democracy of America on the West, Europe may find herself more compressed than she may one day think consistent with her independence and dignity.[1]

Preliminary moves by the American Government to get control of California were started in 1842 by Daniel Webster, whose Massachusetts background identified him with the outlook of the seaboard merchants. Webster's plan necessitated a secret agreement with the British Government, whereby the latter would use its influence in Mexico City in return for a settlement of the perennial Oregon question. To Great Britain would go all of the country north of the Columbia river, a concession that would meet British wishes in full. The British Government would then support the United States in levying a demand upon Mexico to cede her portion of the Pacific coast north of the 36th parallel. By this transaction the United States would have the window on the Pacific that the merchants considered vital to their interests: the section which included Monterey and San Francisco. Webster outlined his ideas to Lord Ashburton, who had come to Washington on a special mission to pacify the Americans on a number of contentious questions, chief among which was the

---

[1] The quotations in this paragraph are borrowed from Norman A. Graebner, *Empire on the Pacific. A Study in American Continental Expansion*, N.Y., 1955, pp. 79–80.

matter of the Northeast boundary. Ashburton favoured the plan at least in principle and apparently encouraged Webster to institute a special return mission on his own part to England to arrange matters. President Tyler favoured the plan too and, according to Mr. Fox, in February 1843 got to the point of drafting a request to Congress for an appropriation to finance Webster's mission. Clearly, if Webster had his way, Mexico would be called upon to make the chief sacrifice, and the devising of a scheme to bring this about seems to have been the practical purpose of his proposed mission.[1]

The plan came to an abrupt end, however, because the Oregon question suddenly erupted into politics and Tyler, not to be caught napping by his Democratic opponents, publicly assumed a pose in December 1843 that was quite different from the policy that he had secretly advocated. Ignoring San Francisco, Tyler had the temerity to say that ' after the most rigid and . . . unbiased examinations of the subject ' he was convinced that the United States was entitled to the *whole* of Oregon. An assembly of Democratic Party politicians, in quest of an issue on which they could unseat the Whig administration, had already declared that ' the rumoured negotiation for a surrender of any part of Oregon for an equivalent in California was *dangerous to peace and a repudiation of Monroe's doctrine* that the American continents are closed to European colonization. . . .'

Even though it came to nothing, Webster's intended excursion into the realm of secret diplomacy deserves a reflection or two. Any deal with the British Government would have involved an agreement over Texas, whose independence Lord Aberdeen, the British Foreign Secretary, was anxious to secure. This, we have reason to believe, would have satisfied Daniel Webster, who was bitterly disappointed at the turn things had taken. Tyler, he told Fox, was ' a man whose conduct is governed by no intelligible motive or principle'. Commenting in March 1845 on the annexation of Texas, which had just been approved by Congress, he informed his son that in his opinion the port of San Francisco was ' twenty times more valuable . . . than all of Texas '.[2] Webster's ideas found an echo in T. O. Larkin, the consul at Monterey, who wrote the influential New York *Journal of Commerce* to say that ' If the Oregon dispute con-

[1] Fox to Aberdeen, Feb. 24, March 4 and 8, 1843. F.O. 5/391. Courtesy of Prof. Galbraith.

[2] Webster to Fletcher Webster, March 11, 1845. *The Private Correspondence of Daniel Webster*, Fletcher Webster, ed., Boston, 1857, II, p. 204.

tinues, let England take eight degrees north of the Columbia, and purchase eight degrees south of forty-two from Mexico, and exchange '. And the *Journal* agreed that California was the real objective and that a boundary at the Columbia would be satisfactory.[1]

The Democrats, however, opportunistically revived the no-colonization formula of Adams and Monroe and, the better to promote their cause, talked about the ' re-occupation of Oregon ' and the ' re-annexation of Texas ' in one breath. This was the equivalent of what the British minister in 1843 had predicted would happen: Southern agitation for Texas would induce an irresistible impulse throughout the northern and eastern states to seek compensation beyond their borders, and a collision with Britain would be the result. Indirectly the American move into Oregon threatened the security of Canada and the other British colonies to the north, especially since it paralleled the contemporary ill-feeling over the boundary in the northeast. Delayed as it was, and modest in numbers by comparison, the immigration to the valley of the Willamette was nevertheless an extension of the United States in a way that the colonization of Texas was not. The immigrants remained self-conscious Americans whose local leaders, notably the Methodist missionaries, were imbued with national feeling and were able, through their church ties at home, to keep Oregon before the American public. Unlike the Texans, therefore, the Oregonians developed no national feeling of their own. They made no move to found an independent republic. On the contrary, finding themselves face to face with the Hudson's Bay Company, whose interests collided with theirs, they felt confident that their democratic homeland would have no trouble in ousting this alien monopoly.[2]

Naturally the agitation at home encouraged this belief, and from the start the settlers behaved as though the country belonged to them and the United States. Senator Linn of Missouri had made the demand in 1839 that a territorial government be erected for all of Oregon, and had expressed himself ready to go to war for it. Daniel Webster's secret attempt to partition the country at the Columbia evidently leaked and gave the Democratic politicians their chance. At the

---

[1] Quoted by Norman A. Graebner, ' Maritime Factors in the Oregon Compromise ', *Pac. Hist. Rev.*, XX, 1950–51, pp. 331–45.

[2] For a full account of the Hudson's Bay Company in the Pacific Northwest and its relation with the British Government, see John S. Galbraith, *The Hudson's Bay Company as an Imperial Factor, 1821–1869*, Berkeley, Calif., 1957, pp. 135–251.

party convention in 1844 George Bancroft, a delegate from Massachusetts (he was also an historian), helped write a platform that contained ' a strong Texas, and still stronger Oregon, resolution'. ' Oregon ' might mean all or only a part of the Pacific Northwest: if all, it embraced the entire coast from 42° North to 54° 40'; if a part, it referred to the country between the 42nd and the 49th parallels. Four times previously the American Government had offered to divide the country at the latter line. But when such men as Bancroft declared that ' Oregon shall ever be American soil ', they were giving the impression that they meant ' all '.

A Whig editor who diagnosed this new issue as a ' fever ', declared that Oregon had been ' wrapped round ' Texas ' just as the nurse disguises a nauseous dose in honey to cheat the palate of a rebellious patient '. The ' Oregon fever ' became dangerously high, however, only after the Democrats had won the election and their candidate, James K. Polk of Tennessee, was safely installed in the White House. The ' ultra friends of Oregon ', led by Senator Hannegan of Indiana, then became exercised lest the President yield to the spirit of compromise; and they began a wordy battle in the Senate out of which came the slogan ' Fifty-four Forty or fight '.[1]

By implication Polk, like Bancroft, was linked with the ultras. In his inaugural address he reiterated the campaign language that ' our title to the country of the Oregon is " clear and unquestionable " ' and he made no public attempt at correction when the adjective ' whole ' was interpolated in the ambiguity. Nevertheless, he and his cabinet soon decided in favour of a retreat; and so early in May 1845 the President directed George Bancroft, who was now acting Secretary of War, to make a secret approach to Martin Van Buren, the ex-President who, though a Democrat, had dissociated himself from the ultras. Bancroft wrote a long, urgent letter to Van Buren pressing upon him the post of Minister to the Court of St. James's on the ground that Van Buren's standing as an ex-President and his reputation for dignity and moderation would serve to temper the indignation that had been aroused in Britain.[2] Of course too the

---

[1] Edwin A. Miles, ' " Fifty-Four Forty or Fight "—an American Political Legend ', *Miss. Valley Hist. Rev.*, XLIV, 1957, pp. 291–309. Mr. Miles has effectively demolished the legend, colourfully embellished by various text writers, that this slogan dominated the election campaign of 1844.

[2] Bancroft to Van Buren, May 5, 1845; Van Buren to Bancroft, May 12, 1845. The Papers of George Bancroft in Library of the Mass. Hist. Soc., Boston, Mass.

appointment would be a signal to public opinion at home. But Van Buren wrote an elaborate refusal; and so in July the Secretary of State, James Buchanan, offered a compromise to the British minister, Richard Pakenham, on the basis of the 49th parallel. Pakenham's refusal even to transmit the proposal to the Foreign Office has sometimes been blamed for the deadlock that continued for almost a year. But this hardly seems a convincing apology for Polk's intransigence —the President withdrew his offer and then, having been informed by his own representative in London, Louis McLane, that the British Government was prepared to accept a compromise, mendaciously informed Congress that such was not the fact. It seems more likely that Polk was playing a very cautious game with his senatorial allies, the ' Fifty-four Forties ', biding his time while the latter gradually lost ground with the public.

Two separate factors must be kept in mind as we discuss this protracted controversy over Oregon: First, the substantial question at issue was the question of the ports. On the American side the one-time importance attached to the Columbia river had been largely discounted, interest having shifted southward to California. James Buchanan's change of attitude is a good case in point. As a partisan Democrat, Buchanan was a ' Fifty-four Forty ' man during the campaign; but once in office as Secretary of State, Buchanan reversed himself and worked persistently thereafter for a compromise with Britain. Part of this change in attitude was due to the sobering effects of office; but part was due also to Buchanan's interest in the Mexican province to the south. The problem of annexing California was henceforth one of the Secretary of State's chief preoccupations.[1]

To the maritime interests of the Atlantic seaboard the cry for ' Fifty-four Forty ' was an unwelcome red herring, although there was a division of opinion on whether to leave everything north of the Columbia to Great Britain or whether to stand firm for a partition of Oregon at the 49th parallel. William Sturgis, the influential Boston merchant, counted himself among the latter and decided to take a hand in the controversy during its early stages. Sturgis was personally familiar with the Northwest coast and with the handicap to navigation offered by the bar at the mouth of the Columbia, but he appreciated the potential importance of Puget Sound and the Strait

---

[1] *The Works of James Buchanan*, John Bassett Moore, ed., 12 vols., Phila., 1908–11, VI, pp. 275–8.

of Juan de Fuca to the north. In a lecture delivered in Boston in January 1845 he publicly condemned American territorial ambitions, fortifying his argument by citing Jefferson on the probability of an independent Pacific republic. Sturgis declared:

The people of this country are both covetous and ambitious in regard to territory. They covet and are ready to grasp at all that lies upon their borders, and are ambitious of extending their empire from sea to sea—from the shores of the Atlantic to the borders of the Pacific. . . .

There can be little doubt that the country in question will be settled at no distant day—probably by the Anglo-Saxon race—and we may find it expedient for a time to extend over a portion of these settlers our protection and our laws; but . . . The Rocky Mountains, and the dreary deserts on either side, form a natural barrier between different nations, rather than a connecting link between parts of the same nations; and I care not how soon they form the boundary between the United States, *as they now are*, and an independent nation, comprising the *whole* of what is now called the ' Territory of Oregon '. . . .[1]

Sturgis's lecture attracted the attention of Lord Ashburton in England, who wrote to express his agreement with the idea of an independent Pacific republic. ' I have personally a high opinion of the future destinies of that portion of the coast of the Pacific ', said Ashburton. ' The Northern Pacific Ocean, and in the course of time probably the Eastern shores of Asia will find their masters in the country North of California '.[2] But James Kirke Paulding of New York, a former Secretary of the Navy under Van Buren, regarded the Northwest as the base for a vast American empire. A crisis was rapidly approaching, wrote Paulding to Bancroft, ' the issue of which is to decide whether the United States or England is to be the dominant power of the New World '. The discovery of the New World was destined to change the commercial relations of the whole world ' and establish a new balance of power, provided we are betimes sensible to the vast advantages of our position, and have spirit and firmness to maintain it. If we do this, nothing is more certain than that we shall succeed to the abdicated diadem of Europe . . . ' At the next meeting of Congress, Paulding declared:

[1] William Sturgis, *The Oregon Question*, Boston, 1845.
[2] Ashburton to Sturgis, April 2, 1845. Sturgis forwarded this letter to Bancroft. Bancroft Papers.

I shall attempt to demonstrate that the New World is entirely independent of the Old, and most especially of Europe; and that causes are in perpetual operation . . . which must inevitably transfer the seat of Empire to the West; and that though it may be delayed by a feeble and pusillanimous policy on the part of the United States, it will come as sure as fate. The subject is so grand, that my only discouragement from making the attempt is the consciousness of being unable to do it justice. . . .[1]

Meanwhile Sturgis had determined to take advantage of his personal friendships in both Britain and America and play the role of an intermediary between the two governments. His own idea of an adjustment was the 49th parallel to the Gulf of Georgia, thence dipping south to extend through the middle of the Strait of Juan de Fuca to the sea; and he learned from his friend Joshua Bates, a Boston banker living in London as a partner in the House of Baring, that Lord Aberdeen was agreeable to this too, provided that both banks of the Fraser river were north of the 49th parallel.[2] Sturgis passed this information along to his friend George Bancroft in Washington, in a letter marked *Private & Confidential* and dated May 25, 1845. The date is important because it establishes that the Polk cabinet knew, more than six weeks in advance of the time when Buchanan made his first overture to the British minister, Pakenham, that the British Government would compromise. Bancroft's reply, dated June 2, is likewise important because it showed the Secretary of the Navy prepared to recommend the proposed compromise to the President. The Fraser river, he acknowledged, was a few miles north of 49°. Sturgis looked to a speedy settlement, and so did Bancroft. With Texas annexed, it was thought, there would be no difficulty about Oregon, ' but had Texas rejected our offer it would (& with good reason) have been ascribed to British influence, & war with G. Britain upon the Oregon dispute would have been almost certain. . . .'[3]

But a sign from London of willingness to compromise did not come, as Sturgis and Bancroft expected, and Sturgis through his correspondent Joshua Bates partly understood the reason. Aberdeen was having difficulties, partly because of the false value put on the Columbia river by many persons, including Lord John Russell, the

---

[1] Paulding to Bancroft, June 14, 1845. But Paulding favoured a peaceful adjustment.

[2] Sturgis to Bancroft, May 25, 1845. Ibid.

[3] Ibid., July 16, 1845.

leader of the Opposition, and partly because of the resentment toward the belligerent tone of President Polk and the 'Fifty-four Forties'. To disillusion the British public of the belief in the Columbia river as a great artery of inland commerce, Aberdeen encouraged the economist, Nassau Senior, to publish articles in the London *Examiner* and the *Edinburgh Review*. Senior agreed with Sturgis on the boundary, and his information in fact came from Sturgis, probably through Joshua Bates.[1] In the meantime, the Hudson's Bay Company which, under Sir George Simpson's management, had made some effort to colonize the country north of the Columbia, had long recognized the impracticability of Canning's dream of the Columbia as an artery for the trade of Asia. But anxious to put more stress on the coastal trade, the Company in 1845 opened its new Fort Victoria on Vancouver Island; and this gave the impression that it too had lost interest in the Columbia.[2] This move, plus the articles inspired by Lord Aberdeen in favour of the 49th, convinced the British public of the comparative worthlessness of the Columbia river.[3]

But the second factor in this controversy was a difficult hurdle to surmount, and it was the one that accounted for the long delay. It was the emotional element that had dominated the stage in American domestic politics since 1843 and that had been kept alive, or at least not discouraged, by the mendacious President Polk. William Sturgis, restless over the long delay, wanted the boundary question submitted to himself and Lord Ashburton for arbitration,[4] but the politics of the question made so sane a move as this impossible. Edward Everett of Boston, who had represented the Tyler administration at the Court of St. James's, wrote to Bancroft in February 1846 to say that the Peel ministry would gladly accept the compromise if it could be done on its merits. But it was not the terms, but the manner that had for a whole year prevented a settlement. 'What could the President & his Cabinet do to preserve peace', he asked, 'if every arrival from England brought from Parliament the Counterpart of the Resolutions, Reports, Speeches which are daily appearing in the

[1] Ibid., Aug. 6, 1845.
[2] W. Kaye Lamb, 'The Founding of Fort Victoria', *Brit. Col. Hist. Quart.*, VII, 1943, pp. 71–92; Galbraith, op. cit., pp. 222–4, 242.
[3] F. Merk, 'British Government Propaganda and the Oregon Treaty', *Amer. Hist. Rev.*, XL, 1934–5, pp. 38–62.
[4] Sturgis to Bancroft, Jan. 20, 1846. Bancroft Papers.

two houses of Congress, from the known friends & representatives of the Adm.?'[1] And Joshua Bates wrote to the Barings' agent in Boston, Thomas Ward, to give his opinion that the British Government had made a great mistake to keep so quiet. 'I think', he added, ' if they had sent a fleet to the Pacific it would have been settled before now. As it is we shall find the Western members will be more extravagant than ever and there is no calculating what they will do '.[2]

As a matter of fact, the Peel ministry decided upon just such a step as this. By making a show of force it intended to make it clear in the United States that it would not retreat north of 49°. On February 3 Louis McLane, the American minister, reported that Lord Aberdeen had informed him that, if necessary to guard against the contingency of war with the United States, preparations would not only be made for defending the Canadas, but also for offensive operations. Included in the latter was ' the immediate equipment of thirty sail of the line besides steamers and other vessels of war. . . .'[3] The receipt of this report prompted Polk to call a cabinet meeting, as a result of which secret instructions were dispatched to McLane to the effect that, if Lord Aberdeen would propose the 49th parallel, the offer would be sent for advice to the Senate.[4] Apparently the President reached the conclusion that he had been bluffing long enough. Nevertheless, he maintained a poker face in public and, when questioned, refused to assume any responsibility. He was afraid of the ' Fifty-four Forties ' in the Senate, to whom he owed his nomination in 1844.[5]

In the meantime Lord Aberdeen refrained from proposing a compromise, as Polk had suggested, until he could be reasonably sure that the offer would be accepted. Since the President would give no leadership, the only recourse was to watch the shifting currents in the Senate. There the debate dragged on over the question raised by Polk of serving notice on the British Government that the joint occupation arrangement would be terminated, as stipulated by treaty, at the end of one year. In this debate the extremists fought hard in defence of their demands, but were gradually crowded into a minority

---

[1] Everett to Bancroft, Feb. 2, 1846. Ibid.
[2] Bates to Ward, Feb. 1, 1846. Thomas W. Ward Papers in Library of Mass. Hist. Soc.
[3] Miller, *Treaties*, V, 57–9. McLane's report was published for the first time in 1937.
[4] Wilbur D. Jones and J. Chal Vinson, ' British Preparedness and the Oregon Settlement ', *Pac. Hist. Rev.*, XXII, 1952–3, pp. 353–64.
[5] Graebner, *Empire on the Pacific*, pp. 143–4.

by a coalition of conservative Northern and Southern Democrats and Whigs. As the *New York Herald* put it: ' The chivalry of the West goes hot and strong for 54–40, while the ardent South, and the calculating East, coalesce, for once, on this point, and quietly and temperately call for 49.'[1]

Thus indirectly the British Government learned that its compromise offer would be accepted. On June 6 the President got the offer in the form of a draft treaty; on June 10 he asked the Senate for advice; on June 12 that body gave its advice; and on June 15 the President signed the treaty, containing substantially the terms that Aberdeen had first proposed in March 1844. Daniel Webster's ironical description of the poker game that the President had been playing sums up the matter well:

> Now, Gentlemen, the remarkable characteristic of the settlement of this Oregon question by treaty is this. In the general operation of the government, treaties are negotiated by the President and ratified by the Senate; but here is the reverse,—here is a treaty negotiated by the Senate, and only agreed to by the President.[2]

The immediate crisis was now over, but victory had gone to the Americans and, it appeared, this was just a beginning. John Quincy Adams's ' law of nature ' was at this point transmuted into ' manifest destiny '—a phrase upon which an Irish-born editor of New York City elaborated in an article which he published in the midst of the Oregon crisis. Declared John L. O'Sullivan in the *Democratic Review*:

> There is a great deal of Annexation yet to take place, within the life of the present generation, along the whole line of our northern border. . . . Whatever progress of population there may be in the British Canadas, is only for their own early severance of their present colonial relation to the little island three thousand miles across the Atlantic; soon to be followed by Annexation, and destined to swell the still accumulating momentum of our progress.[3]

Earl Grey, the British Colonial Secretary, expressed much the same thought from a different point of view at about the same time,

---

[1] Quoted in ibid., p. 137.   [2] Miller, *Treaties*, V, p. 89.
[3] This article, entitled 'Annexation', is reprinted in part in Louis M. Hacker, *The Shaping of the American Tradition*, N.Y., 1947, pp. 563–8. O'Sullivan develops a theory of the natural law of growth, thereby anticipating the social Darwinists, and, despite some flamboyancy of style, writes lucidly and with conviction.

though his mind was fastened on a specific problem—the immediate future of Vancouver Island. Before the House of Lords Grey declared in 1847:

> It is obvious, when an eligible territory is left to be waste, unsubdued to the use of man, [that] it is impossible to prevent persons from taking irregular possession of the land. We have found it impossible in all our dominions to restrain such persons. The government of the United States will be equally unable to prevent such an occurrence, and unless the island is regularly settled and regularly colonized, it is quite certain that it will be irregularly colonized by squatters.[1]

Grey was in this speech re-living the experience of the Hudson's Bay Company, to whom the British Government had entrusted the task of holding the Northwest as far south as the Columbia; and his speech was inspired by warnings from the Company that American penetration beyond the treaty line would sooner or later force a repetition of the Oregon episode. Thus for the first time the British —and the Canadians too, as we shall see—were compelled to take seriously the formula for continental empire Adams and Monroe had propounded in 1823. Irregular colonization by squatters was in fact the established rule in American society.

Two American fingers, V-shaped, pointed north: one extended up the coast to hook in Vancouver Island; the other thrust itself into the valley of the Red River, a grassy, treeless plain stretching from Lake Traverse in Minnesota northward to Lake Winnipeg. Itself under fire and its capacity for colonization doubted, the Bay Company was nevertheless apparently the sole means of blunting either of these fingers. On Vancouver Island it had built Fort Victoria; and the Red River Colony, founded by Lord Selkirk in 1812, belonged to its domain. From Hudson Bay to the Pacific no other British interest existed. Averse to colonization as injurious to its trading interests, the Company through its leaders—J. H. Pelly in London and Sir George Simpson, its superintendent in North America—recognized that it had no choice. Promising to push British colonization, Pelly applied to the Colonial Office for a grant of all the territory north of the 49th parallel and west of the Rockies, to be added to its already large holding over Rupert's Land; but this being refused, it accepted instead a charter authorizing it to establish a colony of British subjects

[1] Quoted by Arthur S. Morton, *A History of the Canadian West to 1870–71,* Toronto, 1939, p. 751.

on Vancouver Island. It did succeed in planting a very small colony of farmers and coal-miners on the island, but the achievement was unimpressive in comparison with the American settlements south of the border. With the discovery of gold on the Fraser and Thompson rivers in 1857, a rush of American immigrants occurred comparable to the great gold rush of '49 to California. The population of Victoria rocketed to 30,948 in 1858; Wells Fargo Express Company of California fame set up assay offices, merchants swarmed in from the south, and the Pacific Mail Steamship Company established a scheduled service from San Francisco, carrying people and goods north and taking back the gold to the mint in San Francisco. Within a year Victoria and New Westminster, the mainland settlement at the mouth of the Fraser, had become economic outposts of the city by the Golden Gate.

The very next year an ominous incident occurred in the San Juan Islands, which had been overlooked by the Oregon treaty. The treaty had stabilized the land, but not the water boundary: there were two channels leading into the Straits of Juan de Fuca, and the treaty was not explicit on which channel constituted the boundary. The islands lay between the channels, and the Hudson's Bay Company maintained a farm upon them. Taking advantage of a trifling incident over the ownership of a pig, General Harney of the Oregon department of the United States army rushed troops to the islands in 1859 to ' protect American property '. A one-time Indian fighter in Florida, Harney pictured himself as the Andrew Jackson of the Northwest, appointed to invade that country as Jackson had in 1818 invaded East Florida. Vancouver Island, he asserted, was ' as important to the Pacific States as Cuba is to those on the Atlantic '. The administration in Washington disagreed, however, and co-operated with the British Government in patching up the affair. But title to the islands remained unresolved and, lest another ' Oregon fever ' develop in the United States, it was mutually agreed not to experiment again with ' joint occupation ' by civilians. Joint military occupation was resorted to instead, each force being assigned to its portion of the islands; and under this regime no further incident occurred until the entire archipelago was awarded to the United States by arbitration in 1872.[1]

[1] Hunter Miller, *San Juan Archipelago. A Study of the Joint Occupation of San Juan Island*, Bellows Falls, Vt., 1943. See also my ' International Rivalries in the Pacific Northwest ', op. cit.

Harney's ambition found an echo in Major-General Henry W. Halleck, commanding officer of the Military Division of the Pacific, who in 1868 gave the War Department in Washington six reasons why ' the British claim to all territory west of the Rocky Mountains' should be extinguished by purchase and treaty. Halleck's opinions remained his own, however, and the tide of miners was by this time receding almost as rapidly as it had surged. Obviously neither the Hudson's Bay Company nor the insignificant little colony of British settlers on Vancouver Island was a match for this flood, had it been accompanied by an annexationist fever. But the miners had come for riches, and the Americans at home were fighting among themselves. In the meantime the Company had found in 1851 an unusually competent governor for Vancouver Island: its chief factor for the western department, James Douglas. Douglas required the miners to purchase licenses and, acting to head off lawlessness and trouble over claims in the diggings, imposed his own authority on the mainland. Out of this extra-legal step emerged in 1858 an Act of Parliament creating the colony of British Columbia; and Douglas, resigning his position with the Hudson's Bay Company, became governor of the two colonies. Eight years later Vancouver Island and the mainland were consolidated into the single Crown colony of British Columbia, and in 1870–71 the new Dominion of Canada induced the local inhabitants to join it much as the Texans had joined the American Union.[1]

Quite different from the scene on the Northwest coast, but more deliberate and calculated to eventuate in annexation was the American push into the valley of the Red River. This valley is the meeting-place of three historic routes into the interior: the Hudson Bay from York Factory, whence had come the first settlers in 1812; the old canoe route from Canada and Lake Superior, pioneered in the eighteenth century by the *voyageurs* but virtually abandoned after 1821 when the Hudson's Bay Company absorbed the North West Company; and the route from Minnesota in the upper Mississippi valley. Neglected by the Bay Company, the scattered settlements of

[1] For a more detailed account of British Columbia than it is possible to offer here, the reader should consult F. W. Howay, W. N. Sage and H. F. Angus, *British Columbia and the United States*, Toronto, 1942; Morton, op. cit.; Galbraith, op. cit., pp. 283–307; and Margaret A. Ormsby, *British Columbia: A History*, the Macmillans of Canada, 1958. The documents are in *Parl. Papers*, Vancouver Island Papers, 1848–1867.

Scots, *Canadiens* and *métis* stagnated for a quarter of a century; but the appearance in 1844–45 of American traders and an American cavalry unit at Pembina, just south of the border, altered the scene with remarkable rapidity. The Bay Company saw its monopoly threatened; the British Government, influenced by Sir George Simpson, identified the Americans at Pembina with the contemporary ' fever ' for conquest in the Pacific Northwest; and the Governor-General of Canada, Sir Charles Metcalfe, thought a showdown with the United States should then and there be forced, Britain to seize control of the Great Lakes and station an army of 50,000 to 100,000 men along the border. The Peel ministry did consent to reopen the fort on Red River on a temporary basis, but even this became unnecessary when the Oregon crisis evaporated. Nevertheless, the trade route from Minnesota, once established, was obviously superior to the other two; and by 1849, a regular cart-freighting service having been introduced, Red River had come to life and St. Paul, the southern terminal of the cart line, was aware of its possibilities as the entrepôt for the country north-westward to the Rockies. Minnesota became a state in 1858, and the census that followed showed an almost thirty-fold growth in population during the decade. Moreover, Red River's reputation abroad as part of the ' frost kingdom ' was changed for the better when an American scientist, Loren Blodget, published a book on climatology which showed that spring and summer temperatures were warm and nearly the same along the immense line of plains from St. Paul to the Mackenzie River. Blodget's book got wide attention in all three countries: it strengthened the case for a Pacific railway, in which Americans, Canadians and British were all interested, and it opened up the prospect of extensive colonization of the northern prairies.

In Canada animosity towards the Bay Company mingled with fear lest the Northwest go by default to the United States. By 1857 Toronto had the capital and the enterprise, and the province had the population, sufficient to compete for the development of Red River. George Brown's Toronto *Globe* denounced the Company and asserted that Rupert's Land belonged by right to Canada; the half-breed, William Kennedy, founded a new North West Company with the privilege of carrying mail to Red River; S. J. Dawson pioneered a new route from Fort William and urged the building of a wagon road; the government sent a party of Royal Canadian Rifles to Fort Garry to impress the local populace; and in 1859 two Canadian newspaper men, who had worked for Brown on the *Globe*, started a newspaper at Red River with the avowed purpose of agitating for annexation to Canada. Meanwhile, the British surveyor, Captain John Palliser, discovered the park belt beyond Red River; but having travelled the American plains and familiarized himself with the route from St. Paul, Palliser discounted the competitive ability of the Canadians.

Over in Britain Parliament appointed a select committee to investigate the affairs of the Hudson's Bay Company; and the committee in a masterly report rendered in 1857 showed its appreciation of the advantages held by the Americans and the necessity to establish colonies all the way from Red River to Vancouver Island, if the country was to be kept British. This was easier said than done, however. There was the posssibility that Red River might be converted into a Crown colony, but both the Bay Company and the Imperial Government backed away from this. Britain looked to Canada to assume the lead in buying out the Company and extending the Canadian borders to the Rockies; but the jealousies of Quebec and the alarming internal political friction that produced a succession of weak governments in Canada after 1857 made such an ambitious move out of the question for the time being. A stalemate set in on Red River, the trade going more and more to St. Paul; but political action from the direction of the United States was deferred by the Civil War.

British North America was by this time approaching its great crisis of the century: either the scattered colonies from sea to sea would be sucked into the United States one by one, or they would federate and develop a transcontinental nation of their own. Of the 'American danger' both the select committee in Westminster and the Canadian leadership in Ottawa were aware; and only Canada, the 'empire province', could furnish the lead. This the governor, Sir Edmund Head, with the knowledge and desire of Canadian conservatives, such as John A. MacDonald, proposed to do in 1858. Federation and westward expansion were regarded as necessary steps complementary to each other. Internal factionalism, however, retarded the movement until the formation of a coalition government in 1864. Recognizing the need for haste, this government sought union with the Maritime Provinces, and from this careful planning emerged the Quebec Conference and the subsequent enactment in

March 1867 of the British North America Act. Sundry expansionist elements in the United States looked sourly on and tried, by various methods, to trip up Canadian federation. General Nathaniel P. Banks sponsored an annexation bill in Congress in 1866; an agent was sent to the Maritime Provinces to spread ' influence ' among the local legislators and induce them to vote against union with Canada; the Senate foreign relations committee reported out a resolution expressing its ' extreme solicitude ' that a rival confederation was about to be formed on the continent and ' founded upon monarchical principles '; and the Maine legislature, under the influence of a railroad promoter who was seeking to bring the neighbouring province of New Brunswick under his control, ' resolved ' that Canadian federation was a ' violation of the Monroe doctrine '.[1]

These futile gestures had their counterpart in the West, where James Wickes Taylor was zealously promoting a plan for a Pacific railroad that would run from St. Paul northwesterly into the valley of the Saskatchewan and complete the process already begun of making the British Northwest an economic tributary of Minnesota. Taylor, with the support of the state legislature, of Oscar Malmros, the American consul in Winnipeg, of several influential senators in Washington, and of various interests in Chicago and Philadephia, viewed annexation and the acquisition of Rupert's Land as steps linked together; but none of these interests was able to prevent the transfer of Rupert's Land to the Dominion of Canada in 1869. They thought their chance had come, however, when [shortly after] the métis of the Red River, mistaking the purposes of the Canadian Government, rebelled. Malmros hoped to procure a subsidy from the United States to finance the insurrection; Taylor hastened to Red River to confer with the insurgents and urge them to vote themselves into the American Union; but Secretary of State Hamilton Fish disappointingly held back and insisted upon non-intervention until such a time as the local inhabitants might themselves petition for annexation. This never came, however, and the métis by their subsequent actions demonstrated their desire to make terms with Canada. They did not intrigue with the Americans, and the MacDonald Government acted so swiftly that the insurrection was not allowed to fester.

[1] Alice R. Stewart, ' The State of Maine and Canadian Confederation ', Can. Hist. Rev., XXXIII, 1952, pp. 148–64; D. G. Creighton, ' The United States and Canadian Confederation ', Ibid., XXXIX, 1958, pp. 209–22.

'It is quite evident to me', declared MacDonald in January 1870, 'that the United States Government are resolved to do all they can, short of war, to get possession of the western territory and we must take immediate and vigorous steps to counteract them.'[1] First, the Manitoba Act was passed by the Canadian Parliament and proclaimed in July, thereby giving to the small population on Red River the status of a province; second, the aid of the Hudson's Bay Company and its chief factor, Donald A. Smith, who well understood the *métis* mentality, was enlisted to explain to them Canada's intentions; and third, a military expedition of mixed British and Canadian troops under the command of Colonel Garnet Wolseley was dispatched to reopen the all-Canadian route from Lake Superior and demonstrate that the difficult topographical handicap separating Canada from the west could be overcome. The formidable barrier of the Laurentian Shield was reason enough to make Canadian success seem improbable; but by these and subsequent measures the Dominion of Canada extended itself *a mare usque ad mare* and thereby demonstrated an unsuspected fallacy in the historic American belief in the law of nature.[2] When Canada, with the encouragement and practical assistance of the United Kingdom, acquired Rupert's Land from the Hudson's Bay Company, she took a step comparable in importance to the American acquisition of Louisiana in 1803 from Napoleon— she ensured her independence as a North American nation.

[1] Quoted by C. P. Stacey, ' The Military Aspect of Canada's Winning of the West, 1870–1885 ', *Can. Hist. Rev.*, XXI, 1940, pp. 1–24.

[2] The best account of the Riel Rebellion on Red River is in W. L. Morton, *Manitoba, a History*, Toronto, 1957, pp. 121–50. The annexationist activities of Taylor *et al.*, are documented by Donald F. Warner, ' Drang nach Norden: the United States and the Riel Rebellion ', *Miss. Valley Hist. Rev.*, XXXIX, 1953, pp. 693–712, and by Paul F. Sharp, *Whoop-Up Country. The Canadian-American West, 1865–1885*, Minneapolis, 1955. Mr. Sharp's book is a fascinating and authoritative account of the activities of the Royal Northwest Mounted Police in keeping the country Canadian.

Chapter VI

EMPIRE OF COMMERCE AND RELIGION IN THE PACIFIC

'The empire of the seas . . . alone is real empire'

UNTIL the voyages of the English mariner, Captain James Cook, the Pacific Ocean was virtually an unknown sea. Cook inspired a long series of explorations—British, French, Russian and American—that kept up until the middle of the nineteenth century. His third voyage especially aroused interest in the seaboard United States, although it took place during the bitterest years of the War of Independence, 1776–1780. In spite of the hostilities, Yankee naval vessels had orders that, should they happen upon the English explorer, they were not to treat him as an enemy, but on the contrary were to pay him honour and respect. These orders originated with Franklin, who called the attention of the commanders to the immense benefits, commercial and otherwise, likely to result from the voyage of the celebrated navigator. In April 1780 Franklin received from Sir Joseph Banks, then President of the Royal Society, a warm letter of appreciation for his thoughtfulness.[1] French warships, it should be added, had similar orders.

The first account of the voyage (by Lieutenant John Rickman) appeared in London in 1781, and an American edition of this account was published in Philadelphia two years later. John Ledyard, the Yankee seaman who served as a corporal of marines under Cook, also wrote an account, borrowed partly from Rickman's, which was published in Hartford, Connecticut the same year. Ledyard is commonly given the credit for creating this new interest in America, but clearly both the interest and the expectation were already there.[2] And the information carried home by Cook's men of the profitable trade in sea otter skins with the Chinese justified the expectation. The new China trade via Cape Horn, linking the American ports with the Pacific Northwest, with Hawaii and the islands of the Southwest

---

[1] Banks to Franklin, March 29, 1780. Franklin Coll.

[2] An account of Cook's first voyage had been published in New York in 1774. For evidence of widespread interest in Cook see Sir Maurice Holmes, *Captain James Cook, R.N., F.R.S. A Bibliographical Excursion*, London, 1952.

Pacific, and with Macao and Canton, marked out the path of empire to the Pacific.

We must not, however, make the mistake of narrowing this movement to the dimensions of a path. Merchants, missionaries, adventurers, sea captains, naval officers and consular officials crowded into the Pacific during the nineteenth century and spun a web whose strands extended to every part of the ocean. The history of this movement has yet to be written.[1] There is an epic story still to be told of this American penetration of the Pacific basin, undertaken by private traders seeking furs and other things that would attract the Chinese. So keen was the spirit of rivalry among themselves that Yankee captains, finding an island which contained something that looked promising for the Chinese market, kept their discovery secret, sometimes not even recording the event in the ship's log. Captain Joseph Ingraham of Boston reached the Marquesas Islands in April 1791; Captain Edmund Fanning of Connecticut discovered Kingman Reef in 1798; a trading firm of Stonington, Connecticut decided in 1820 to send out an expedition primarily for the purpose of making new discoveries; and in 1824 Captain Coffin from the same state discovered (or rediscovered) six islands of the Bonin group. These are just a few examples of the energy and speculative inclinations of New England shipowners. Beginning about 1820 New England congressmen began to show an interest in inducing the navy department to send out an official exploring party.

Nor has the part taken by the American navy been properly evaluated. Captain David Porter, entering the Pacific in the hope of capturing stray British merchantmen, temporarily occupied and annexed an island in the Marquesas group in 1813; and on his return to the United States at the end of the war, Porter showed his imaginativeness in a letter to President Madison. ' We border on Russia, on Japan, on China ', he insisted. (His use of the word ' border ' is interesting.) ' We border on islands which bear the same relation to the N.W. Coast as those of the West Indies bear to the Atlantic States. . . . The important trade of Japan has been shut to every nation except the Dutch. . . . Great changes have since taken place in the world—changes which may have effected [sic] even Japan. The time may be favourable, and it would be a glory beyond that acquired

---

[1] Samuel Eliot Morison, *Maritime History of Massachusetts, 1783–1860* (Boston, 1923) is a fascinating introduction to the subject.

by any other nation for us, a nation of only 40 years standing, to beat down their rooted prejudices, secure to ourselves a valuable trade, and make that people known to the world '.[1] Porter's communication went into the presidential pigeon-hole, but it was not long before others took up the same plea. In 1821 the navy began operating a squadron off the west coast of South America; and by 1835 intercourse with China and the East Indies reached the point where it justified the establishment of a separate East India squadron.

Meanwhile in 1828 Representative J. N. Reynolds of New York submitted a long communication to the Secretary of the Navy, giving information about the Pacific that he had gathered on his own responsibility. Reynolds had been talking to the whaling captains of New London and Stonington, Connecticut, of Newport, Rhode Island, and of New Bedford, Nantucket and other places in Massachusetts. These navigators, he said, know more about the Pacific and the South Seas than those of any other country. At least two hundred ships are employed in whaling and sealing alone. Reynolds's object was to learn all he could concerning the navigation, geography and topography of the whole range of seas from the Pacific to the Indian and Chinese oceans. The navy department, he declared, was now better informed than any other admiralty, ' for those seas are truly our field of fame. Too much credit cannot be given to our whalers, sealers, and traffickers for the information they have acquired. But after all their exertions, justice to ourselves, as a great people, requires that this mass of information should be reviewed, analyzed, classified, and preserved in careful literary labours for the benefit of mankind '.[2]

Ten years of pressure from New England finally brought about the United States Exploring Expedition, commanded by Lieutenant Charles Wilkes. The expedition was to blanket the Pacific, sailing from Valparaiso to the Society Islands and thence to the Fijis where, it was hoped, a safe harbour could be selected. It was to take in Hawaii and the Pacific Coast, where it was to make surveys with special attention paid to San Francisco Bay. From the northwest coast it was to sail by the great circle route for Japan and thence south to the Straits of Sunda and the port of Singapore. Wilkes has told the story of his expedition in five ponderous tomes, published in 1845, the year of the Oregon crisis and the year too when the

---

[1] Porter's letter is edited by A. B. Cole in the *Pac. Hist. Rev.*, IX, 1940, pp. 61-5.
[2] *Amer. St. Papers.* Naval Affairs, vol. 4, pp. 688-700.

government of President Polk was making preparations to take California. Like Webster and others, Wilkes, with a mariner's sense of distance from the United States, seems to have thought of the Pacific coast as the home of a new sovereign republic, ' possessed as it must be by the Anglo-Norman race '. But he singled out the Strait of Juan de Fuca and San Francisco as ' two of the finest ports in the world ', and declared:

> These two regions have, in fact, within themselves everything to make them increase, and keep up an intercourse with the whole of Polynesia, as well as the countries of South America on the one side, and China, the Philippines, New Holland, and New Zealand, on the other. Among the latter, before many years, may be included Japan. Such various climates will furnish the materials for a beneficial exchange of products, and an intercourse that must, in time, become immense, while this western coast . . . is evidently destined to fill a large space in the world's future history.[1]

But many years before Wilkes and others began praising San Francisco Bay, the native Polynesian kingdom of Hawaii had come under American influence and Honolulu had grown into a thriving town. The Sandwich Islands, the name bestowed by Captain Cook, became very early in the nineteenth century an international frontier, a crossroads in mid-Pacific where British, French, Russian and American vessels rendezvoused. Vancouver paid five visits to the islands, the first two times as a junior officer under Cook, the other three as leader in his own right of exploring expeditions in 1792, 1793 and 1794 respectively. On his last visit Vancouver got King Kamehameha I to cede the islands to Great Britain, but the home government in London never acknowledged the cession and never showed any interest other than to state in 1814 that, in view of the victory over France, the native kingdom would continue to enjoy freedom from foreign molestation. Whenever a British vessel called at the islands, however, the king would inquire ' how his cousin George was '.

Russian contacts with Hawaii began in 1804 with the visit of some Russian vessels, and a trade started between the islands and Sitka in Alaska. The Russian governor, Baranov, conceived of a

---

[1] Charles Wilkes, U.S.N., *Narrative of the United States Exploring Expedition during the Years 1838, 1839, 1840, 1841, 1842*, 5 vols., Philadelphia, 1845, V, pp. 182–3. A second edition was published in 1849 and a third in 1851.

Russian empire in the North Pacific pivoting upon Sitka and Hawaii, and in 1815–16 he sent a German, Dr. Scheffer, to establish an ascendancy over the native monarch. But St. Petersburg, like London, ignored the opportunity. By this time the fur trade, over which the Americans had gained control, had passed its zenith, but the advantages of Honolulu as an entrepôt for goods and ships passing to and fro across the Pacific were well established. It was a permanent town by 1810, its economy linking it with China, the American Atlantic ports, Russian America and Spanish America, not to mention western Europe and the islands of the south-west Pacific. The new native Hawaiian sandalwood trade with China, another monopoly won by the Yankee traders, gave the town a boost, and in 1821 a direct trade started between Honolulu and California. The sandalwood trade did not last long, but its place was taken by the whalers, who yielded second place to no one until the advent of the sugar plantation in the 1850s. Sometimes the whaling fleets from the United States, *en route* to Japanese and Alaskan waters, spent six weeks in the harbour. After 1835 the American East India squadron paid regular calls.

The French explorer, Duflot de Mofras, regarded the islands as an appendage of California, and predicted that the nation which controlled the one would also control the other, a point of view with which Lieutenant Wilkes concurred. But one of the best appraisals of the strategic value of Hawaii comes from the pen of Sir George Simpson, from whose *Journey Round the World* I quote in part. Said Simpson:

> For all practical purposes, the Sandwich Islanders are on the direct route from Cape Horn to all the coasts of the Northern Pacific. With respect to Kamchatka and the Sea of Ochotsk this is evident at a glance . . . with respect to California and the north-west coast, the apparently inconvenient deviation to the left is rendered not only expedient, but almost necessary, by the prevailing breezes . . . .
>
> But the group as naturally connects the east and the west, as the south and the north. . . . It crosses the shortest road from Mexico to China; while . . . it may . . . be regarded as a stepping-stone from the whole of the American coast to the Celestial Empire. . . .[1]

[1] Sir George Simpson, *Narrative of a Journey Round the World during the Years 1841 and 1842*, 2 vols., London, 1847, II, pp. 132–3.

But the most unusual group of foreigners to settle in the islands and establish their ascendancy were the Congregational missionaries from New England. ' The Boston missionaries arrived in the nick of time partially to offset the demoralization introduced by Boston traders and Nantucket whalers ', slyly remarks Morison in his *Maritime History of Massachusetts*. The American Board of Commissioners for Foreign Missions, established in Boston, was the directing agency, and the first missionaries arrived in Honolulu in 1820. Honolulu was the central mission station in the islands and the hub of American missionary enterprise in the Pacific. Ten years later the American missionaries extended their operations to China. How firmly the New England conscience obtained a grip on the life of Honolulu; how successfully it imposed Sabbatarianism in the teeth of resistance from the traders and seamen; with what persistence Calvinist doctrines were taught to the native chiefs and the native population; how the missionaries gained temporal as well as spiritual ascendancy over the chiefs to the point where they became the controlling element in the king's government; how they kept French Catholics from obtaining a foothold in the islands—all of these make up a remarkable and almost inexplicable story.[1] Gradually the missionary inclined to change first into a governmental official, and thence into a landowner and speculator. Thus the Reverend Richard Armstrong exchanged a meagre mission pittance for $3,000 a year from the king, which he proceeded to use toward the purchase of land. By 1849 Armstrong held 600 acres, tripled his holdings during the next year, and was eagerly searching for funds to use in further speculations. By 1852 ten missionaries had acquired land, averaging 400 acres apiece. From the landowner the missionary (or his son) developed into the sugar planter, with an agricultural revolution based upon sugar well under way during the 1850s. From then on the American sugar planter and his ally, the Honolulu merchant, dominated the Hawaiian scene.[2]

The American Hawaiian, however, was no annexationist. Nor was he a republican. He took his oath of allegiance to the king seriously, his object being to Christianize and improve the native

[1] For a lengthy and scholarly account of the missionaries and their work see Harold Whitman Bradley, *The American Frontier in Hawaii. The Pioneers 1789–1843*, Stanford, Calif., 1942, pp. 168–270.

[2] Sylvester K. Stevens, *American Expansion in Hawaii, 1842–1898*, Harrisburg, Pa., 1945, p. 30.

monarchy and to obtain for it international recognition as an independent, sovereign State. A secret approach to the American Government in 1838 met with a rebuff. But in 1842 a diplomatic mission was dispatched to negotiate treaties of friendship and commerce with the United States, Great Britain and France. The mission was only partially successful: from the British and French it got a declaration that neither Government would ever take possession directly or indirectly of the islands; from the American Government it got a statement that it was ' more interested in the fate of the islands . . . than any other nation can be ', and a warning that ' no power ought . . . to take possession or to seek for any undue control over the existing Government. . . .'[1]

Thus under missionary governance the islands were neutralized in a *de facto* sense, but they held their tenure precariously. The declared policy of their governments to the contrary, both the French and the British consuls and their respective supporters in the islands were jealous of the Americans and determined to assert themselves. The British were irked at seeing the Americans get ahead of them— there had been a time when the king preferred their counsel; and the French were angry over the failure of their Catholic missions and over the duties on brandy and other spirituous liquors which the prohibition-minded American missionaries wanted kept out.

The French protectorate over Tahiti, proclaimed in this same year 1842, set a precedent for Hawaii; and despite the comparative success of its mission abroad, the Hawaiian Government believed that its days were numbered. The very next year the irate British consul engineered a naval intervention which lasted five months; a commission appointed by the commanding officer, Lord George Paulet, took over; but in due course King Kamehameha got his independence back at the hands of Paulet's superior officer, Admiral Thomas, who appreciated Whitehall's real attitude. A more severe test, however, arose in 1849 when a touchy new French consul, Patrice Dillon, fresh from Newcastle, England, opened up old sores and demanded a share in the administration of the schools which the Protestant missionaries had thoughtfully reserved for themselves. Dillon had French gunboats at his back, and though the Government of Louis Napoleon disavowed him, the troubles continued during the ensuing two years.

[1] Miller, *Treaties*, V, pp. 601–02, 623–8.

Dillon's intermeddling caused the native government to dispatch a second mission abroad in quest of diplomatic support and reassurance on the part of the three maritime powers, Britain, France and the United States. By this time a Scotsman, Robert C. Wyllie, had become Kamehameha's minister of foreign affairs; and he, Dr. Gerritt P. Judd, an American medical missionary, and the Reverend Richard Armstrong, were the king's chief counsellors. All three, together with the young Prince Alexander Liholiho, who in 1854 was to become King Kamehameha IV, were devoted believers in Hawaiian independence, though they knew this could only be maintained through the goodwill of the maritime powers. They preferred a joint guarantee from all three powers, but were prepared to accept almost anything that would promise continuation of Hawaiian self-government. An Anglo-American guarantee would be acceptable, or even a guarantee from the United States alone. But, as a last resort, they were reconciled to advising the king to abdicate in favour of the United States. Even Robert Wyllie, the least disposed of the Caucasians toward annexation, confessed that in the long run he could see no alternative.

Toward these Hawaiian problems the Whig administration in Washington behaved complacently, merely reiterating the statement made in 1842 and taking no action to checkmate the French. But, on the other hand, the Hawaiians' dilemma found an answering chord among the Democrats, especially those on the Pacific coast. The leading newspaper of San Francisco, the *Alta California*, revived the ' ripe pear ' theory which had formerly been applied to Cuba, and described the islands as ' luscious fruit ' ready to fall into the American lap; and a California congressman in 1852 built the argument for annexation by insisting that Hawaii was needed both for defence of the Pacific coast and for the advancement of the trade with Asia. More important still were the possibilities of a filibustering descent from San Francisco upon the islands. William Walker, the ' grey-eyed man of destiny ' who had launched private invasions of Mexico, had already given San Francisco a reputation as a filibustering centre; and with the continued French pressure on Hawaii as an incentive, rumours of a similar attempt on Honolulu circulated freely in San Francisco. These in turn gave rise to a sense of crisis in Hawaii, where a small annexation-minded party, composed chiefly of sugar planters who wanted a free market on the Pacific coast, took shape.

A new empire has, as by magic, sprung into existence. San Francisco promises, at no distant day, to become another New York, and our prosperous trade in the Pacific, amid the wonders of commerce, [promises] to bear the same relationship to China and Japan which that of the Atlantic coast bears to the continent of Europe and Great Britain.

Thoughts like this, expressed by the Secretary of the Navy in his annual report for 1853, lay behind the forward policy projected by the incoming Democratic Government of Franklin Pierce. Pierce planned to resume where James K. Polk had left off in 1848. His policy, he declared would ' not be controlled by any timid forebodings of evil from expansion '; and though it does not appear that the new administration had thought things through in advance, it is clear from the steps undertaken what it hoped to accomplish. Confident that overseas expansion would heal the wounds of internal conflict, and believing that Cuba and Hawaii were ' ripe pears ' waiting to be plucked, Pierce and his cabinet set out to forge a chain of dependencies connecting the Atlantic with the Pacific. Nicaragua and its transit route in Central America made up the link between the two island extremities. Tentative in nature, blundering in execution, and unsuccessful as we shall see, the Pierce plan charted a course that the American empire would resume decisively at a later period in the century. The southward thrust into the Caribbean, described in the next chapter, the thrust across the continent, and finally the drive toward Asia were related and contemporaneous parts of the same movement. Pierce and his associates, not comprehending the forces of disintegration within, did perceive these external forces, though through a glass darkly.

In Hawaii meanwhile an explosive situation had developed, serious enough to place the throne in jeopardy. A ' committee of thirteen ' talked insurrection and expressed readiness to welcome filibusters from California, but aimed its shafts principally at Dr. Judd and his prohibitionist policies. When, in September 1853, Judd was replaced as minister of finance by Elisha Allen, the former American consul, the committee became more conservative. Its interests were in sugar and free trade, but the United States was its only feasible market. The government now consisted of Robert Wyllie, who clung to his hope of a three-power protectorate but who by now was reconciled to annexation *provided* that Hawaii could be treated, like Texas, as a state; of William L. Lee, a recent immigrant from the States who had risen to be chief justice; and of Elisha Allen. Lee was lukewarm on the subject of annexation and critical of the Pierce Government; Allen was for annexation, but only in terms of statehood. As an alternative Allen would co-operate with Wyllie in asking for British and French protection against the country's falling into anarchy. King Kamehameha III was amiable and co-operative, though at times the victim of alcohol; but his son, the Prince Alexander, young, vigorous, intelligent, and repelled by the Sabbatarianism of the missionaries who had subjected him to their discipline, was a sustaining influence of great importance. To Alexander the native Hawaiians looked as a saviour from the ever-encroaching whites.

This then in a word was the situation in the islands at the close of the year 1853 as David L. Gregg, the new emissary from Washington found it; continued unrest, mutual distrust, and division of opinion among the whites; chronic reports of a filibustering party on the way from California embellishing the general talk of annexation; fears of enslavement or dispossession among the natives; and apprehension within the government lest it be overthrown either by a local insurrection or by a sudden assault from without. In these circumstances Messrs. Wyllie, Lee and Allen, with the knowledge and consent of the king and the prince, turned to Gregg with proposals for annexation. It was, they agreed, the one remedy against anarchy. Gregg on his part had come to the islands uncommitted. The Secretary of State, William L. Marcy, had taken pains to impress the envoy with the commercial and strategic value of Hawaii and with the importance of keeping it out of British or French hands, but otherwise had left the matter of policy open. Gregg therefore responded favourably to the Hawaiian appeal, and Marcy encouraged him to go ahead with a treaty. Knowing that Britain and France were opposed to the United States having the islands, and apprehensive of the pressure they might bring to bear on the king's government, the Secretary of State was anxious to present them with a speedy *fait accompli*.

But things did not move as fast as expected and, moreover, there were hidden rocks. The Secretary of State had specified a complete surrender of Hawaiian sovereignty, reserving the question of the political rights of the inhabitants for future determination.

Statehood, however, was the fixed objective of even the most committed of the American Hawaiians; nor were the latter opposed to the insistence of Prince Alexander upon a liberal financial settlement for the royal family and the chiefs. Upon these conditions, and not upon Marcy's, the treaty negotiations went slowly ahead in Honolulu. Meanwhile the British and French consuls laboured to stimulate native fear of racial degradation; the warships of all three powers haunted the harbour, while the British consul argued in favour of a three-power protectorate in lieu of annexation; and the British and French Governments, conscious of common ground in opposition to Russia on the one hand and the United States on the other, deliberated the wisdom of a formal diplomatic protest to Washington. The British Foreign Office did send a solemn note in October, but it was unnecessary—annexation was by then a dead issue. Gregg had accepted a treaty granting immediate statehood to Hawaii and pledging generous annuity payments to the royal family and the chiefs. This killed the treaty so far as the United States was concerned; but in the meantime Prince Alexander succeeded to the throne as Kamehameha IV, and in January 1855 he formally terminated the negotiations. David Gregg subsequently resigned his diplomatic post and settled down in Honolulu as minister of finance; Robert Wyllie remained in the government as foreign minister; while William Lee departed for Washington to ask for a reciprocity treaty which would help the island economy, and for a guaranty treaty which would stabilize the political independence of the island kingdom. To the commercial interests on the Pacific coast reciprocity was a satisfactory substitute for annexation, but it failed nevertheless to pass the test of Senate approval. Refusing to negotiate a formal treaty of recognition and guarantee, the administration reverted, however, to the position of 1842 and in addition obliged with a written statement that it would exert all its power to protect the islands from filibusters. In a word, it conceded that it had miscalculated the ripeness of the ' pear '. Hawaiian independence was better grounded than had been supposed.[1]

We have now moved some years ahead in our story and so must

[1] For the above account of Hawaii and annexation I am indebted to Ralph S. Kuykendall, *The Hawaiian Kingdom, 1778–1854. Foundation and Transformation*, Honolulu, 1938, pp. 185–428, and to Stevens, op. cit., pp. 1–107. See also my article, ' Great Britain, the United States, and Hawaiian Independence, 1850–1855 ', *Pac. Hist. Rev.*, IV, 1935, pp. 15–24.

return to the Pacific coast. The determination of the American missionaries and others in Hawaii to save the island kingdom from annexation stands out in sharp contrast to the desires and expectations of the small American minority who had settled in California during the early 1840s and who were exerting themselves to the best of their ability in favour of the United States. ' Once let the tide flow toward California ', wrote Alfred Robinson, the resident agent of Bryant and Sturgis in Monterey, ' and the American population will be sufficiently numerous to play the Texas game '. At the time he wrote this, Robinson was in New York preparing for the publication of his book, *Life in California*, one of several such volumes appearing in the States and widely read. With Thomas O. Larkin, the well-to-do Yankee merchant who had settled previously in Monterey, Robinson shared fears of the British or French getting the province. Larkin was now United States consul, and in 1845 he started a series of letters to the *New York Herald* and to the *Journal of Commerce*, which were published. ' The progress of California is onward ', he declared, 'but the British Government, on the pretext that the American settlers want to revolutionize the country, is aiding Mexico in preparing to send an army of thieving soldiers and rapacious officers to subdue the province.'[1] Larkin was especially afraid of the Hudson's Bay Company, which he pictured as making common cause with the British Government. The Bay Company had furnished the local government with arms and money apparently with the purpose of making it independent; but since that attempt had failed, another Mexican force was expected, financed, according to rumour, by two English houses in Mexico. None of Larkin's accusations has been verified—neither the British nor the French had developed plans for action, although the prospect of California and its harbours going to the United States was viewed openly with distaste. Said *The Times*, for example:

England must think of her own interests, and secure the Bay of Francisco and Monterey . . . to prevent those noble ports from becoming ports of exportation for brother Jonathan for the Chinese market.[2]

[1] *The Larkin Papers*, George P. Hammond, ed., 4 vols., Berkeley and Los Angeles, 1952, III, pp. 265–8, 292–6.

[2] Quoted by Graebner, op. cit., p. 82. See also Ephraim Douglas Adams, ' English Interest in the Annexation of California ', *Amer. Hist. Rev.*, XIV, 1909, p. 746.

The Americans have all of the foreign trade of California in their hands, Larkin averred. There are 500 to 1000 whalers with 20,000 American seamen in the Pacific, half of whom are within twenty days sail of San Francisco. The bay there will hold all the ships in the United States. And if Congress wishes the extension of the navy, of our naval power or of our commerce San Francisco must be obtained, or else Oregon and California must become a nation within themselves. Perhaps an 'independent' California, influenced by Britain, was Larkin's real fear. In this Mexican province, inhabited by about 12,000 whites, of whom nearly 11,000 were native-born, Spanish-speaking Californians, there was a strange absence of constituted authority. An attempt by Mexico to re-establish her authority failed ludicrously at the hands of the Californians. There were two rival governors, neither of whom exercised much power: Pio Pico in Los Angeles, General Castro at Monterey. Pico desired to offer the province to Great Britain as a protection against the United States, but Castro hoped for more help from Mexico with which to keep alien influences under control.

Since 1841 small parties of American immigrants had been filtering through the passes of the High Sierra, many of them taking up lands in the Great Valley of the Sacramento and the San Joaquin, which lay between the Sierra and the Coast Range. The German Swiss, Johann August Sutter, entering the province by sea, had already acquired a huge barony of 60,000 acres for himself on the banks of the Sacramento River. Like Austin of Texas, Sutter became a naturalized Mexican in order to secure title to his grant, and the Americans who settled in the Great Valley followed suit. In California to-day there is an attractive legend dramatized by the frequent showing at festive occasions and on public buildings of a large white flag in the centre of which is an artistic, kindly-looking bear standing on all-fours. This is the emblem of the 'Bear Flag Republic', a republic that existed only in fantasy. California is naturally a land of romance, and the Bear Flag has in recent years become a necessary part of the pageantry of the state. In 1846 some ranchers, alarmed at seeing a party of armed horsemen dispatched from Monterey by Castro, and fearing lest this was a move to deprive them of their lands, attacked the party and raised a flag with the rough figure of a bear upon it. But, though a few keenly observant visitors, such as Sir George Simpson, had suggested that California could become another Texas, the Bear Flaggers were not of revolutionary timber and entertained no political ambitions. Such aspirations would have been futile in their case anyway, *because United States forces were already poised to take control of California.*

It is now evident that the California scene in 1845–46 bore no resemblance to either Texas or Hawaii. California within itself possessed no element capable of self-determination. The Spanish-speaking Californians, easily in the majority, were indifferent to Mexico but at the same time were ill disposed towards political action. Between the American ranchers of the interior and the merchants on the coast, with their Eastern connections, there was little if any bond of sympathy. The merchants, however, were keenly aware of the rising tide of interest abroad in the future of the province, of the frequent visits of British and French agents and travellers and of the calls paid by British ships of war. And by long experience California was linked by sea not only with the United States, but with the islands of the Pacific and with China. And now that relations with the Chinese Empire had been placed on a firm foundation by the treaties forced upon the Chinese in 1842–44, the China trade appeared more dazzling than ever. We remember how the Bay of San Francisco had been spotted as the great harbour of the future that would hold the key to the wealth of the Pacific. Simpson, de Mofras, Wilkes, and many others had pointed this out. Webster had intended in 1842 to bargain for it. Consul Larkin at Monterey declared that ' it must, will be, the medium stopping place from New Orleans and New York to the China Ports now open to all the world '. And in the same year, 1845, the project of building a transcontinental railroad to San Francisco to shorten the route to Hawaii and China was given serious consideration.

In the spring of that year, the Polk administration being seated in power in Washington, a complicated situation began to unfold, involving Texas, Oregon and California all at the same time. Polk had made political commitments to annex Texas and all of Oregon, but his real objective was California, which had not been mentioned by either of the parties in the election campaign. Partly to put himself in a better position to manoeuvre for California, Polk, we remember, began secretly sounding the retreat from Oregon. But in order to get what he wanted from Mexico he began treading two divergent paths simultaneously, the one leading toward war, the other toward peace. The obscure and relatively unimportant issue of the Texan boundary was fixed upon as the final test between the two.

Agents sent to Texas by both Polk and his predecessor, John Tyler, to promote the cause of annexation with the people of that state, tried to foster a war between Texas and Mexico. The agents were told that the Rio Grande was the indisputable boundary, so far as the United States was concerned, and that Texas would be ' protected ' accordingly. Apparently on their own responsibility, these emissaries planned an armed expedition to the Rio Grande and beyond, the seizure of the northern states of Mexico being the ultimate objective. Commodore Stockton, the commander of an American squadron stationed at Galveston, was one of these agents; and a private letter, dated May 27, 1845, from him to George Bancroft, the Secretary of the Navy, confirms our suspicion that the Polk Government was aware of the plot. This letter reads:

> Since my last letter I have seen Mr. Mayfield late [Texan] Secretary of State, who says that if the people here did not feel assured that the Boundary line would be the Rio Grande three fourths and himself amongst the number would oppose the annexation—But I need hardly say another word on that subject; its importance is apparent. But it may perhaps be as well for me *in this way* to let you know how I propose to settle the matter without committing the U. States. The Major Genl will call out Three Thousand Men & " B. F. Stockton Esq." will supply them in a private way with [arms?] & ammunition.
>   Yours
>
>   R. F. Stockton[1]

Stockton's letter reveals intentions, but it was written in too optimistic a vein. The proposed expedition never materialized, perhaps because of the opposition of President Anson Jones of Texas who, on May 30, received the draft treaty of recognition that Captain Elliott, the British chargé, had procured for him in Mexico. Jones was bitterly opposed to Polk, whom he accused of trying to inveigle him into manufacturing a war for the United States.[2] Stockton's activities certainly make it difficult to refute the accusation. It is difficult too to justify the continued American insistence on the Rio Grande as the boundary. No practical issue was at stake, since the

---

[1] Bancroft Papers.

[2] Anson Jones, *Memoranda and Official Correspondence relating to the Republic of Texas, Its History and Annexation*, N.Y., 1859, pp. 46–7.

country between the Nueces and the Rio Grande was at the time unsettled. Polk now issued a cautious order to General Zachary Taylor to defend Texas as far as the Rio Grande but to remain ' near ' the Nueces. Taylor, a Whig in politics and an opponent of Polk, chose to define this adverb literally, for he took up his station on the banks of the Nueces and remained there until ordered to advance. It can be said that there was a war party in Mexico rashly eager for an armed clash with the United States. But the intelligence received by the Polk administration was to the effect that the Mexicans would make no trouble so long as the Americans confined themselves to Texas proper. ' The Mexican governments are in a dilemma ', Bancroft was told, ' from which they would gladly escape & expect to receive money in payment for adjusting the boundary, which I presume it would be greatly for our interest to pay '. Bancroft's informant was a New York merchant, Mr. W. Kemble, whose knowledge came from a correspondent in Mexico City. ' I keep no copy of my letter ', Mr. Kemble added in a postscript, ' & shall destroy yours lest either should get in improper hands '.[1]

Kemble's intelligence confirmed the advices that Polk had received from another source, and led to the conclusion that war could be avoided and perhaps even a large cession of territory secured by means of a money transaction. No Mexican government had ever lent an ear to any American proposal to barter away territory, although it had been approached repeatedly on the subject through a quarter of a century. An attempt by President Tyler in 1844 to buy a slice of California met with the usual rebuff. No matter how impecunious a Mexican regime might be, and no matter how lightly its hand rested on its outlying provinces, it dared not bargain with the *Yanqui* over the national domain. Still the American faith in the ultimate power of the dollar remained undimmed; and this time it was thought that a handsome cash offer would bring the greatest prize of all: California. As Congressman Charles J. Ingersoll of Massachusetts wrote Bancroft:

... as I formerly took leave to intimate to you and to Mr. Buchanan our whole course to Mexico has been most injudicious and impolitic. They are people easily bought, but [impervious?] to threats. Instead of menaces we should have a great mission

---

[1] Kemble to Bancroft, Private, Aug. 29 and Sept. 3, 1845. Bancroft sent a copy of the first letter to Buchanan. Bancroft Papers.

there to give them almost any price they ask for S Francisco and peace.[1]

This renewed enthusiasm for resorting to the dollar was spurred by fresh rumours, confirmed by Consul Larkin, of European interference in California. The British had opened a vice-consulate, the French a consulate, he reported, although neither one shared noticeably in the trade of the province. These fears, finding their way into print in the summer of 1845, inspired a newspaper campaign demanding that the President either try to buy California or warn off Europe by the Monroe Doctrine. The Polk Government took a series of steps. On June 24 Bancroft sent orders to Commodore Sloat, in command of the Pacific squadron, to seize Monterey and San Francisco Bay if and when war broke out with Mexico. On October 17 Buchanan sent word to Larkin to foster a local insurrection in California, with annexation as the ultimate end in view. Larkin, especially commissioned as confidential agent and rewarded with extra pay of six dollars per day, would have no trouble in reading between the lines. In his best fox-like manner Buchanan proceeded:

In the contest between Mexico and California we can take no part, unless the former should commence hostilities against the United States; but should California assert and maintain her independence, we shall render her all the kind offices in our power as a Sister Republic. This Government has no ambitious aspirations to gratify and no desire to extend our Federal system over more Territory than we already possess, unless by the free and spontaneous wish of the Independent people of adjoining Territories. . . .[2]

Meanwhile Captain Frémont, leading a band of sixty-two men, was sent west from St. Louis on his third overland journey to California. Frémont's ostensible mission was to explore, but his temporizing movements, once he arrived in the Sacramento valley, throw this wide open to doubt. 'My private instructions', he himself asserted, 'were, if needed, to foil England by carrying the war now imminent with Mexico into the territory of California'.[3] And in the following May 1846 Frémont had a chance meeting with the Bear

---

[1] Ingersoll to Bancroft, May 24, 1845, ibid. Graebner, op. cit., pp. 108–11.
[2] *Larkin Papers*, IV, pp. 44–7.
[3] Quoted in Allan Nevins, *Fremont, Pathmarker of the West*, N.Y., 1939, p. 204.

Flag insurgents, took them into his command and marched on Monterey. The British Admiral Seymour was the immediate object of these suspicions, the Americans all fearing that Seymour, in command of the British Pacific squadron, would step in and declare California a protectorate.

While these moves were being made on the chessboard, Polk undertook a fourth move which he hoped would have a happy ending. Encouraged to believe that the Mexicans were reconciled to receiving an envoy, the President dispatched John Slidell to Mexico City with orders to get a boundary at the Rio Grande and to offer sums ranging from $5,000,000 to $30,000,000 in payment for territory, depending on how much land the Mexicans would agree to sell. The smaller amount was to be compensation for New Mexico, the territory outside of Texas north of the Rio Grande; and the reason why the American Government was such a stickler for this river now becomes clear—any boundary short of the Rio Grande would fail to give the United States possession of this important wedge of territory driven into the heart of the Mexican southwest. The maximum amount was to be offered if the Mexicans could be tempted to sell California, including San Francisco Bay. The possession of this bay, Slidell was told, was all important to the United States.

The President gave his envoy no advice on what to do, if the Mexicans should slam the door in his face. Slidell was not to resort to threats. Polk, it appears, with the concurrence of the pacific-minded Buchanan, really hoped that the Mexicans would see for themselves the handwriting on the wall. On the one hand they were confronted with a show of force; on the other, they could choose peace and acceptance of a liberal offer of cash. Moreover, in addition to the cash, Polk offered to forgive them the full amount of unpaid claims the United States held against them. Such magnanimity, however, did not deter him from injecting a note of anger against Mexico in his annual message to Congress on December 2, 1845. Furthermore, in this same message Polk aimed his parting shot at Britain and France. The United States, he asserted, ' cannot in silence permit European interference on the North American continent; and should any such interference be attempted will be ready to resist it at any and all hazards '.

We know, and Polk knew, what action he premeditated in the event of an actual British attempt at intervention. But since no such intervention transpired, nor was even threatened, the succession of steps taken following his presidential message cannot be attributed to fear of foreign interference. Very early in January 1846 Polk learned from Slidell of the utter failure of the latter's mission: fearing internal repercussions, the feeble Mexican regime refused even to receive him. On the 13th orders were dispatched to General Taylor to cross the disputed ground and take up a position on the Rio Grande. Meanwhile, in the preceding October, Bancroft had sent Commodore Stockton to reinforce Sloat in the Pacific; and the orders to the latter to seize San Francisco Bay and Monterey, immediately upon receiving news of war, were now repeated. Taylor's advance to the Rio Grande met with the expected results. Appearing in full view of the Mexican army stationed at Matamoros on the opposite bank, he gave the Mexican commander no choice short of a humiliating retreat. A Mexican demand that the Americans evacuate the territory was countered by an American blockade of the river. This brought an armed clash, the first shots of which occurred on the *north* bank of the river although the main battle (Palo Alto) was fought on the *south* bank.

This successful manoeuvring of the Mexicans into firing the first shot worked out extremely well for President Polk. The date of the battle was April 24; the date on which news of it arrived in Washington was May 9; an entry in Polk's private diary under May 8, the day preceding, reveals that the President had already made up his mind to go to war. With an air of injured innocence Polk wrote, with apparent sincerity, of his ' duty ' to ' act with promptness and energy '; but still he and his cabinet were ludicrously anxious that the Mexicans commit the first hostility. When the good news finally arrived, he had his cabinet all assembled within the hour, and with their blessing he was now able to tell Congress that Mexico

> has passed the boundary of the United States, has invaded our territory and shed American blood upon the American soil . . . war exists, and notwithstanding all our efforts to avoid it, exists by the act of Mexico. . . .[1]

A cool judgment on Polk can be found in a speech delivered by Abraham Lincoln in the House of Representatives in January 1848,

[1] *The Diary of James K. Polk during his Presidency, 1845–1849*, Milo Milton Quaife, ed., 4 vols., Chicago, 1910, I, pp. 382–6. Richardson, *Messages and Papers of the Presidents*, V, pp. 2288–93.

after the war was all over. The evidence that the President had offered to prove that Mexico had begun hostilities on American soil, said Lincoln, was ' the sheerest deception ', and, he added:

> My way of living leads me to be about the courts of justice; and there I have sometimes seen a good lawyer, struggling for his client's neck, in a desperate case, employing every artifice to work round, befog, and cover up with many words some position pressed upon him by the prosecution, which he dared not admit, and yet could not deny. . . . A true issue made by the President would be about as follows: I say the soil was *ours* on which the first blood was shed; there are those who say it was not.[1]

Now it is apparent that the Texan boundary issue, in itself of no immediate practical importance and of doubtful merit, was the *casus belli* decided upon by James K. Polk and his cabinet. But the real objective was the coastal province of California. The manoeuvring during the preceding year leaves no doubt about this, although Polk characteristically kept it concealed. California was to be got and got without delay, by one of three methods: (1) bargaining for it over the counter, (2) incitement of a local insurrection, (3) outright seizure, if necessary. After Slidell's bootless mission to Mexico City the third alternative was the only one left.

Congress on May 13, 1846 accepted Polk's story and declared war. A month later George Bancroft wrote his friend Samuel Hooper, a Massachusetts merchant banker, as follows:

> From the best judgment I can form, Commodore Sloat could not have heard of hostilities before May 17, perhaps not so soon. Within three weeks after that, our flag ought to have been flying at Monterey and San Francisco; and the customhouse of Mexico would of course become an antiquity. I hope California is now in our possession, never to be given up. We were driven reluctantly to war; we must make a solid peace; that shall open the far west to religious freedom, political rights, schools, commerce and industry. The time will come when you may pass on railroads and steamers from Boston to San Francisco.[2]

---

[1] *Cong. Globe*, 30th cong., 1 sess., app. pp. 93–5.

[2] Bancroft to Hooper, June 16, 1846. Bancroft Papers. Bancroft's timing was remarkably accurate: Sloat wrote to Larkin from Mazatlán, May 18, that he had just heard of the battle and was sailing immediately for Monterey with a squadron of seven ships. One of these ships, apparently faster, was sent on ahead with the message. ' I do not think it necessary to write more particular ', added Sloat, ' as I am confident you will understand my object '. *Larkin Papers*, IV, p. 378.

Having business interests in California, Hooper lost no time in replying with an inquiry respecting the boundary. Would it be extended as far south as ' St. Diego ', and so take in all the good harbours of California? Hooper's letter attracted Bancroft's immediate attention, for he replied on June 22:

Write to me exactly your views about California, what orders it would be for the mercantile interest to give now, what line to insist upon in the event of a treaty of peace. . . .

I had not enumerated in the orders San Diego, but said ' San Francisco ', ' Monterey ', ' Mazatlan ' and ' Guymas ' and such other ports as he [Sloat] can. I can bid him send a brig into San Diego. Write me fully, giving information and suggestions.

If Mexico makes peace this month the Rio del Norte and the parallel of 35 may do as a boundary; after that 32 which will include San Diego.

Hooper was the first to advocate conquering all of California, and his arguments were easily accepted. Prior to this time the Americans intended to limit the conquest to the country north of 35. But, said Hooper, the settled part of California is a narrow strip extending about 300 miles on the coast north of 32. If 35 should be made the dividing line, about one-third of the population would be left subject to Mexico, although isolated from that country by hundreds of miles of impassable country. Revolts would be a constant source of annoyance. On the other hand, south of 32 there is no fine country, and if that line is made the boundary, it would continue for centuries to leave an almost impassable country between Mexico and the United States on the Pacific. Moreover, it was important to the mercantile interest to have San Diego and the pueblo de Los Angeles, the largest single settlement in the province, as well as Monterey and San Francisco, ' as it would insure a peaceful state of things through the whole country and enable them to continue their trade as before along the whole coast and to collect their debts as they expected from the crops of this year. . . .'[1]

The whole of California fell as the prize of war before the end of August 1846, Bancroft having followed Hooper's advice and ordered Sloat to take San Diego. But the Polk Government did not get the short war and quick peace that it wanted. Bancroft even hoped that,

[1] Hooper to Bancroft, June 19; Bancroft to Hooper, June 22; Hooper to Bancroft, June 25, 1846. Bancroft Papers.

now that the Oregon issue was settled, Britain would use her influence with the Mexicans to settle up.[1] But since the Mexicans would not treat, Polk to his embarrassment came to the conclusion that the one way to get a treaty was to dictate it in Mexico City. As Webster said: ' Mexico is an ugly enemy. She will not fight—& will not treat '. An amphibious expedition under General Winfield Scott, disembarking at Vera Cruz, penetrated to the vicinity of the capital and forced an armistice in August 1847. But since Mexico had been the ' aggressor ', the formula for peace required that she ' indemnify ' the United States by ceding California and New Mexico. Polk's agent, Nicholas P. Trist, who was dispatched from Washington in great secrecy to catch up with Scott's army, had difficulty in convincing the Mexicans that they ought to do this, even though Trist was authorized to offer a money compensation of as much as $25,000,000. Trist's first diplomatic contact in Mexico was Charles Bankhead, the British minister, who helped persuade the Mexicans to agree to an armistice on the basis of the Nueces River and the cession of San Francisco.

News of this armistice threw Polk into a rage; moreover, with Mexico showing signs of collapse, the President began to think in terms of dismemberment, the ' indemnity ' to be increased so as to include Lower California and Mexico's northern states. The United States might even be forced into annexing *all* of Mexico to satisfy a rising chorus of newspaper opinion that raised its voice after Scott had entered Mexico City.[2] Such demands, however, alarmed the more conservative politicians of both parties, for the war was already embittering the internal controversy over slavery. If the war continued indefinitely, the Mexicans refusing to come to terms, the whole cause might be lost. In his December 1847 annual message, Polk, for the first time, publicly admitted what he had had in mind all along: his desire for California. The latter's harbours, he said ' would afford shelter for our navy, for our numerous whale ships, and other merchant vessels employed in the Pacific ocean, [and] would in a short period become the marts of an extensive and profitable commerce with China, and other countries of the East '.[3]

[1] Bancroft to Hooper, June 16, 1846. Ibid.
[2] J. D. P. Fuller, *The Movement for the Acquisition of All Mexico, 1846–1848*, Johns Hopkins University Studies in Historical and Political Science, LIV, Baltimore, 1936, *passim*.
[3] *Cong. Globe*, 30th cong., 1 sess., app. pp. 2–3. For the effects of the war upon internal politics see Graebner, op. cit., pp. 171–90.

Whether peace could be made, however, rested upon the shoulders of Nicholas P. Trist, whom Polk had ordered home. Trist remained in spite of the order, resting his decision upon the advice of General Scott and Mr. Bankhead, the British minister. The British legation now laboured with the Mexicans to meet the American demands, which included San Diego, for British diplomacy too recognized the threat of political disaster if the war were not brought to a close. The end result of this combined diplomatic effort in Mexico City was a treaty of peace signed by Trist at Guadalupe Hidalgo, February 2, 1848, yielding the Rio Grande and the line of the 32nd parallel as the boundary, the United States to compensate Mexico with a money payment of $15,000,000. According to Polk, Trist was ' an impudent and unqualified scoundrel', but the ' scoundrel' nevertheless got the President exactly what he had set out in the war to get. The United States now had its Pacific Ocean frontage.

Speaking in the Senate two years later, William H. Seward, the rising senator from New York State, gave free play to his imagination in depicting the dazzling future he saw for the United States. Said Seward:

The world contains no seat of empire so magnificent as this, which, while it embraces all the varying climates of the temperate zone, and is traversed by the wide-expanding lakes and long branching rivers, offers supplies on the Atlantic shores to the over-crowded nations of Europe, while on the Pacific coast it intercepts the commerce of the Indies. The nation thus situated, and enjoying forest, mineral, and agricultural resources unequalled, if endowed also with a government adapted to their character and condition, must command the empire of the seas, which alone is real empire...

... The Atlantic States, through their commercial, social, and political affinities and sympathies, are steadily renovating the Governments and social constitutions of Europe and Africa; the Pacific States must necessarily perform the same sublime and beneficent functions in Asia. If, then, the American people shall remain an undivided nation, the ripening civilization of the West, after a separation growing wider and wider for four thousand years, will in its circuit of the world, meet again, and mingle with the declining civilization of the East on our own free soil, and a new and more perfect civilization will arise to bless the earth, under the sway of our own cherished and beneficent democratic institutions. . . .[1]

[1] Ibid., app., p. 267.

CHAPTER VII

THE THRUST INTO THE CARIBBEAN, 1848–1917

'A Basin of Water belonging to the United States'

THE American *Drang nach Süden*—the pull to the south— had its origins, like the thrusts to the west and the north, in the seventeenth century. It belongs with the British push into the Caribbean, which started even before Cromwell, and it grew with the successive British attempts to invalidate the Spanish claims to that sea as a closed Spanish lake. In the next century Colonial leaders welcomed the War of Jenkins's Ear for the trade benefits that it would bring, and in 1741 an expeditionary force of 3,600 men, mostly from Pennsylvania, joined the British in the abortive siege of Cartagena. Benjamin Franklin, at that time editing his weekly newspaper, the *Pennsylvania Gazette*, shared the enthusiasm of the provincial governor for this expedition and lent a hand in the latter's recruiting campaign. Freebooting voyages to the Spanish Main by vessels from Philadelphia and other Colonial ports were already an old story; and if the Americans gained no other benefits from this war, their privateers reaped the profits from the capture of nearly 2,500 Spanish and French merchantmen. Moreover, by the time this war was over, the Colonial merchants had obtained almost a monopoly of the West Indian business: they owned and operated the ships, and marketed in the French and Spanish as well as in the British islands the large surplus of products which the mainland colonies had for export. In exchange they brought back sugar and molasses to supply the innumerable distilleries scattered along the thousand-mile coast from Maine to Georgia. Every mainland port and nearly every mainland merchant had ties in the West Indies— family ties and property holdings, such as the Livingstons of New York and the Dickensons of ·Philadelphia; speculators like the Beekmans of New York; general exporters and ship-owners like the Browns of Providence; agencies like that of Peter Faneuil of Boston and Richard Derby of Salem who dealt in enemy sugar during the Seven Years War, handling the affairs of Frenchmen as well as their own. In short, the West Indian trade permeated all parts of the main-land economy and contributed substantially to the wealth of the sea-board merchants.[1]

Benjamin Franklin gave candid expression to this pull to the south in 1761, when he suggested Cuba and Mexico as the next objects of aggression. Spain would thus vanish from the region and her lake become British or, more realistically, American. This was about the same time that Russia began her quest for the Turkish Straits. The history of warfare in the Caribbean shows that it has been very difficult for any one power to gain, or keep, control of this American Mediterranean. Writing in *The Federalist* in 1787, Alex-ander Hamilton set forth in terse language how he thought it might be done. A small American navy, he reasoned, could easily turn the scales between the rival European powers and enable the United States to control the balance of power in the Caribbean.

Cuba being looked upon as an appendage to the Florida coast, it was generally assumed that the island would sooner or later be absorbed into the American Union. John Quincy Adams expressed the current notion of his generation when he likened it to a ripening apple which ' cannot choose but fall to the ground '. But, though it was policy to encourage the independence movements on the main-land against Spain, neither the Monroe administration nor its successors desired an insurrection on the island. Preservation of Spanish authority for the time being suited American purposes, as it did Britain's. There was one difference between British and Ameri-can policy, however. The British were prepared to neutralize Cuba under Spain, provided the United States and France would join them in a formal guarantee. A proposal to this effect met with a refusal: the Adams administration preferred to keep an eye on the apple tree.

As a last desperate resort, the United States in 1823 was even prepared to fight in defence of Cuba, if John Quincy Adams is to be taken at his word. The island, he declared, had ' an importance in the sum of our national interests, with which that of no other foreign territory can be compared, and little inferior to that which binds the

[1] This paragraph is based mainly on the works of Richard Pares, *War and Trade in the West Indies, 1739–1763*, Oxford, 1936, and especially his *Yankees and Creoles. The Trade between North America and the West Indies before the American Revolution*, Cambridge, Mass., 1956. See also Robert L. D. Davidson, *War Comes to Quaker Pennsylvania, 1682–1756*, N.Y., 1957, pp. 24–48.

different members of this Union together '.[1] But Adams did not believe his own threat, for he gambled on Britain too being concerned with the *status quo*. British zeal against slavery and the slave trade led subsequently, however, to the belief readily accepted in the United States that Britain intended to 'Africanize ' the island and treat it as a protectorate. Lord George Bentinck, the Tory leader in Parliament, lent support to this belief when in 1848 he publicly advocated Spain's hypothecating Cuba as security for the debts on which she had defaulted.

By this time the American rumour factory was already hard at work over alleged British designs on Central America and the Yucatan peninsula. An agent from Bogotá and another agent from Yucatan, each seeking American intervention, fed these rumours, if indeed they did not originate them. Señor Sierra spread tall tales among congressmen of the British putting arms into the hands of Indians in Yucatan with the object of instigating a massacre of the whites. Sierra's mission was to try to persuade the Polk government to declare a protectorate over his country and so free it from Mexico; and the best way to accomplish this, so he apparently concluded, was to excite American suspicions of the British. This propaganda succeeded admirably, for it touched off another round of fiery speeches in the Senate and a request from Polk to Congress to give him authority to intervene in Yucatan with troops.[2] England, cried Senator Hannegan of Indiana (one of the old 'Fifty-four Forties'), is hastening ' with race-horse speed ', to seize the entire isthmus of Central America, Yucatan, and then Cuba. This encouraged Jefferson Davis of Mississippi to declare himself in favour of the United States taking Yucatan and Cuba. These are ' the salient points on the Gulf of Mexico ', he explained,

> which I hold to be a basin of water belonging to the United States.
> . . . I am ready for one, to declare that my step will be forward, and
> that the cape of Yucatan and the island of Cuba must be ours.[3]

Suspicion of Great Britain—morbid suspicion, to put it candidly —was a stimulus for the forward movement into the Caribbean

[1] John Quincy Adams, *Memoirs, Comprising Portions of His Diary from 1795 to 1848*, C. F. Adams, ed., 12 vols., Phila., 1874–77, VI, pp. 112, 138; *Writings*, W. C. Ford, ed., 7 vols., N.Y., 1913–17, VII, p. 372.

[2] The documentation on this matter is to be found in Richard W. Van Alstyne, ' The Central American Policy of Lord Palmerston, 1846–1848 ', *Hisp. Am. Hist. Rev.*, XVI, 1936, pp. 341–59.

[3] *Cong. Globe*, 30th cong., 1 sess., part II, app., p. 596.

which now began. But it was only a stimulus, never the cause; and the new position of power gained by the United States from the war with Mexico made the time ripe, or at least so it seemed. It was time to start converting the negatives of the Monroe Doctrine, the formulae prepared for invocation against Europe, into positives, embodying first of all steps toward turning the Caribbean into an American lake. But for popularizing the movement, for explaining and justifying it, recourse was henceforth had in increasing measure to the dogmas of Monroe. It is to be remembered that the Monroe Doctrine gathered dust during the first twenty-five years after its pronouncement, that it did not gain fame until the era of President Polk. Furthermore, it was the very men who demanded a forward movement of annexations who vociferously exploited the name of Monroe. The Prophet was at last coming into his own. Like Holy Writ, his doctrine was something to be believed, but not to be criticized.

Grist for this mill came also from John L. O'Sullivan, the editor of the *Democratic Review* who, we recall, had brilliantly restated John Quincy Adams's law of nature, and from Moses Yale Beach, the editor of the *New York Sun*, who had been in Mexico during the war intriguing for President Polk. O'Sullivan had family ties in Cuba, and had persuaded himself that the sugar planters, attracted by the prospect of an American guarantee of slavery, would put up the money for buying the island. The American Consul-General in Havana, Robert Campbell, seconded these arguments, as did the United States Mail Steamship Company of New York and its Havana agents, Drake Brothers. To compensate for the extra slave state, O'Sullivan pointed out, the North would renew its thrust against Canada, an object desirable for its own sake. Beach broke out in his paper with a leader declaring that, if the government would offer a hundred millions for Cuba, ' with one week's notice, the whole amount will be raised and paid over by the inhabitants of the Island '. ' Give us Cuba ', he demanded, ' and our possessions are complete.'

O'Sullivan, Beach, Campbell and Jefferson Davis all urged their arguments on Polk and Buchanan, and persuaded them that the Cuban planters were indeed ready to revolt; and when the Secretary of the Treasury, Robert J. Walker, who had been influential in getting Texas, declared himself convinced, Polk's mind was made up. Borrowing the ideas of O'Sullivan and Beach, he would undertake to buy Spain's 'Ever Faithful Isle' without consulting Congress in advance, much less asking it for funds. Moreover, he had a secret report that Queen Isabella II wanted to sell the island, and so Romulus M. Saunders, the American minister in Madrid, was told to start with an offer of $50,000,000 and go up to $100,000,000 if necessary. These are large sums when compared to the paltry amounts Polk had held out to Mexico for California, though even the larger amount was in this case looked upon as a bargain.

Monroe Doctrine language, though not the Monroe Doctrine by name, was employed by James Buchanan, the Secretary of State, in composing this note of June 1848 to be used by Saunders in his secret talks with the ministers of the Spanish Crown. Alluding to the uprising which he had been told would soon occur in Cuba, Buchanan proceeds on the assumption that Britain wants the island, though he is understandably vague in submitting evidence thereto. But he is not vague in calculating the benefits possession of Cuba would bring to the United States. It would give command of the Gulf of Mexico, render the British West Indies valueless, and gain vast new markets for the United States, especially in the area of tropical products. We are, says the Secretary of State, Britain's chief commercial rival; our tonnage is now almost equal to hers, and it will soon be greater, if nothing should occur to arrest our progress. ' Of what vast importance would it, then, be to her to obtain possession of an island from which she could at any time destroy a very large portion of our foreign and coasting trade? '

But the most surprising feature of this dispatch is the bland assumption that Cuba could be annexed as a State. ' Under our government', asserts Buchanan, 'it would speedily be *Americanized*, as Louisiana has been.' And then he added, confidently: ' Cuba, justly appreciating the advantages of annexation, is now ready to rush into our arms.' Flushed with such hopes, Buchanan must have had a shock at the snubbing his emissary received from the Spaniards. They would rather see the isle sunk in the sea, was the response. Nevertheless, Buchanan had strong feelings on the subject. ' We can't do without Cuba ', he wrote privately to his successor in the State Department, John M. Clayton. 'And above all we must not suffer its transfer to Great Britain. We shall acquire it by a *coup d'état* at some propitious moment, which from the present state of Europe, may not be far distant.'

Now it is evident that President Polk and his Cabinet hoped, by a sudden, dramatic stroke, to crown the victory over Mexico with an annexation that would make American hegemony to the south a certainty. From this point on, the internal controversy over slavery breaks fiercely into the open and draws attention away from the otherwise strong and persistent forces seeking expansion. The unity of these forces and their meaning in terms of a universal American empire was perceived and succinctly, though colourfully, described by J. D. B. DeBow, a South Carolinian who had in 1846 moved to New Orleans and begun publication of a monthly review that bore his name. This is what DeBow had to say in 1850:

> *We have a destiny to perform*, a ' manifest destiny ' over all Mexico, over South America, over the West Indies and Canada. The Sandwich Islands are as necessary to our eastern, as the isles of the gulf to our western commerce. The gates of the Chinese empire must be thrown down by the men from the Sacramento and the Oregon, and the haughty Japanese tramplers upon the cross be enlightened in the doctrines of republicanism and the ballot box. The eagle of the republic shall poise itself over the field of Waterloo, after tracing its flight among the gorges of the Himalaya or the Ural mountains, and a successor of Washington ascend the chair of universal empire! . . . The people stand ready to hail tomorrow . . . a collision with the proudest and the mightiest empire upon earth.

Northern, Southern, and Middle Western interests united at this time in a common desire for Cuba. But for the internal quarrel, the pressure exerted by these interests was strong enough to bring results. From New York the firm of Drake Brothers and Company dealt in the Cuban sugar trade and owned one of the best plantations in the island; while the United States Mail Steamship Company, collaborating with Drake Brothers and possessing diversified interests in shipping, sugar and slave labour functioned as an intermediary between revolutionists in the island and the junta in New York. New Orleans—the Crescent City—was still more directly concerned. Cotton, grain and cattle from the Mississippi valley passed through it *en route* to foreign markets; by the mid-century it was second only to New York in the value of its foreign trade; possession of Cuba, declared DeBow, would make New Orleans the leading port of the world; and as a future slave state, the island was looked upon as a bulwark of strength for the South. Similar interests in the upper Mississippi valley regarded Cuba with great favour. Thus the Illinois Central Railroad anticipated bringing Cuban sugar to the Chicago market and carrying wheat and pork south for export to the West Indies. Chicago, New Orleans, Havana and New York were tied together in a web of banking, trading and transportation interests; and politicians like Stephen A. Douglas of Illinois, George N. Sanders of Kentucky, Judah P. Benjamin of Louisiana, and George Law of New York, each of whom was active in business, identified themselves as ' Young Americans ', eager proponents of expansion.

'Young America', Ralph Waldo Emerson had written in 1844, is the land of the future: ' the development of our American internal resources, the extension to the utmost of the commercial system, and the appearance of new moral causes which are to modify the State, are giving an aspect of greatness to the Future, which the imagination fears to open. One thing is plain for all men of common sense and common conscience, that here, here in America, is the home of man.' The sentiment, Utopian as Emerson expressed it, made a wide appeal—to all patriots, of course, and to the refugees from the European revolutions who believed the United States would overthrow Old World institutions and establish a ' republic of the world '. Thus Louis Kossuth, the Hungarian patriot, hoped and believed he would get American help in the liberation of Hungary. But while the practical leaders of ' Young America ' could declaim in terms of world ' liberation ', and while some of them appear to have believed their own rhetoric, they gave their main attention to the southward drive, Cuba being the immediate object.

President Polk's hopeful intrigue having met with failure, New York and New Orleans interests seized the opportunity to collaborate with Cuban revolutionaries in overthrowing Spanish rule. The filibustering adventurer, Narciso Lopez, made three armed attempts on the island, 1849–51, his men, like their Italian counterparts in Europe under Guiseppe Garibaldi, wearing red shirts. O'Sullivan, Sanders, Jefferson Davis and many others came to the aid of Lopez with arms and money; and New Orleans, the romantic city of bygone pirates, became the headquarters. Veterans of the Mexican war offered their services, the arsenals of Louisiana and Mississippi furnished some of the guns, and the port authorities, accepting the story that the expeditions consisted of peaceful emigrants *en route* to

California, cleared the filibustering vessels for Panama. The Spanish consul complained to the Federal Government in Washington, and the latter tried to stop the expeditions from sailing; but indifference on the part of the Federal district attorney and collusion with the filibusters on the part of the city and state authorities defeated these efforts. Lopez, however, was a failure: his landings in Cuba did not lead to an uprising, and on his third attempt his entire band was captured and the leader himself executed.

Meanwhile, prodded by Spain to come to her assistance, the British and French Governments had approached the conservative Whig administration of President Fillmore in the hope of inducing it to join in a tripartite pact guaranteeing the *status quo*. The pact was meant as a disclaimer by all three powers of any designs on the island and as a binding pledge to discountenance filibustering, something which the Fillmore Government had already attempted, though without success. The administration gave the proposal serious thought, but finally, having lost the presidential election to the Democrats, decided against embarrassing its own party by declaring itself opposed to annexation. Edward Everett, the Secretary of State, wrote a reply of extraordinary length and detail in which he reverted to the position of John Quincy Adams. Territorially and commercially, he admitted, Cuba would be an extremely valuable possession. Its condition was mainly an American question, and its acquisition might take place ' in the natural order of things '.

The incoming administration of Franklin Pierce and its supporters of Young America, however, were disinclined to await the slow operation of the ' forces of nature '. They wanted action, and in their eyes Texas still stood as the shining example of how a valuable territory could be acquired. If a general advance was to be made, moreover, as Pierce implied and as his supporters demanded, Cuba was a prerequisite. Without this island the dreams of a greater American empire would be futile. The Pierce Government worked along two parallel lines of policy. August Belmont, a thirty-eight year old banker from the Palatinate, initiated the first; Governor John A. Quitman of Mississippi, a veteran of Texan annexation and of the Mexican war, promoted the second. Belmont had made his mark working in Naples and Havana for the German branch of the Rothschild family. He then moved to New York, took out citizenship, acquired a fortune of his own, and became infected with the enthusiasms and ambitions of Young America. The young banker was a party to the intrigue of 1848 and, retaining his faith in the power of money, was confident of his own ability to procure Cuba for the United States. He proposed to work through the Rothschilds, bankers to the Spanish Crown and to the Spanish royal family. Spanish bonds were in default and the royal family impoverished. If the Rothschilds could be won over, Spanish intransigence over Cuba could be overcome. Belmont and Buchanan concurred on the feasibility of this approach; the former went to The Hague as United States minister, the latter to London. To London also went two other Young Americans: George N. Sanders, who was privy to Belmont's scheme, took the consular post, while Daniel Sickles attached himself to the legation as secretary. This is as far as our factual knowledge goes. What Belmont did in The Hague and what Buchanan and his associates did in London to mobilize the bankers against Spain remain an unknown quantity. The scheme fell through, but the idea of buying Cuba continued as a fixation in the American mind.

Governor Quitman proposed resuming where Lopez had left off: he would personally organize and lead a filibustering attack large enough to succeed. Quitman had regarded Lopez as his protégé and had put his own funds into Lopez' expeditions. After Cuba, in Quitman's mind, would come Mexico and Central America, and the result would be a powerful empire of the Southern states, which would then break their union with the North. The militant governor began laying his plans almost immediately after Pierce became President, and made no secret of his intentions. He had powerful and willing support: Caleb Cushing, the Attorney-General; John L. O'Sullivan, whom Pierce appointed to the diplomatic post in Lisbon; Pierre Soulé, the fiery exile from France who got to be senator for Louisiana and who now prevailed upon President Pierce to make him United States minister to Spain; George Law of the New York Mail Steamship Company; John Slidell, who succeeded to Soulé's seat in the Senate; Robert J. Walker, whose name was a hardy perennial in the history of American filibustering; and many others. All the evidence points to the conclusion that the Pierce Government, or at least certain members of it, knew and approved of Quitman's plans. The President even obliged by sending a personal friend of Quitman to fill the consular post in Havana. In August 1853 the governor signed an agreement with the Cuban junta of New York, by which they made him their chieftain and handed him absolute power.

In the meantime Soulé set out for Madrid via Paris with the one object of inducing Spain to part with Cuba. Hopefully the administration waited upon the expected uprising. Soulé, Sanders, and their friends were so optimistic as to think they could stimulate revolutionary outbreaks in Europe. Then Cuba, free and independent, would knock for admission to the Union and enter as Texas had done. The word for Soulé to pass on to Spain was that the island would either ' release itself, or be released '. But Quitman was not yet ready, and the Cubans themselves were cowed by the size of the Spanish garrison. The captain-general set a backfire with threats to free the slaves, a move calculated to bring about the dreaded Africanization; and then in February 1854 he audaciously called the bluff of the Pierce Government by seizing an American vessel, the *Black Warrior*, on a technical charge of violating the port regulations. But President Pierce was incapable of meeting the challenge—he may have been waiting for Quitman, although that worthy in spite of proffers of help kept on procrastinating. The Secretary of State, William L. Marcy, who looked on all these activities with something less than enthusiasm, sent fresh instructions to Soulé to demand a $300,000 indemnity from Spain; but when the reckless minister turned this into a 48-hour ultimatum, he found his own bluff called by the Spanish Foreign Minister. But the administration in Washington continued to harbour the illusion that somehow or other the prize could be won. Soulé was authorized to tempt the Spaniards with a fresh offer of $130,000,000; but should they be unreceptive (as Marcy anticipated they would) he was then to direct his efforts ' to the next most desirable object which is to *detach* that island from the Spanish dominion and from all dependence on any European power '. Historians have spilled ink over this word ' detach '. What did the Secretary of State mean? Taken in context with the *Black Warrior* affair, which could have furnished a pretext for war, it seems certain that the administration lacked resolution, that in its Micawber-like fashion it was waiting and hoping for something to turn up.

Soulé, Buchanan and John Y. Mason, the American minister to France, held a meeting and put their names to a document asserting that, should Cuba become a menace (meaning Africanization), and should Spain still refuse to sell, 'then, by every law, human and divine, we shall be justified in wresting it from Spain if we possess the power'. The text of this paper was not intended to be scanned by the public, but, having been carried secretly to Washington, it 'leaked' to the *New York Herald* and earned the sobriquet of the Ostend Manifesto, by which it has been known ever since. Actually it is of slight importance, since it is an expression of attitudes previously formed and is an admission of failure. The Pierce Government likewise had to confess failure: its hopes of leading the nation away from sectional conflict through the panacea of 'popular sovereignty' in the Territories were already dashed. Ironically Quitman was ready at last. He had been laying the groundwork for his invasion with great care, and by February 1855 he was satisfied the job could be done. The Cuban conspirators let him know they would rise on the 12th and would assassinate the Spanish officials. Then the filibusters would come in four thousand strong at various points. But the captain-general nipped the plot in the bud and Quitman, after talking privately with President Pierce, decided to bury his part of the scheme. Franklin Pierce's dream of being a second President Polk thus ended in humiliation. Cuba was now more than ever out of reach, though James Buchanan, who succeeded Pierce in the presidency, from time to time put out feeble feelers in the hope of realizing a miracle.[1]

The problem which the Americans desired to solve painlessly of how to gain an ascendancy in Nicaragua, and eventually in the other Central American republics, turned out to be equally baffling. In this area too James K. Polk started certain preliminary moves which, like

[1] For this section on Cuba I am chiefly indebted to the penetrating monograph by Basil Rauch, *American Interest in Cuba: 1848-1855*, N.Y., 1948. See also: Amos A. Ettinger, *The Mission to Spain of Pierre Soulé, 1853-1855. A Study in the Cuban Diplomacy of the United States*, New Haven, 1932; Roy Franklin Nichols *Franklin Pierce, Young Hickory of the Granite Hills*, Phila., 1958; Ivor D. Spencer, *The Victor and the Spoils. A Life of William L. Marcy*, Providence, R.I., 1959. The editorial by DeBow is in his *Review*, IX, Aug., 1850, pp. 167-8. Emerson's essay on the Young American may be found in any edition of his collected works. Buchanan's dispatch of June 17, 1848, to Saunders and his private letter of 1849 to Clayton are in his *Works*, John Bassett Moore, ed., 12 vols., Phila., 1908-11, VIII, pp. 90-102, 360-1. Marcy's dispatch of April 3, 1854, containing the ill-fated word 'detach', is printed in Rauch, p. 282. (This word was deleted from the printed government document). Everett's state paper of Dec. 1, 1852, is by no means limited to saying 'no' to the Anglo-French proposal for a tripartite convention; for reasons subject only to surmise, it ranges far and wide through American history. It is worth reading as a study in basic attitudes and in historical interpretation. It is printed in full in 32nd cong., 2nd sess., *sen. ex. doc.* 13, pp. 15-23.

the pressure on Spain, registered the beginning of the general forward movement into the Caribbean set going by the war with Mexico. Here, as in California, Cuba and elsewhere, symptoms of British interest furnished the stimulus for the advance. British interests in Central America during the 1840s centred around two men: Alexander MacDonald, the superintendent of the flourishing logwood and mahogany settlement of Belize, and Frederick Chatfield, the chargé accredited to Guatemala. In 1844 the Colonial Office, acting upon MacDonald's urging, sent a resident agent to the Mosquito Coast to investigate the activities of certain speculators who were British subjects. The agent charged the latter with committing a fraud against the Mosquito Indians, whose chief had been previously declared 'king' with MacDonald's knowledge and consent. MacDonald hoped to promote a progressive group of British colonies clustered about Belize, with the Mosquito 'kingdom' an example of an enlightened British protectorate. It was the sort of relationship that Governor Hobson of New South Wales had already established with the Maori tribes of New Zealand. In 1845 Lord Aberdeen, prompted by MacDonald, declared a protectorate over the Indian 'kingdom', a move that aroused protests from New Granada, Nicaragua and Honduras, each of whom laid claim to all or portions of the Mosquito Coast. Vigorous action followed in 1847–8 under orders from Lord Palmerston, and the British Government now stood committed to defend the Mosquito 'kingdom' and the 800 miles of coast that it theoretically occupied. These steps were taken upon the advice of Frederick Chatfield, who was trying to resuscitate the defunct Central American Federation. Alarmed by the collapse of Mexico, Chatfield aimed at a *pax Britannica* in Central America, with Guatemala as the northern buffer against a further American advance and British naval stations erected on either side of the Central American isthmus.

The sum total of these activities spelled out a British sphere of influence over Central America and the inner Caribbean, including Jamaica, with the ostensible purpose of making a stand against the United States. Lord Palmerston himself was favourably disposed to the general plan, but not to the point of pushing matters to their logical extreme. Unfortunately, however, here was one case where the British Government permitted itself to be pulled along by its subordinates to a point where there was an implied challenge to the

. But of course neither government wished to draw lines over
arge and indefinite issues. Each was disposed to keep the
sion at the purely local level; and each aimed to convince the
that it harboured no large ambitions to dominate the area. A
acted negotiation in Washington between Sir Henry Bulwer
John M. Clayton led to the adoption in April 1850 of a lengthy
elusively worded formula designed to neutralize Central America.
ther country would seek to obtain exclusive control over the
roceanic trade route; neither would colonize or exercise dominion
r any part of Central America; neither would make use of any
iance or of any intimacy that it might have with any Central
merican state to get the advantage over the other. In short, the
layton-Bulwer treaty required a completely hands-off policy on the
art of both powers.[1]

When it came to practice, this requirement proved very difficult,
fundamentally because, as Sir Henry Bulwer himself admitted, the
Clayton-Bulwer treaty ' tacitly set aside the Munro doctrine, viz.,
that the States of Europe have nothing to do with the States of
America '.[2] In reality Central America was a power vacuum of weak
and jealous local republics situated strategically on a potentially
valuable interoceanic route, which had peculiar importance to the
United States. On her part, Britain possessed certain old and well-
established interests, which included the historic tie with Belize and
its dependencies, the Bay Islands, as well as the prestige matter at
stake in the issue over the Mosquito protectorate.[3]

The Democrats, who had already under Polk identified themselves
as the party of the Monroe Doctrine, recognized the political value
to themselves of challenging the treaty, and lost little time in doing so.

---

[1] See the following of my articles: ' The Central American Policy of Lord
Palmerston, 1846–1848 ', op. cit.; ' British diplomacy and the Clayton-Bulwer
Treaty, 1850–1860 ', Journ. of Mod. Hist., XI, 1939, pp. 149–183; ' John F.
Crampton, Conspirator or Dupe? ' Amer. Hist. Rev., XLI, 1935–6, pp. 492–502;
'Anglo-American Relations, 1853–1857. British Statesmen on the Clayton-Bulwer
Treaty and American Expansion ', ibid., XLII, 1936–7, pp. 491–500; 'American
Filibustering and the British Navy: a Caribbean Analogue of Mediterranean
" Piracy " ', Amer. Journ. Int. Law, XXXII, 1938, pp. 138–42. And for a brief
treatment of same see my Amer. Dipl. in Action, pp. 141–55.

[2] Quoted in my ' British Diplomacy and the Clayton-Bulwer Treaty ', op. cit.,
p. 156.

[3] David Waddell of University College of the West Indies is the author of two
excellent studies: ' British Honduras and Anglo-American Relations ' in the
Caribbean Quarterly, V, 1957, 50–9; and ' Great Britain and the Bay Islands, 1821–
61 ' in the Hist. Journ., II, I, 1959, pp. 59–77.

United States, especially now that the latter h̶
in developing a trade route across the isthmus.
Central America with orders only to investigate,
with commendable caution; but the agent, a K̶
matched Chatfield by negotiating an alliance with
lated to bring the two powers into direct collision.
administration of General Taylor repudiated this m̶
agent, Ephraim George Squier, an amateur archaeo̶
in a similar fashion. Belatedly the two governments t̶
out of the hands of their subordinates; but both Sq̶
predecessor subsequently made themselves thorns in th̶
Taylor administration by supplying its Democratic oppo̶
ammunition against the British based upon their reaction̶
field. In 1852 Squier published a two-volume book on N̶
which he depicted as ' the key to the continent, destined t̶
the riches of two hemispheres, and which eager nations even ̶
aiming to snatch, with felon hand, from its rightful posses̶
Squier declared:

> To us is given, in this modern time, the ability . . . of acqui̶
> the rule of the East, . . . of transferring into our unarmed ha̶
> that passage for which Columbus strove in vain, . . . that vast a̶
> incalculable trade upon which is mainly based the maritime powe̶
> of England. . . . The fortune of war has planted our eagles on the
> Pacific: across the entire continent . . . our Republic is supreme.
> Our trim built fairies of the deep . . . sweep in the trade of Europe
> on one hand, and on the other bring to the mouth of the Sacra-
> mento the treasures of the Oriental world. . . . To gird the world as
> with a hoop, to pass a current of American Republicanism . . .
> over the continents of the earth, it needs but one small spot should
> be left free from foreign threats and aggression. . . .[1]

Thus the innocent-looking Mosquito question contained some very
large implications: the question of a British sphere of influence in the
Caribbean that would collide with the American aspiration to exercise
the sole voice over the affairs of Latin America; the question of the
control of the interoceanic passageway; and the general question of
the commercial rivalry of the two powers on a global scale. Here was
material for a conflict between the two empires over fundamental

---

[1] E. G. Squier, *Nicaragua; its people, scenery, monuments, and the proposed inter-oceanic canal*, 2 vols., N.Y., 1852, I, pp. 7–8.

To be implemented properly, the Clayton-Bulwer Treaty required co-operation, or at least a close understanding between the two governments; but the very opposite was of the essence of the Monroe Doctrine. When the Pierce administration came into power in 1853, an extremely complicated situation developed and continued to hover over the Clayton-Bulwer Treaty until the end of the decade. Except in a Pickwickian sense, the treaty ceased to function: officially the administration bombarded the British Government with arguments to prove that it should abandon all of its interests in Central America, and it became so argumentative after the Crimean war began that it was suspected of trying to exploit this war for its own ends; and by 1855 in Central America, with the swarming of the filibusters from the United States the scene was given over to anarchy. But in spite of its argumentative attitude and its disposition to harass, the Pierce administration was basically one of inaction. Nor was its successor, the Buchanan Government, any different. In their hands the Monroe Doctrine was still a straw sword, and the increasing shrillness of the internal controversy guaranteed that it would remain so. Finally in 1859, after Buchanan had agreed to step aside, Britain implemented the treaty in a series of agreements with the local states which disposed of the several local issues, including the reduction of the Mosquito protectorate and an agreement on the boundaries of Belize. As a final gesture in 1860 she converted the latter from a ' settlement ' into a Crown Colony. This formal act of colonization failed to excite a Monroe Doctrine protest from the man in the White House.

The War between the States was barely over before the forward movement into the Caribbean was resumed. But for thirty years it was more like an underground river than a surface stream. The wartime occupation of Mexico by the soldiers of Napoleon III provided a temporary stimulus in 1865, but in less than two years the French had liquidated this adventure, giving the Monroe Doctrine in American eyes an easy and bloodless victory. Other considerations besides American pressure, we now know, influenced the Emperor of the French to abandon this ill-starred enterprise; but the timing of the withdrawal led to the universal belief in the United States that the Monroe Doctrine had brought it about. From Polk to Buchanan the Doctrine had been utilized by the Democrats for party purposes; some Whigs, including Seward himself, had denied their belief in it. Moreover, when Seward as Secretary of State addressed Napoleon III on the advisability of his withdrawing from Mexico, he carefully refrained from offending French suscepti-bilities by thrusting the Doctrine upon them. But public opinion assumed that the Monroe Doctrine had accomplished the feat, and henceforth the Doctrine was endowed in the popular mind with supernatural qualities. From being a piece of stage property flaunted by the Democrats it emerged after the Civil War as the central creed of American nationalism, receiving as such universal affirmation.

A minority of belligerent nationalists at first tried to force the pace, sweeping south through the Caribbean and north over Canada. Ephraim George Squier organized a ' Monroe Doctrine Committee ', and tried to arouse enthusiasm with the jingle:

> If the old-world minions on our Continent remain,
> We'll take the old familiar guns, and go with Grant again!

General Nathaniel P. Banks, a fighting politician from Massachusetts though not a fighting general, proposed invoking the Monroe Doc-trine against the newly-formed Canadian Federation and, while chairman of the House committee on foreign affairs, lobbied inten-sively in the legislatures of Nova Scotia and New Brunswick to bring about a vote against joining the Dominion. Nothing daunted by the outcome in those provinces, Banks joined in the hue and cry raised in 1869 for the cession of Canada as indemnity for the alleged misdeeds of Britain against the North during the war. But Banks was equally eager for annexations in the Caribbean, the Danish West Indies, Haiti and Santo Domingo being his choice. ' I want to iden-tify my name ', he declared, ' with the acquisition of the Gulf of Mexico as a Sea of the United States. The day is near when Every European State will withdraw from this Continent; that is what I want to see done and to help to do '.[1] When in 1868 an insurrection broke out in Cuba, Banks tried to arouse popular passions against the Spaniards. But Congressional resolutions sponsored by him demanding intervention in Cuba and annexation of the Dominican Republic fell flat. The times were not ripe for further adventures abroad. Meanwhile the efforts of Seward and President Grant to

[1] Fred Harvey Harrington, *Fighting Politician. Major General N. P. Banks*, Phila., 1948. p. 186.

resume the southward march came to nothing. Seward negotiated a treaty with Denmark for the purchase of the Virgin Islands, but the Senate tabled it. Grant in 1869 made a dubious arrangement with the incumbent Dominican president for the annexation of that country, and then brought all the pressure he could bring to bear in the Senate to get his treaty ratified. A personal feud with the powerful Senator Sumner was a strong factor in defeating this treaty by a vote that fell just short of the necessary two-thirds.

New signs of preparations for a southward thrust appeared in 1879, when the American public led by President Hayes reacted unfavourably to the project of the French engineer, Ferdinand de Lesseps, to build an isthmian canal with private capital. De Lesseps's scheme was fully in line with the Clayton-Bulwer treaty—a waterway constructed and financed by private enterprise and encouraged by governments. But Hayes took the public position that any isthmian canal built would be ' virtually a part of the coast line of the United States ', and that it should be American-owned and controlled. De Lesseps tried, but failed to enlist the support of American private capital. Then in 1881 James G. Blaine, the Secretary of State, re-opened the argument with the British Government over the Clayton-Bulwer Treaty. The practical effect of the treaty, he insisted, was to leave Great Britain in control of the isthmus because of her preponderance in naval power. Hence the treaty did not really neutralize the region. But Blaine had a ' more comprehensive objection to the treaty ' than this. He wrote:

Its provisions embody a misconception of the relative positions of Great Britain and the United States with respect to the interests of each government in questions pertaining to this continent. The Government of the United States has no occasion to disavow an aggressive disposition. . . . At the same time, this government, with respect to European states, will not consent to perpetuate any treaty that impeaches our right and long-established claim to priority on the American continent. . . .[1]

Blaine's argument was a refinement of the one used by Buchanan at an earlier date, a demand this time that Great Britain recognize the changed power position of the United States. ' The military power of the United States, as shown by the recent civil war ', he

[1] 56th cong., 1st sess., *sen. ex. doc.* 161, pp. 178–84.

wrote, ' is without limit, and in any conflict on the American continent altogether irresistible.' But the Gladstone ministry was not impressed. It could conceive of ' no more melancholy spectacle ', than an arms race among the nations with West Indian possessions. Nor could it believe that, since the United States had openly insisted that any canal built was ' part of her coastline ', the Latin American states in the vicinity of the canal could ' retain as independent a position as that which they now enjoy '.[1] This cool reply terminated the debate for the time being, but in that very year, 1881, the United States began the construction of a new navy; Alfred Thayer Mahan started his lectures on the lessons of sea power at the newly-created Naval War College three years later; and in 1890 the Secretary of the Navy, Benjamin F. Tracy, recommended an increase in the number of battleships sufficient to command the western Atlantic, the eastern Pacific and the Caribbean Sea.[2] The navy also wanted coaling stations in the West Indies, and moving in its behalf Secretary Blaine made a secret approach to the Haitian Government for a lease of the harbour of Môle St. Nicolas.[3] The Haitians managed to evade the demand, however, and when next the question of a West Indian coaling station arose, American interest shifted to Guantanamo on the south side of the island of Cuba.

Chauvinism, directed at Great Britain and centring of course around the Monroe Doctrine, forced these undercurrents to the surface during the 1890s. There was a loud noise from a small explosion over a British intervention in Nicaragua in 1894, followed by a vigorous charge of dynamite set off the next year by Richard Olney over a long-standing question of a boundary between Venezuela and British Guiana. 'To-day', insisted Olney, 'the United States is practically sovereign on this continent, and its fiat is law upon the subjects to which it confines its interposition.' Thus in 1895 Olney bared the hidden purpose of the Monroe Doctrine, the assertion of a right of unlimited intervention in any issue concerning the two American continents. This time the British Government conceded the right, but subsequently won the boundary award on the merits of the case. The testiness of Olney, the Democrat, was

[1] Ibid., pp. 191–4.
[2] Harold and Margaret Sprout, *The Rise of American Naval Power, 1776–1918*, Princeton, N.J., 1939, pp. 205 ff.
[3] Rayford W. Logan, *The Diplomatic Relations of the United States with Haiti, 1776–1891*, Chapel Hill, N.C., 1941, pp. 411–57.

meanwhile outmatched the very same year by Henry Cabot Lodge, the Republican. Recommending that the United States add Canada, the Nicaraguan canal, Hawaii and Samoa to its dominions, Lodge assumed a threatening attitude toward Britain because of her West Indian possessions. ' We should have among those islands at least one strong naval station, and when the Nicaraguan canal is built, the island of Cuba . . . will become to us a necessity '.[1] The American public during this decade was feeling its oats, and the pose struck by Olney and Lodge showed that the stream of imperialism was once more in full view and flowing along at a rapid pace.

Spain, not Britain, was caught in this stream, however, and her few remaining possessions made the object of conquest. Like a number of other short wars of the latter part of the nineteenth century —the Franco-German war of 1870-71, the Sino-Japanese war of 1894, the South African war of 1899-1901, the Russo-Japanese war of 1904-05 are cases in point—the Spanish-American war of 1898 was a little war with big consequences. Ostensibly the issue was Cuba, but the Americans committed the overt act with a blow against the Spanish fleet in far-away Manila Bay. Cuban insurgents had started a second war for independence in 1894, and this time they found a receptive ear in the United States to their appeals for sympathy and assistance. Demands for intervention, fed by an awareness of how a liberated Cuba would subserve American ambitions, pressed in upon the administrations of Presidents Cleveland and McKinley.[2] For unlike the shrewd moves of James K. Polk against Mexico, the executive arm of the American Government followed a do-nothing policy until it was overwhelmed by popular demand. Belatedly the Spanish Government, counselled by the Holy See, announced a suspension of hostilities against the insurgents; but though this move promised domestic peace on the island, it did not halt the war demand in the United States. On April 11 President McKinley, with knowledge of the armistice already proclaimed in Cuba, asked Congress for authority to bring the war there to a stop!

The war that thus began between the United States and Spain,

---

[1] Quoted in Julius W. Pratt, *Expansionists of 1898. The Acquisition of Hawaii and the Spanish Islands*, Baltimore, 1936, p. 207.
[2] See, for example, George W. Auxier, ' Middle Western Newspapers and the Spanish-American War, 1895-1898 ', *Miss. Valley Hist. Rev.*, XXVI, 1939-40, pp. 523-34.

after the ostensible cause for it had disappeared, made the United States the dominant power in the Caribbean. Cuba was converted into a protectorate in 1901; Puerto Rico, where there had been no insurrection against Spanish authority and which had not been involved in the original controversy, was taken during the war by an army of occupation dispatched by the commanding general in Cuba. Spain ceded it to the United States, and it became an American dependency. There was, as I have hinted, a counterpart to these conquests on the farther side of the Pacific. The Spanish-American war was an expression of two powerful historic drives: the pull to the south, and the pull across the Pacific toward Asia. Its Pacific phase will be reviewed in the final lecture of this series.

That the Caribbean was now an American lake Great Britain characteristically recognized by coming to terms in 1901 over the long pending question of the isthmian canal. Not only did the United States get all that it wanted in the matter of ownership and control of the proposed waterway, subject to the use of the canal by the vessels of other nations on terms of equality; but it got the implied right to garrison the canal and fortify it at its own discretion. Perhaps the most significant feature of the new treaty, however, is the omission of any reference to an obligation to refrain from taking territory, making alliances, or exercising political influence. The neutralization formula, which was the very heart of the Clayton-Bulwer Treaty, was silently repealed.[1] The United States now had a blank cheque to treat the region of the Caribbean as its exclusive sphere of influence; and it proceeded to do so, using either or both of two arguments as justification—the Monroe Doctrine and the defence requirements of the canal. This meant that whatever independence (or 'self-determination') was enjoyed by the local republics situated on the islands and along the littoral of the Caribbean Sea was henceforth mortgaged to the foreign policy of the United States. There are a great many facets to this problem which make it difficult to generalize, though I am inclined to regard the first two decades of the twentieth century as a period of consolidation. Superficially American policy softened after 1920, but the basic consideration as I have just stated it remains fixed. The Caribbean

[1] Of the many discussions of the Hay-Pauncefote Treaty the following are to be especially recommended: Charles S. Campbell, Jr., *Anglo-American Understanding, 1898–1903*, Baltimore, 1957; J. A. S. Grenville, 'Great Britain and the Isthmian Canal, 1898–1901', *Amer. Hist. Rev.*, LXI, 1955, pp. 48–69.

republics are satellites of their powerful neighbour. The Monroe Doctrine throws a curtain over them, as it was originally intended to do, although it is not exactly an iron curtain.

The Platt Amendment, imposed on Cuba in 1903, served as a norm in the development of a policy applicable to all the Caribbean states according to the circumstances. Among other things, the amendment granted to the United States ' the right to intervene for the preservation of Cuban independence, [and] the maintenance of a government adequate for the protection of life, property, and individual liberty '. Lest I be misunderstood, let me repeat that the Platt Amendment conferred a statutory right of intervention in Cuba alone, but that it was assimilated to the treatment of the other Caribbean states. Elihu Root, the real author of this amend- ment, intended according to his own admission to spell out the Monroe Doctrine in detail, taking into account all possible contin- gencies. To put the matter in another way, the Platt Amendment is a bill of particulars regarding the Monroe Doctrine. And the basic attitude adopted by the United States was that the Caribbean was its exclusive preserve. It did not want the collaboration of outside powers, even small ones. Thus when Belgium in 1903 proposed an international debt commission to manage the affairs of the bankrupt and anarchical Dominican Republic, the proposal was ignored. The case of the Dominican Republic is especially interesting because it furnished the closest parallel to Egypt of any of the countries of the Caribbean. But whereas Egyptian finances had come in 1876 under the management of the international *Caisse de la Dette*, and whereas the Belgian Government suggested a similar procedure where the debt was likewise international, the United States in 1905 proceeded unilaterally with its own Receiver-General of Dominican customs.

This policy of exclusiveness was the one generally followed, the American Government expecting (and getting) silent consent from Europe. Nevertheless it did not hesitate to solicit European co- operation, if the occasion demanded. The illustration that comes to mind concerns steps taken secretly in 1909 to keep an exiled dictator from returning to his own country. In March of that year Cipriano Castro, one time president of Venezuela, embarked at Bordeaux with the announced intention of repeating Napoleon's feat of ' returning from Elba '. But Castro never got a chance to mimic Bonaparte—an ignominious voyage back to France was his fate. While he was on the high seas, the American Government made preparations for shadowing his ship, when it entered Caribbean waters. It sent two warships to Trinidad to intercept a disembarkation, and it procured the advance promise of the British, French and Dutch Governments not to allow him to land on any of their islands. Castro did get ashore once during the voyage—on Martinique island where, after five days, he was literally carried in his night-clothes to ship-side, while an American cruiser stood by in the harbour observing the spectacle. Lest he escape in a small boat, the cruiser then followed his ship until it was safely out in the Atlantic.[1]

Oftentimes Theodore Roosevelt and his successor, William Howard Taft, are singled out for pursuing a ' big stick ' policy in the Caribbean, with compliments paid to President Wilson for repudiating the ' imperialism ' of the Republicans. Actually the reverse is true, for the American grip on the Caribbean states tightened to the point of a stranglehold during the era of World War I. Thus a puppet government set up in Nicaragua in 1911 was continued by Wilson and the right of intervention strengthened by a new canal convention with that country; Haiti was converted into a protectorate in 1915; an American Military Government assumed the reins in the Dominican Republic in 1916; and a military occupation of Cuba took place in 1917. Although Wilson had a penchant for ' teaching democracy ' to the Latin Americans and for encouraging what he called ' constitutional government ', the Cuban president whom he maintained in office, General Menocal, had been elected as a result of a fraud. Various motives have been attributed to Wilson in his Latin American policies, but they all pointed straight in the direction of a *Pax Americana*. Thus his administration hoped to exclude even European private capital not merely from the Caribbean area, but from all Latin America, and to establish an American financial hegemony over the countries to the south.[2] To what extent fear of Germany served as a stimulus for these strong-arm policies it is difficult to say. At the end of the war, when Wilson's Caribbean policies came under fire (at the hands of the Republicans), his

[1] J. Fred Rippy and Clyde E. Hewitt, ' Cipriano Castro, " Man Without a Country " ', *Amer. Hist. Rev.*, LV, 1949–50, pp. 22–35.

[2] The policy of making financial vassals of the Latin American republics is set forth by Robert Lansing in a confidential memorandum on the Monroe Doctrine, Nov. 24, 1915. *For. Rel. U.S.*, *The Lansing Papers*, 2 vols., Washington, D.C., 1940, II, pp. 468–70. President Wilson's acknowledgment of this memo. indicates his endorsement.

defenders pleaded the danger of German aggression as justification. Yet there is a lack of tangible evidence of German activity in the Caribbean during World War I. Whatever the stimuli, it remains a fact that by 1917 the United States was truly the mistress of the Caribbean.

CHAPTER VIII

THE LURE OF EAST ASIA

' The World has assigned this duty to us '

IN point of time the China trade was the first of the American expansionist movements. China was the magnet which accounted for the path of empire into the Pacific broken by Yankee shipping in the 1780s. It frequently involved round-the-world voyages and, beginning with Thomas Jefferson, it stimulated a new search for trade routes. William Sturgis, the Boston merchant whom we previously encountered on the Pacific northwest coast, was in Canton in 1800, in command of a vessel when he was only eighteen years of age. Within the next eight years Sturgis made four voyages round the world, Canton being the principal destination of each voyage. In 1810 he formed a partnership with John Bryant, also of Boston, and from that date to 1840 more than half of the American trade between the Pacific coast and China was in the hands of this one firm. From Portsmouth, New Hampshire, to Charleston, South Carolina, there was hardly a port on the Atlantic seaboard that did not have its China merchants; but Boston, Salem and New York came to have the lion's share of the business. Sealskins from the Falkland Islands, sea-otter pelts from the Pacific northwest, natural sandalwood from the Sandwich Islands, ginseng from the Pacific southwest, opium from Turkey and India, kegs of Spanish silver dollars, and finally cotton-piece goods from the new New England mill towns furnished the bulk of the cargoes with which the American China merchants maintained a balance of payments for their purchases in China.

But it is not the purpose of this chapter to linger over this rich and fascinating commerce. Congregational missionaries from the American Board of Commissioners for Foreign Missions, notably Elijah C. Bridgman, Peter Parker and Samuel Wells Williams, entered upon the scene during the 1830s. The first two were medical missionaries, the third a printer who became the secretary of the mission station at Canton. All three were career missionaries whose influence in shaping governmental policies came to be considerable.

Between the missionaries and the China merchants there emerged a fund of interest and knowledge upon which the American Government drew in formulating its policies. Thus it was Senator Woodbury of Connecticut, an advocate of an official exploring expedition to the Pacific, who engineered the first diplomatic mission to the Far East and got Edmund Roberts, a New Hampshire merchant captain, appointed to the post; and it was Caleb Cushing, a Yankee lawyer and cousin of John P. Cushing, who at one time had been the most influential of the foreign resident agents in China, whom the Tyler administration dispatched in 1842 to negotiate a treaty with the Celestial Empire. None of these men could be accused of being Anglophiles, least of all Caleb Cushing; but they were all agreed on one thing—the desirability of wresting from the Chinese whatever advantages and privileges the British were extracting in consequence of the so-called Opium War. Nor were they conscience-stricken or hostile to the British because of the connection between the war and the opium trade. The merchants from whom the government elicited information dismissed the opium problem as unimportant, and urged the government to send a respectable fleet to back up its demands, a move that for some reason it failed to undertake. And though Bridgman and Parker were appalled by what they saw of the opium trade in China, they did not allow their emotions to becloud their verdict that the Anglo-Chinese war was necessary. The war, they reported, was ' not so much an opium or an English affair, as the result of a great design of Providence to make the wickedness of men subserve his purposes of mercy toward China, in breaking through her wall of exclusion, and bringing the empire into more immediate contact with western and christian nations .'[1] Returning to China in 1842 after a visit to Boston, Parker further reported that the opportunities for missionary labour were now better than at any previous time.[2]

With his usual gift for rationalizing, John Quincy Adams delivered a lecture in Boston which was printed in full in *Niles Weekly Register*, a Baltimore newspaper which was jealously anti-British. Adams drew upon the Christian religion and upon the Swiss publicist, Vattel, for a philosophical tirade against the Chinese. Their exclusion

---

[1] American Board of Commissioners for Foreign Missions, 32nd ann. rept. (1841).

[2] Ibid., 33rd. ann rept. (1842).

policy, he asserted, is contrary to the law of nature (an old favourite of his); it is anti-social, unrighteous because it violates the Christian principle of ' love thy neighbour ', anti-commercial and therefore immoral. It is ' an enormous outrage upon the rights of human nature, and upon the first principles of the rights of nations . . . .' And then added Adams:

I cannot forbear to express the hope that Britain, after taking the lead in the abolition of the African slave trade and of slavery, . . . will extend her liberating arm to the farthest bounds of Asia, and at the close of the present contest insist upon concluding the peace on terms of perfect equality with the Chinese empire. . . .[1]

Caleb Cushing did not need a fleet to get what he wanted, because the Treaty of Nanking already contained a safeguarding clause permitting merchants of the various nations to trade in the same ports as the British. Moreover, the American merchants resident in China had already expressed their satisfaction with the British instrument providing for the opening of the five treaty ports. So in a sense Cushing's treaty was superfluous, though it came in for undeserved praise on the ground that it was superior in legal phraseology and in a superficially more considerate moral approach to the Chinese. But Cushing's masterpiece assumed no obligation to be borne by the United States, and in fact none was assumed subsequently. Thus Cushing agreed to outlaw the opium trade, but the Boston firm of Russell & Company continued to prosper on the business. Members of this house were at the same time serving as American consuls at Canton and Shanghai.[2]

Subsequently the establishment by the British consul at Shanghai of the Imperial Chinese Customs Service, with which the Americans co-operated, led to the effective operation of the treaties. These became, after the Second China War ,' the perfected legal basis ' of the Sino-Western relationship. As Professor John K. Fairbank writes:

The aim of the Western trading powers in China was to trade but not to govern. Free trade and most-favored-nation treatment, expressive of this commercial interest, were the raison d'être of the Customs Service, whose constant purpose was to provide equal

[1] *Niles Weekly Register*, vol. 61, Jan. 22, 1842, pp. 326–30.
[2] John King Fairbank, *Trade and Diplomacy on the China Coast. The Opening of the Treaty Ports, 1842–1854*, 2 vols., Cambridge, Mass., 1953, I, p. 208.

terms of competition both among individual traders and among the trading nations in China. This was the spirit of the Open Door, a British doctrine long before John Hay voiced it.[1]

Meanwhile, the foreign community in Shanghai having been established and the United States having annexed California on the other side of the Pacific, projects for a trans-pacific steamship line operating between San Francisco and Shanghai came to the fore. Since the Japanese islands lay on the flank of this route, they naturally attracted attention. American whaling men were already familiar with Japanese waters, and needed ports for re-provisioning their vessels before doubling back on the long voyage to Nantucket. Japan, declared Daniel Webster, was 'the last link in that great chain, which unites all the world, by the early establishment of a line of Steamers from California to China.' Webster inspired the expedition of Commodore Matthew C. Perry, which set forth from the United States in 1852; but Perry, with a background of first-hand knowledge of the Orient, intended to put on a naval demonstration in Japan calculated to bring firmer results than Webster had planned. Perry would employ force, if necessary, to bring the Japanese to terms, as the British had done with the Chinese. And he could make the phrases of Manifest Destiny ring. 'The World has assigned this duty to us,' he declared: 'we have assumed the responsibility and undertaken the task, and can not now hold back.' Basic to his objectives was his appraisal of the strategy of the Pacific Ocean, and his belief that Britain and the United States, the two leading commercial powers, were fated to have a war over the Pacific. Britain had done much for China, Perry conceded, but she will take advantage of the positions she has gained to exclude her rivals from the trade of southeast Asia. She was

> already in possession of the most important points in the East India and China Seas. . . . Singapore commanding the South Western while Hong Kong covers the North Eastern Entrance, with the Island of Labuan on the Eastern Coast of Borneo, an intermediate point, she will have the power of shutting up at will, and controlling, the enormous trade of those seas. . . .[2]

The commodore had plans for converting the island of Okinawa into a depot for American commerce and for initiating treaty relations

[1] Ibid., p. 463. Quoted by permission of Harvard University Press.
[2] Miller, *Treaties*, VI, pp. 555–6.

with Japan equivalent to those previously imposed upon China. But he did not persist in his intentions, and the net result of his expedition was a mere shipwreck convention which opened two small Japanese ports for the purchase of provisions. Considering the breadth of Perry's ambitions, the distrust he felt for rival European powers, and the spirited way in which he pursued his mission, his treaty of March 31 1854, with the Japanese Shogun seems like a pale result of the elaborate planning and activity that had gone on for nearly two years.

Less familiar to history, but perhaps more important, was the United States Surveying Expedition to the North Pacific Ocean, 1853–56. This expedition started out under the command of Lieutenant Cadwallader Ringgold, who had sailed with Wilkes; but Ringgold broke down of a fever and was replaced, at Perry's direction, by Lieutenant John Rodgers. The mission of this expedition was to explore the waters of Japan and North China which, it was explained, were of ' uncommon interest to the United States '. These waters would ' soon become the preferred route of the immense commerce that is now anticipated to grow up between the Eastern Coasts of Asia and the Western coast of America '. Rodgers performed his task with consummate tact and ability, but he left the secretary in Washington in no doubt over the attitude of the Japanese. In Porpoise Sound (near Hakodate), he reported, ' we asked for water, and the authorities sent off about five gallons. We asked for provisions and they gave us a bunch of turnips. The people are jealous, and timid, and very poor. They regret doubtless that the world had found them.'

From the north of Japan Rodgers proposed to sail for San Francisco via the Arctic; and from San Francisco he would survey a route to Shanghai, ' because interesting points lie on the route, and because opinion points to that as the Chinese Emporium of American Commerce '. Then, after outlining his homeward course from Shanghai, Rodgers closed his dispatch with an evaluation of his cruise. ' It will devote our labours ', he said, ' to the Ocean upon which we have important possessions, and are the only powerful race; to the Ocean in which we of all the world have the deepest interest '. Unfortunately Rodgers was not permitted to complete his survey. He was notified, when he reached San Francisco, that his funds were exhausted. But he clung to his conviction that the survey should be made. ' I think that the Pacific Railroad, and Steamers to China, will turn the tide of commerce this way ', he declared in a final dispatch in January 1856. ' We shall carry to Europe their teas and silks from New York. I believe this result is inevitable; and I also think the time of its attainment will be shortened by accelerating as far as possible the passage to China. The results are so vast as to dazzle sober calculation. . . .'[1] The reader will remember that Rodgers was merely echoing ideas that had been gaining ground since the beginning of the century. But what Rodgers and other Americans who had so much confidence in this new trade route could not foresee was that Western Europe would forestall it. The Suez Canal, opened to shipping only thirteen years after Rodgers wrote, prevented this American dream from coming true.

Rodgers' experience at Hakodate, one of Perry's treaty ports, showed that Perry's treaty was ineffective. Nevertheless, Perry had got a foot in the door by requiring the Japanese to accept a consul if the United States chose. Townsend Harris, a China merchant of New York City with an indifferent record of commercial success behind him, opened the first American consular post in Japan in 1856; and two years later Harris succeeded in getting a comprehensive treaty fully equal to the treaties with China. Six Japanese ports were opened, with the Americans holding the vital rights to trade, establish residence, and maintain consulates. Harris regarded Japan as a sort of an ally against Great Britain or Russia, and he went as far as he could toward binding the country to the United States. The United States was pledged to act as ' friendly Mediator ' in any disputes that might arise between Japan and any of the Western powers, a clause that hinted that Japan could be taken under the American protective wing. She was ' the spot of all others ', declared Harris, ' in which the Naval depots of the United States in Asia, should be established ', and he suited the action to the word by getting naval depots at Nagasaki, Kanagawa (near Yokohama), and Hakodate.[2] In short, his purpose was to utilize Japan as a spearhead for American commercial penetration of northeast Asia.

This initiative was almost lost during the War between the States, which broke out shortly thereafter and which coincided with

[1] Allan B. Cole., ed., *Yankee Surveyors in the Shogun's Seas. Records of the United States Surveying Expedition to the North Pacific Ocean, 1853–1865*, Princeton, N. J., 1947.
[2] Miller, *Treaties*, VII, p. 1070.

an outbreak of anti-foreignism among the Japanese daimyos, who resisted the treaties. In 1864 the British organized a joint naval demonstration calculated to impress the recalcitrant daimyos. There were nine British, four Dutch, and three French war vessels in this expedition, from which the Americans, preoccupied with blockading the South, were afraid of being left out. But Secretary Seward managed to rent a little steamer which trailed along, and so, when the Mikado ratified the treaties, the American flag did not disappear from Japan.

Seward is the central figure of nineteenth-century American imperialism. He understood the nature and the directions which American expansion historically strove to follow—the effort to absorb British North America, which was to come to a head between 1867 and 1871; the drive southward into the Caribbean; and the trans-Pacific thrust into northeast Asia. With the suppression of the Southern rebellion in 1865 Seward acted adroitly to set these forces again in motion. He threw out several lines in the Caribbean, hoping (though in vain) for at least one island; and he boldly seized the bait Russia suddenly held out in 1867 in letting him know she was ready to sell Alaska. This deal was a master stroke, comparable to Jefferson's deal with Napoleon over Louisiana. Alaska is the north star of the American empire, shedding its light on two continents. It was the back door to the British Northwest, a hint that the Hudson's Bay Company would do well to allow its vast holdings in Rupert's Land to go by default to the advancing Americans. But Seward and his contemporaries overlooked the potentialities of the new Canadian Federation, consummated in the same year that the United States purchased Alaska from the Russians; and the speed with which the Canadian leaders acted, in co-operation with Her Majesty's Government, to buy out the Bay Company and annex the Crown Colony of British Columbia on the coast, meant that by 1871 the United States was confronted with an accomplished fact. There can be no doubt but that the Dominion of Canada is the great surprise of North America. Its long period of gestation had gone unnoticed, and while still in swaddling clothes it placed a permanent barrier against the American northward advance.

But Seward also meant that Alaska and its dependent island chain, the Aleutians, should be the finger pointed at northeast Asia; and the demagogic General Nathaniel P. Banks undertook to make the finger wag. Alaska, declaimed Banks, was the key to the Pacific. Through it ' we have in our grasp the control of the Pacific ocean, and may make this great theatre of action for the future whatever we may choose it shall be '.[1] Seward, meanwhile, had made a futile gesture at annexing Hawaii, long since Americanized by New England merchants and missionaries; but he got Midway Island, thus registering the trend toward Asia. But like the pull to the south, this current of American imperialism went temporarily underground, to surface again after the Sino-Japanese War of 1894.

The stream continued to wear down its own channel, however, and to find it only a little digging was needed. With the conclusion of a reciprocity treaty in 1875 Hawaii came at last under American influence. The treaty was a triumph for the Hawaiian sugar planters, who speedily rose thereafter as the ruling class in the islands: but in the United States, where the economic advantages of reciprocity fell mainly to the west coast, political factors prevailed. Britain had annexed the Fijis the year before, and Hawaiian reciprocity was in a measure the American response. The islands' new status as an American outpost was underscored by a clause whereby the native government agreed never to ' lease or otherwise dispose of or create any lien upon any port, harbour, or other territory ' in its dominion to any other power. Senator Sargent, the Californian who steered the treaty through the Senate, expressed his confidence in the certainty of future annexation by bringing up the old analogy of Texas; and six years later Secretary of State James G. Blaine characteristically pointed to Hawaii as the ' key to the dominion of the American Pacific ', the door to which Blaine was already trying to fling wide open. In this same year 1881, we remember, he importuned the British Government to give up its rights to an isthmian canal and leave to the United States a free hand in the Caribbean. Finally, in the year 1887, through the initiative of a group of senators in revising the reciprocity treaty, the Hawaiian Government consented to hand over Pearl Harbour to the United States as a coaling station and naval base. This was many years before there were sufficient ships in the navy to make use of it.[2]

The Hawaiian planter aristocracy hoped to remain both inde-

---

[1] *Cong. Globe*, 40th cong., 2 sess., June 20, 1868, app., p. 388.

[2] For an excellent account of the Hawaiian reciprocity treaty and its sequel see Sylvester K. Stevens, *American Expansion in Hawaii, 1842–1898*, Harrisburg, Pa., 1945, pp. 108–86.

pendent and prosperous, and the treaty of 1887 gave them grounds
for confidence. A privileged market in the United States, their only
possible outlet, might now fairly be regarded as permanent. But
within three years reciprocity was nullified by opposing interests
in the United States: Cuban sugar, in which, we recall, American
capital had a vested interest, was given the same privilege of free
entry and then, as compensation, domestic American producers were
granted a bounty of two cents a pound. Two other disturbing elements put in an appearance: a nativist movement, aroused by
encroachments on the monarchy, developed among the half-castes
and found a strong-willed leader in the Princess Liliuokalani, who
became Queen in 1891; and a radical agitation, opposed both to the
Queen and to the large planters, sprang up among the smaller
American planters, business and professional men of Honolulu. In
the minds of this element revolution and annexation went along
together. A reform party organized and put itself under the direction
of the Annexation Club, which was dominated by seventeen members,
citizens of Honolulu. Ostensibly a secret society, the Annexation
Club established relations with American naval officers on duty in
the islands and with the American minister, John L. Stevens, whom
Blaine had sent over in 1889. By February 1893, Stevens was in a
position to tell Blaine: ' The Hawaiian pear is now fully ripe, and
this is the golden hour for the United States to pluck it '.

Meanwhile the large planters, in control of the government, had
sent a minister to Washington to try to defeat the pending tariff
changes. If they could get the proposed sugar bounty, they would
agree to Hawaii becoming a protectorate; if they were rebuffed,
they argued rather futilely, they would seek other connections,
notably Canada. The management of the Canadian Pacific Railway,
completed to the west coast in 1885, wanted to outdistance the
Americans in the trans-Pacific trade, and it might easily be attracted
to Hawaii. Furthermore, Australia and New Zealand disliked the
hold the Americans had obtained over the island, and hoped to set
it back by a return to the former British programme of neutralization.
These ideas Stevens and Blaine magnified in their own minds until,
like Buchanan in the middle of the century, they saw the covert
hand of Great Britain working against them.

The Annexation Club in May 1892 sent its leader Lorrin Thurston, a lawyer and small planter, to Washington to apprise the right

people of its intentions. Thurston saw, among others, the Secretary of State, the Secretary of the Navy, and the chairman of the House committee on foreign affairs, and gave them to understand that the Annexation Club was preparing to take advantage of the existing internal tension and manoeuvre Hawaii into annexation. Inspired articles, published in important organs of American expansionist opinion, notably Albert Shaw's *Review of Reviews* and Whitelaw Reid's *New York Tribune*, helped get his message across to the public. Upon his return the Queen, chafing at finding herself more and more the helpless toy of the whites, attempted a *coup d'état* which played right into their hands. The annexationists immediately responded by appointing a ' committee of safety ', and the next day, January 16, 1893, the American naval commander ordered his sailors ashore to support the committee. A provisional revolutionary government assumed power and the Queen and her supporters, imprisoned in the government buildings, capitulated saying truthfully that they ' surrendered to the superior force of the United States of America '. Three days later Thurston and his colleagues were on their way to Washington, and on February 14 the Secretary of State, John W. Foster, who had succeeded the deceased Blaine, concluded a treaty of annexation.

Unexpected obstacles developed, however. The Republican administration which had made all the arrangements had less than a month to run, and the Senate declined to accommodate itself to this timetable. Upon the advice of his Secretary of State, Walter Q. Gresham, who viewed the enterprise as 'a selfish and dishonourable scheme of a lot of adventurers', President Grover Cleveland withdrew the treaty from the Senate. Gresham thought the Queen should be restored to her throne, but this turned out to be impracticable; the revolutionary provisional government had meanwhile transformed itself into a permanent constitutional republic, in which the large planters collaborated with the annexationists. The ill-favour with which the former had hitherto looked upon annexation had arisen in part out of fear that the contract labour system of the sugar plantations would be jeopardized under United States law; but another change in the American tariff in 1894, restoring Hawaiian sugar to its former position of preference, helped to alter this attitude. Furthermore, the American Hawaiians found themselves getting into trouble with Japan after 1894 over the status of Japanese immigrants. Henceforth, therefore, the American element in the islands stood solidly united in favour of annexation.

In the United States the issue became a *cause célèbre* over which controversy remained heated during the ensuing four years. The domestic beet sugar industry organized to protect itself against annexation, and its lobby in Washington was strong enough at all times to prevent any treaty of annexation from gaining the necessary two-thirds approval in the Senate. In terms of party politics the Republicans were in general proponents of annexation, the Democrats opponents. But there were important exceptions: Richard Olney, the tendentious Boston lawyer who succeeded Gresham and who in 1895, we remember, asserted sovereignty over South America, took a practical view of the question and influenced President Cleveland to modify his attitude too; and the influential Democratic senator, John T. Morgan, was an ambitious and outspoken annexationist. To the side of annexation too came the Protestant church press and the missionaries, who felt very strongly that Christian missions to the heathen had their own manifest destiny in the Pacific. John R. Mott, head of the Student Volunteers for Foreign Missions and one of the most prominent of the missionaries, agreed that Hawaii was ' the cross-roads of the Pacific ', ' a great lighthouse and a base of operations for the enterprise of universal evangelization'. Against these many different pressures, all of which implied that Hawaii, once annexed, would become the stepping-stone for further advances, stood a determined group of anti-imperialists, among whom the Republican Carl Schurz counted himself. The upshot of this was that in 1897 President McKinley commissioned John W. Foster to negotiate a new annexation treaty but, the beet sugar lobby and the anti-annexationists proving too strong for them in the Senate, the proponents of the treaty suddenly in March 1898, during the last days of the crisis with Spain, changed their tactics in favour of a joint resolution by both houses of Congress. A large favourable vote ensued and Hawaii, the symbol of empire, became an American dependency in the midst of the preparations for depriving Spain of her remaining island colonies.[1]

---

[1] For this account I have relied upon Stevens, pp. 187–299, and upon Julius W. Pratt, *Expansionists of 1898*, Baltimore, 1936, pp. 34–229. The direct quotations are from Stevens. For the remarkable outburst of missionary fervour in the 1890s and its identity with American imperialism in the Pacific and the Orient, see Paul A. Varg. *Missionaries, Chinese and Diplomats. The American Protestant Missionary Movement in China, 1890–1952*, Princeton, 1958, pp. 3–85.

Toward China, business interests began during these same decades to show a fresh interest, and in 1885 they prevailed upon President Cleveland to appoint Charles Denby, a Middle Western lawyer with a knowledge of railroads, to the diplomatic post in Peking. Denby held his post for thirteen years, and showed himself eager and able to push American interests to the fore. General James Wilson, president of the New England Railroad Company, followed him to Peking; but their joint efforts to procure a concession for a line to be built with American capital, employing American engineers and American materials, proved premature. Denby formed the opinion, however, that China was ' a vast market for commerce not satisfactorily exploited ', and that construction of a rail network was indispensable to this end. Railroads, moreover, would aid in checking the political disintegration of the empire which Denby, a keen observer, saw had already set in. (Great Britain annexed Upper Burma and France Annam in the *same* year of his arrival in China.) The continued political independence and territorial integrity of the country, he reported, was all-important to American interests, but, he added, the United States must stand with the other treaty powers in exacting rights from the Chinese for its nationals. ' There is no room for doubt ', he told the Secretary of State in 1889, ' that foreigners hold their place in China by force and force alone. . . . The fear of interfering with international rights or offending China should not for a moment be allowed to stand in the way of ordering immediate, and armed protection to . . . all foreigners in China.' The minister was an early witness to the anti-foreign riots chronic in China after 1885; and to discourage them ' a gunboat policy should be resumed '. Armed vessels patrolling the inland waterways and ready to move to danger spots at a moment's notice were greatly to be desired. The Christian missionaries, whose numbers in China were rapidly increasing, especially after 1890, aroused his criticism— he believed them responsible for causing some of the riots—but nevertheless he advocated full protection for them and their property as American citizens. Furthermore, though he disliked their ' intemperate zeal ' and discounted the value of their religious work, he recognized them as ' pioneers of trade and commerce ', a function which the missionaries themselves candidly admitted in putting forth their demands for armed protection. ' Fancy what would happen to the cotton trade if every Chinese wore a shirt! ' exclaimed the minister at one point. ' Well, the missionaries are teaching them to wear shirts ! '

Denby's activities, and those of the interests who supported him, anticipated by almost two decades the aggressiveness the American Government was to demonstrate in its China policy during the 1900s. Lacking professional diplomatic experience, the minister nevertheless took in brilliantly the nature of the Chinese situation and, despite occasional admonitions to the contrary from home, pursued a line of policy based on practical considerations rather than on the abstractions which the Department of State used repetitively in its instructions. Luminaries in the British Diplomatic Service (Stratford Canning comes to mind) could hardly have done better. Formosa attracted his interest almost immediately—his reports on this island in 1887 foreshadowed the desire for an entrepôt to China which motivated American policy a dozen years later. Formosa, he advised, ' formed a portal to the southern China Sea and could be used as a link in the trade with China '. Japan's seizure of this island and defeat of the Celestial Empire in 1894 found Denby alert to the economic gains that the United States could extract from the war. The conflict marked ' the crumbling of the Chinese wall '. China's war indemnity could not be paid from taxation, but it could be met by selling franchises to foreign railway, banking and mining enterprises. Denby urged the establishment of an American bank in China, and attempted to steer the loan which the latter required into the hands of an American syndicate. This brought an admonition from Washington. The loan went to Russia, and Denby, aware of the advance of the Trans-Siberian Railroad through Manchuria, resumed his activities on behalf of American railroad building. American enterprise, he argued, should collaborate with the Trans-Siberian, providing the latter with an entry into north China. General Wilson adopted this argument and circularized various concerns in the United States in the hope of forming a syndicate. Wilson even tried, without success, to get himself appointed to the diplomatic post in St. Petersburg. Wilson's activities came to naught, but in 1898 another syndicate, the American China Development Company, came forward with the purpose of constructing a bridge line running from Peking to Hankow, thence on to Canton, and joining Russian interests in the north with French in the south. From backing these various activities the government in Washington refrained, much to the disappointment of Mr. Denby; but, as we shall see, the business interests on their part followed up the American war with Spain with demands upon the administration to abandon its hands-off policy and come to their support.[1]

Meanwhile in 1876 Japan had pried open the Hermit Kingdom of Korea, with the United States and the other principal treaty powers following her lead in 1882-83. There then appeared in Seoul a sharp-witted Presbyterian minister from Ohio named Horace N. Allen. Allen's personality was a remarkable blend of the missionary, the politician, the trader, the entrepreneur, the military strategist and, one is tempted to add, the rogue. Using his medical knowledge to ingratiate himself with the Hermit King, Allen turned to politics and concession-hunting. His smartest piece of work was his landing of a gold-mining concession in the Chusan district, north of the 38th parallel. This he accomplished in 1895 for James R. Morse and the Oriental Consolidated Mining Company, whose operations proved to be the most profitable of their kind in all of Asia. It was ' a Cripple Creek all our own ', chirped Allen.[2] Meanwhile he had taken over the job of leading the first Korean diplomatic delegation to Washington; and from the McKinley administration he received in 1897 the post of Minister to Korea, which he held until 1905. His official instructions enjoined him against intermeddling in Korean domestic affairs, but Allen was too influential a figure to be embarrassed by such restraint. Korea, it appears, was headed under his guidance toward becoming an American protectorate; but Japan, by her victory over China in 1894, established the priority of her own claims. Henceforth Allen was anti-Japanese, and in conjunction with certain officers sent out by the navy department he wanted naval bases for the United States in the Gulf of Chihli or on the south coast of Korea opposite the Japanese island of Kyushu. Feeling certain of the coming war between Japan and Russia, he hoped to persuade Theodore Roosevelt to seize the latter base as soon as the

[1] For this account of Minister Denby and the accompanying quotations I am greatly indebted to John Wm. Cassey, ' The mission of Charles Denby and International Rivalries in the Far East, 1885-1898 ', unpublished dissertation, 1959, in the University of Southern California Library, based upon archival material of the Department of State and other important manuscript collections. This long background of interest in China on the part of special business groups in the United States, and the persistent role of Mr. Denby in attracting attention to China, have gone unnoticed by historians.

[2] The reference is to the rich gold-mining district of Colorado.

war broke out. But Roosevelt favoured Japan, and in spite of Allen's arguments he gave her a free hand in Korea.[1]

The ambitions of Charles Denby and Horace N. Allen in the Orient fitted in with the reviving imperialism at home, account of which we have already taken. Literary men like John Fiske, the well-known New England historian, and Josiah Strong, an energetic Congregational minister who had made his weight felt in the West from Wyoming to Ohio, expounded a philosophy of empire on a global scale. Strong headed the American Home Missionary Society which, in its ardour for winning converts in America foreshadowed the outburst of missionary zeal in Asia. In 1885 he published a book, *Our Country*, which sold more than 167,000 copies. For centuries to come, he argued, ' the progress of Christ's kingdom in the world ' would depend on what the United States did during the next few years. Synthesizing Anglo-Saxonry, Protestant Christianity, the teachings of Darwin, and economic acquisitiveness, the embattled clergyman arrived at the conclusion that the United States—' the representative of the largest liberty, the purest Christianity, the highest civilization '—would soon take over the world. ' If I read not amiss ', he declared, ' this powerful race will move down upon Mexico, down upon Central and South America, out upon the islands of the sea, over upon Africa and beyond. . . .'[2] No sooner had war been declared against Spain, April 21, 1898, than the excitable Senator Albert Beveridge of Indiana seized the occasion for a speech in Boston which made him the mouthpiece of the imperialists. He declaimed:

> American factories are making more than the American people can use; American soil is producing more than they can consume. Fate has written our policy for us; the trade of the world must and shall be ours. . . . We will cover the ocean with our merchant marine. We will build a navy to the measure of our greatness. . . .

And he wound up with the assertion: ' The Philippines are logically our first target '.[3] At the very moment Beveridge was speaking, an

---

[1] Fred Harvey Harrington, *God, Mammon and the Japanese. Dr. Horace N. Allen and Korean-American Relations, 1884–1905*, Madison, Wisc., 1944, *passim*. Seward W. Livermore, 'American Naval Base Policy in the Far East, 1850–1914 ', *Pac. Hist. Rev.*, XIII, 1944, pp. 113–35.

[2] Rev. Josiah Strong, *Our Country. Its Possible Future and its Present Crisis*, N.Y., 1885 and 1891, pp. 222–3. John Fiske echoed these ideas in an article on ' Manifest Destiny ' for *Harper's Magazine*, March 1885.

[3] Quoted by Pratt, op. cit., p. 228. Beveridge, a friend of Lodge, was probably

American squadron under Commodore Dewey was on its way from
Hong Kong to strike the first blow of the war at the Spaniards in
Manila Bay. What an unusual coincidence!

There has never been a satisfactory explanation as to why this
attack took place. The direct order to attack was given, February 25,
1898, by Theodore Roosevelt, who was temporarily occupying the
Secretary of the Navy's chair in Washington. This was ten days after
the mysterious sinking of the battleship *Maine* in Havana harbour,
but nearly two months before the start of hostilities. Obviously there
was ample time for the order to be rescinded, had the administration
been so inclined. During the preceding year Roosevelt had said
repeatedly that he wanted a war with Spain as a means of turning all
of the European powers out of the West Indies. Manila too came in
for mention as a desirable object of attack, though in this case
Roosevelt failed to give a reason, an omission which was not according
to his custom. To his friend Senator Henry Cabot Lodge he had
written, for instance, in September 1897: ' Our Asiatic squadron
should blockade, and if possible, take Manila.'[1] And the order of
February 25, 1898, was the result of several weeks of reflection and
consultation with Lodge and probably others. Secretary of the Navy
John D. Long, Roosevelt's superior, professed himself shocked with
the order; but since Long took no steps to change it, he was apparently quite content with what the younger man had done. Furthermore, Dewey's squadron had been previously prepared for war, and
Manila, its only possible objective, was peculiarly located to serve
American designs in the Far East.

How well informed were Roosevelt, Lodge, and even their
great friend Alfred Thayer Mahan on the situation in the Far East
is a question which begs for an answer. Whether they put a value
at the time on a naval base calculated to facilitate American economic
penetration of China is something we do not know. Lodge, the
politician, was the friend or acquaintance of James Wilson, the rail-

in on the secret of this premeditated attack. And the N.Y. *Sun*, a rabidly imperialist
paper, had thrice ' predicted ' that it would take place. Ibid., footnote. What more
likely than that the ' prediction ' had been deliberately inspired?

[1] Elting E. Morison, ed., *The Letters of Theodore Roosevelt*, 8 vols., Cambridge,
Mass., 1951–, I, p. 681. For a good discussion of Roosevelt's imperialist ideology
see Howard K. Beale, *Theodore Roosevelt and the Rise of America to World Power*,
Baltimore, 1956, pp. 14–80. But Mr. Beale's discussion of the order of Feb. 25,
1898 is by no means definitive. See also John A. Garraty, *Henry Cabot Lodge. A
Biography*, N.Y., 1953, pp. 146–65, 180–202.

road promoter, who in turn shared the knowledge of Charles Denby. However that may be, American naval forces on duty in the Far East had always been obliged to make use of British facilities, although there had been a desire for a separate American base ever since 1850.[1] That was a fact that could hardly have escaped Roosevelt, Lodge or a good many others. Manila was a natural choice, indeed it was the only choice, and therefore the conclusion is inescapable that it was selected in advance; the coming war with Spain over Cuba was to furnish the opportunity. As in 1845-46, the cards were stacked so as to wrest the utmost advantages out of a war that the American public was loudly demanding, ostensibly for humanitarian reasons, but the question of who stacked the cards can be only partially answered. After Commodore Dewey had won his victory, but before the fall of the city, Mr. E. H. Conger, who was now filling Denby's shoes in Peking, put a value on the conquest. ' Next to controlling a desirable port and commodious harbour in China ', he observed, ' the permanent ownership or possession of Manila and vicinity would be most invaluable to us in securing and holding our share of influence and trade in the new era just beginning in this country.' ' It would ', he continued, ' give a convenient and essential base of supplies, where American trade, capital and brains could and would be massed ready for the commercial conquests, which Americans ought to accomplish in China '.[2]

In the meantime the Americans were not content with the mere destruction of the Spanish squadron. An expeditionary force was soon thereafter dispatched, with the capture of Manila as its objective. Incidental to this expedition, but determined upon in advance, was the occupation of the vacant island of Wake and of the Spanish-owned island of Guam, nicely spaced on the shipping lane between Honolulu and Manila; and during the same summer months of 1898 the long-deferred annexation of the Hawaiian islands was engineered. The naval life-line between San Francisco and Manila was thus completed, although the acquisitive spirit was by no means appeased. In November 1900 Secretary of State John Hay started a negotiation for a base and territorial concession at Samsah Bay in Fukien province, opposite Formosa; and the navy, disappointed there,

[1] Livermore, op. cit.
[2] Conger to Secretary of State Wm. R. Day, Aug. 26, 1898, quoted by Varg., op. cit., pp. 42-3.

continued to look for a base in Korean waters. These moves, however, remained unfinished, partly because of Japanese opposition.[1]

Meanwhile the irrepressible Senator Beveridge arose in the Senate to fill out his picture of 'God's American Israel', as Reinhold Niebuhr has so well characterized the American conception of destiny. The Philippines, he declared, are ours. Beyond them are China's illimitable markets.

> We will not retreat from either. We will not repudiate our duty. . . . We will not abandon our opportunity in the Orient. We will not renounce our part in the mission of our race, trustee under God, of the civilization of the world. . . . We will move forward to our work . . . with gratitude . . . and thanksgiving to Almighty God that He has marked us as His chosen people, henceforth to lead in the regeneration of the world. . . .
>
> Our largest trade henceforth must be with Asia. The Pacific is our ocean. More and more Europe will manufacture the most it needs. . . . Where shall we turn for consumers of our surplus? Geography answers the question. China is our natural customer. . . . The Philippines give us a base at the door of all the East.
>
> . . . The power that rules the Pacific . . . is the power that rules the world. And, with the Philippines, that power is and will forever be the American Republic.[2]

Paralleling this piece of senatorial extravaganza were the works of Alfred Thayer Mahan and Brooks Adams, the two ablest of the American philosophical imperialists of this generation. Mahan's great works of course were his histories. But his didactic interpretations and generalizations are to be found in his collected essays that appeared in book form in 1898 and 1900. Unlike Strong, Beveridge and other lesser lights, Mahan never became effusive over the cults of race, religion and superior civilization. He recognized that the United States was a member of the complex of national states, and he saw its survival in terms of sea power collaborating with the British Empire. But he did not preach mastery of the world, or even of the Pacific, and in China he would share the Yangtse valley with Britain, leaving Manchuria to Russia.[3]

Like Mahan, Brooks Adams of the famous Boston family was a

[1] Livermore, op. cit. A. Whitney Griswold, *The Far Eastern Policy of the United States*, N.Y., 1938, pp. 83–4.

[2] Excerpts printed in Ruhl J. Bartlett, *The Record of American Diplomacy*, 3rd ed., N.Y., 1956, pp. 385–8.

[3] Beale, op. cit., p. 258.

determinist in his interpretation of history, but the resemblance stops there. In his book, *Law of Civilization and Decay*, he taught that economic competition would eventually reach the breaking point and bring about the collapse of society. In order to put off this calamity as long as possible, he declared the United States should seek empire in Asia:

> Our geographical position, our wealth, and our energy preeminently fit us to enter upon the development of eastern Asia, and to reduce it to a part of our economic system. . . . The Chinese question must therefore be accepted as the great problem of the future, as a problem from which there is no escape; and as these great struggles for supremacy sometimes involve an appeal to force, safety lies in being armed and organized against all emergencies.[1]

The hidden purpose of the attack on Spain in the Pacific was to put the United States in a position to participate effectively in the scramble for China. Nor was this the result of a wild outburst of imperialism during the 1890s, a 'great aberration', as it has sometimes been called. It was, rather, the climax to the drive for wealth and influence in east Asia that had started in the eighteenth century. Under the treaty system this drive prospered, for the treaties as administered by the Imperial Chinese Customs Service kept the door genuinely open; and during this golden age of Western intercourse with China, American commerce, shipping and missionary activity had little of which to complain. But the treaty system was not capable of adjustment to the forces of industrialism and finance capitalism that appeared on the scene in the latter part of the nineteenth century. The treaties had provided the means for a simple exchange of consumers' goods between China and the West. These new forces aimed at the one-sided sale of capital goods to the Chinese, and hence pointed at an imbalance of trade which the West proposed to redress by exporting capital to China in the form of loans and speculative investments.

Beveridge, Brooks Adams, John Hay, Mark Hanna and many others in politics and in business firmly believed that American industry was faced with a saturated market at home and in Europe, and that it must turn to China to dispose of its surplus. China, they

---

[1] Brooks Adams develops this theme in a second book, *America's Economic Supremacy*, published in 1900. See pp. 104–5 and p. 194 of the 1947 edition.

held, provided a vast potential market; and the construction of an isthmian canal, the laying of a cable across the Pacific, the annexation of Hawaii and the retention of the Philippines would give the United States the needed advantage over the other powers in securing this market. Two businesses in particular fostered this movement: the cotton goods industry and the American China Development Company. The former had a substantial foothold in north China and Manchuria, where it was beginning to fear competition from Russia; the American China Development Company had been organized we recall, in 1895, with the intention of seeking railway concessions in China. Other special interests were the oil, flour, iron and steel businesses and the exporting houses. Early in 1898, before the Spanish war broke out, these interests organized to bear down on Washington to formulate a policy calculated to counteract Germany and Russia in the Far East. The American Asiatic Association, as their organization was called, supported the movement to annex Hawaii and retain the Philippines, but realized that island acquisitions would not by themselves bring the desired results in China. The association won its first victory in September when President McKinley appointed John Hay Secretary of State; and Hay soon made a pleasing gesture by ordering two gunboats to proceed to the Taku forts, commanding the entrance to Peking. Shortly thereafter Lord Charles Beresford, M.P., representing the Associated Chambers of Commerce of Great Britain, disembarked at San Francisco after a tour of China. Beresford was a strong advocate of the open door, and with the support of the American Asiatic Association he made a speaking tour across the United States which, in the words of the New York *Journal of Commerce*, contributed much to the ' education of the mercantile community '.[1]

Two other persons enter into this complicated story. They are William W. Rockhill, a New Yorker who had spent years of his life in China and who was now Assistant Secretary of State, and Alfred Hippisley, an English friend of Rockhill with a record of thirty years of service in the Imperial Chinese Customs. Like Beresford, Rockhill and Hippisley saw the treaty system, which had been the bulwark of China, vanishing before their eyes; and it was they who devised the plan for the American Government to address the Powers,

---

[1] Charles S. Campbell, Jr., *Special Business Interests and the Open Door Policy*, New Haven, Conn., 1951, *passim*.

asking them to respect the treaties and allow the Customs Service to function in their several spheres of influence. Each Power was also asked—and this was a point of great importance—to apply open door principles in the matter of harbour dues and railway rates in its own sphere of influence. These stipulations provided the substance of the so-called open door notes, which John Hay dispatched to six governments on September 6, 1899. The notes were followed in July, 1900, by a circular letter announcing that the United States wished to preserve the 'territorial and administrative entity' of China. These moves pleased American business interests which had been concerned with the situation, especially since they were led to believe that Hay's propositions had been accepted. Ironically, however, nothing of the sort had happened. Hay made a fine gesture toward bringing the open door up to date. Publicly he behaved as though the Powers had all subscribed to his declaration; privately he showed his own lack of confidence in his announced policy by entering into the abortive negotiation for a leasehold in Fukien province which we have already mentioned.[1]

By this time North China was well on the road to partition. The Germans had taken over Shantung province, while Manchuria, an almost vacant country in 1890, was steadily being absorbed into the network of Russia's Trans-Siberian Railway. The construction of the Chinese Eastern Railway across north Manchuria, begun in 1896, was supplemented by a branch line running south from Harbin to the tip of the Liaotung peninsula, where in 1898 Russia obtained concession rights to Port Arthur as a naval base and to the neighbouring port of Dairen (Dalny) as a commercial seaport. Thus bisected on an east-west, north-south axis, and isolated geographically and historically from China, Manchuria was about to become a Russian province, especially since, as a result of the Boxer Uprising, it was under Russian military occupation after 1900. Theodore Roosevelt's representative at Peking, Mr. E. H. Conger, took the attitude, formerly assumed by Charles Denby, that Manchuria was a frontier that should be opened up to American economic penetration, as well as Russian. Dairen, he reported in September 1901, would soon be made the main terminal of the Trans-Siberian and, he continued:

[1] For an illuminating, virtually definitive treatment of the 'open door' see Charles S. Campbell, *Anglo-American Understanding, 1898–1903*, Baltimore, 1957, pp. 151–79. Mr. Campbell disposes, once for all, of the several historical legends associated with this phrase.

This will open up to settlement and development the only great territory, still left on the globe, so favored with soil and climate as to promise great agricultural development and its concomitant of a strong people and resultant great trade progress. Its contiguity to the United States and the possibility of connecting its great railroad system by direct lines of steamers across the Pacific with our own transcontinental routes make friendly political and trade relations between the two peoples most desirable and important. . . .[1]

St. Petersburg, however, showed no desire to collaborate, not even in the matter of opening the door in Manchuria, although the Russian Ambassador in Washington, Count Cassini, reported his own opinion that, if the United States were granted full trading rights, it would not hinder Russian domination of Manchuria. Russia, it will be remembered, dragged her feet in meeting the Japanese demands that she evacuate her forces, and by September 1903 it was apparent that she had no intention of doing so. Meanwhile, ever since 1898 with the American war with Spain and the Russian leasehold on the Liaotung peninsula, the British and the Americans had been rallying around Japan. Her alliance with Britain, signed in 1902, was Japan's chief bulwark, though in Russian eyes it was actually the United States who was playing the trump card. Both Roosevelt and John Hay desired to join the Anglo-Japanese Alliance openly, but knew it was not practical politics to try. The utmost they could do was to bombard St. Petersburg with open door notes, and to sign a commercial treaty with China in October 1903 under which *China*, the nominal sovereign in the three Eastern Provinces, opened the ports of Mukden and Antung to American trade and consular residence. Possession by Russia being nine points of the law, however, these ports remained closed. In St. Petersburg and Berlin the Sino-American agreement was interpreted as a Trojan horse from whose belly the United States could emerge in aid of Japan. The interpretation was at least partly correct, for thirty days prior to the Japanese night attack on the Russian fleet in Port Arthur Theodore Roosevelt notified Japan that he would be neutral in case of war.[2] By this gesture the Japanese knew they had friends in their

[1] Quoted in Edward H. Zabriskie, *American–Russian Rivalry in the Far East. A Study in Diplomacy and Power Politics*, 1895–1914, Philadelphia, 1946, p. 76.
[2] Ibid., pp. 65–100; Tyler Dennett, *Roosevelt and the Russo-Japanese War*, N.Y., 1925, *passim*.

rear. Their surprise attack on Port Arthur on the night of February 8, 1904, met with applause from the American newspaper press, and throughout the war Japan was regarded in the United States as ' fighting our battle '. An article written by Professor Paul Reinsch of the University of Wisconsin and published in the January 1905 number of the *North American Review* under the heading, ' Japan and Asiatic Leadership ', argued the viewpoint popular at the time that Japan was the chosen representative of ' the Anglo-Saxon races ' in the Orient, and that the least those ' races ' could do was to counter-act the French and German diplomatic influence that had been thrown to the support of Russia.[1] The son of a Lutheran clergyman, Reinsch was a significant figure because he was destined to be President Wilson's minister to China during the years of the First World War. As such Reinsch was still an advocate of the open door for American enterprise and investments, but an outright opponent of the Japanese.

To try to extend this chapter into the ever-growing complex scene of the Far East in the twentieth century would be to attempt the impossible. But this I would say by way of an epilogue. The lure of East Asia, planted in the American mind in the eighteenth century, continued to provide fascination in the twentieth. The conditions, however, which during the nineteenth century made the lure sub-stantial and profitable passed out of existence before that century was over. It is one of the supreme ironies of American history that, at the very time when the United States dedicated itself to the policy of the open door, that door was being effectively shut. To meet the new situation of the twentieth century, dominated as it was by powerful forces contending against one another all over the world, the Americans deluded themselves with an innocuous formula devised by William Rockhill and Alfred Hippisley and immortalized by John Hay. The secretary himself never believed in his ' doctrine ', although he erected an elaborate pretence that developed into a national legend. Theodore Roosevelt dismissed it as unworkable.

Like the dogmas of Monroe, the open door, in reality a British conception put to work in the classical period of the ' unequal treaties ', was taken into the theology of American nationalism,

---

[1] Quoted in Zabriskie, op. cit., p. 112. For a searching study of American attitudes during this war see Winston B. Thorson, 'American Public Opinion and the Portsmouth Peace Conference ', *Amer. Hist. Rev.*, LIII, April 1948, pp. 439–64.

believed in but not susceptible of practice. Moreover, it seems to have been assimilated to the idea of duty, which perhaps helped it to acquire the fascination of a fixed idea. Thus Woodrow Wilson adopted a viewpoint not really any different from Albert J. Beveridge's. 'We might not have seen our duty', he remarked in 1901, 'had not the Philippines fallen to us by the wilful fortune of war'. To instil moral standards in the Oriental peoples and to protect American commercial interests in the Orient at the same time were, to Wilson, two parts of the same thing. The China market, he declared, was the ' market for which statesmen as well as merchants must plan and play their game of competition, the market which diplomacy, and if need be power, must make an open way '.[1] Such scanty practical knowledge of the Orient as Wilson possessed came mostly through correspondence with certain missionary friends, notably that with a cousin named S. I. Woodbridge, a career missionary and editor in China. In selecting a minister to China Wilson made membership in an evangelical Christian church the primary qualification, and so, after several others had rejected the invitation, it was extended to Dr. Paul Reinsch.[2]

Wilson *believed* in the open door, but there is little evidence that he understood it. The Taft administration had tried to implement the open door for American trade and investments by inducing a group of New York bankers to join the international banking consortium in China.[3] Even more, this administration aspired to an ascendancy in the field of transportation. Here Mr. Taft got his ideas from Edward H. Harriman, the chairman of the Union Pacific. Harriman controlled a trans-Pacific shipping company and, by buying into the Japanese and Russian railways in Asia, hoped eventually to have a round-the-world transportation system. The function of the banking consortium was theoretically to provide the machinery through which the investing nations might compete on equal terms for the loan business of China. But unlike its prototype, the Imperial Chinese Customs, the international banking consortium stimulated rather than allayed national jealousies. In 1913 Wilson reversed the

[1] Woodrow Wilson, *A History of the American People*, 5 vols., N.Y. and London, 1902, V, p. 296.
[2] Tien-Yi Li, *Woodrow Wilson's China Policy, 1913–1917*, N.Y., 1952, pp. 7 ff.
[3] Charles Vevier, *The United States and China, 1906–1913. A Study of Finance and Diplomacy*, New Brunswick, N.J., 1955, *passim*; William Appleman Williams, *American-Russian Relations, 1781–1917*, N.Y. and Toronto, 1952, pp. 49–80.

Taft policy of promoting American membership in the consortium; but his reversal stemmed from ignorance and sentiment rather than from a desire to ' abandon ' China. In 1917 he insisted on reviving the consortium, the same for which he had previously condemned his predecessor; and he proposed to intervene, by means of the consortium, even in territory, such as South Manchuria, long since pre-empted by the Japanese. At the Peace Conference of Paris in 1919 Wilson headed into a direct collision with the Japanese over the concession areas in Shantung that the latter had taken from the Germans. The ensuing quarrels, transferred to the Senate and aggravated by the isolationist senators, notably William E. Borah and Hiram Johnson, elevated to a new plane of emotion the hoary dogmas of the open door and the territorial integrity of China. At the Washington Conference in 1921 these formulae were sanctified afresh by the Nine Power Treaty; but neither the internal condition of China, given over to civil war, nor the external conditions relating to trade and investment provided the means for transforming the Nine Power Treaty from a parchment agreement into a functioning international system.

CHAPTER IX

APOTHEOSIS

' We ourselves are becoming, owing to our strength and geographical situation, more and more the balance of power of the whole world '

BORN an imperial republic in the eighteenth century, the United States joined the coveted circle of great powers at the beginning of the twentieth. From its inception it demonstrated a remarkable sense of direction and purpose, acquired from 150 years of practical experience as British colonies. Even in infancy these Colonies showed a capacity for growth, readily comprehended when we remember their assets. They faced the sea, and they possessed a hinterland of inestimable value; from Britain they attracted both labour and capital. Hubs of empire emerged in various localities: in New England, Boston; on the Hudson River, New York; on the Delaware, Philadelphia; on Chesapeake Bay, the tobacco colonies, where every plantation had access to deep water; and in the south, Charleston. Each of these hubs was, to change the figure, a nucleus and each nucleus fattened on its rapidly and methodically expanding cell. Commerce and agriculture, in perfect balance with each other, supplied the nutriment. In the course of the eighteenth century these cells—partially formed, autonomous empires—amalgamated under the impact of revolution into a single organism. Thus, when the United States started on its career as an independent state, its growth pattern was fully established and visible to its imaginative and far-seeing leaders, who regarded its ' proper dominion ' as bounded only by the shores of the continent.

Beyond this ' dominion ' stretched a potential, but indefinite sphere of influence figuratively defined in 1823 as ' the western hemisphere '. This new doctrine rode along on the wave of nationalism that surged in the mid-nineteenth century, by which time familiarity and intercourse with the coastal lands and islands of the Pacific basin had reached the point where it was natural to boast of the coming commercial empire on that ocean. Meanwhile the wave broke over the British in the northwest and the Mexicans in the southwest, but scattered in confusion thereafter. The United States finished building its continental homeland by 1848, when the acquisition of California fulfilled the ancient tradition laid down by the sea-to-sea charters. Then ensued the great War between the States, which threatened destruction of the whole edifice. The long-range effects of this war were incalculable. Success for the South would have meant the rise of a new, but weak and backward nation. If the Southern states did not get their supply of capital from the North, they would have to borrow it from Europe. A tendency to balkanize North America would have been the result, which in turn would have exerted a profound influence on the state system of Western Europe. The problem of dealing with two separate and mutually hostile American nations, while supporting the Dominion of Canada, would have strained the resources of British foreign policy to the breaking point and smoothed the road for Imperial Germany. But victory for the North led to the consolidation of the Union, the expiration of the compact theory relating to the Constitution which implied that the nation was subordinate to the states, and the development of integral nationalism.

This second wave of American nationalism began forming as the Civil War came to a close. At the end of the century it rose high, carrying on its crest the Monroe Doctrine, with open expressions of hegemony over Latin America; renewed aspirations for annexing Canada, thereby making dominion over the continent a reality; demands for an island chain across the Pacific; and preparations for the economic and religious penetration of China. This wave levelled off after the war with Spain, but it did not break and scatter like the previous wave. It drove on, guided by the fiercely competitive forces of industrialism and its by-product, finance capitalism, which by this time had subordinated the individualistic agrarian society of the nineteenth century, with its sense of isolation from the world, to the tempo and pressures of urban civilization.

The nationalist wave, moreover, carried to the fore a new emphasis on the power and duty of the State to protect and promote the welfare of its citizens at home and abroad. Woodrow Wilson in 1898 published a book on *The State* in which he abandoned the social compact theory of the eighteenth century in favour of the biological and historical findings of Charles Darwin, Sir Henry Maine and others. Wilson praised ' the efficient races ' of Europe for originating the principle of authority and, after a long, rambling discourse, left the reader with the impression that the State was the highest possible institution that society could develop. More direct, and probably more influential at the time, was John W. Burgess of Columbia University, whose teaching reflected the powerful intellectual currents then emanating from Germany. German trained, like scores of other American academicians of his generation, Burgess blended the authoritarian concept of the State which he derived from the English theorist, John Austin, with the philosophy of Hegel. 'A State,' asserts Hegel, ' is then well constituted and internally powerful, when the private interest of its citizens is one with the common interest of the State'. The State, taught Burgess, was endowed with supernatural powers; it was ' the apotheosis of man ', the ultimate expression of reason and morality, and the *ne plus ultra* of political society.[1] Theodore Roosevelt, who insisted that the war with Spain was 'the most absolutely righteous war' of the nineteenth century, carried this worship of the State into the realm of patriotic emotion by branding as ' impertinent ' any European ' whether Pope, Kaiser, Czar or President ', who dared to criticize ' any American because of his action or nonaction as regards any question between America and an outside nation '.[2] And Wilson was not far behind in his justification of *raisons d'état* for the actions of statesmen in the past. In his five-volume *History of the American People*, published in 1902, Wilson praised Secretary Olney for the latter's absolutist version of the Monroe Doctrine and upheld the war with Spain for putting America into ' the open arena of the world '. The war had ' awakened us to our real relationship to the rest of mankind ', he declared; our frontiers were now ' beyond the seas '. And, unconsciously echoing Josiah Strong, Wilson moralized that it was ' our peculiar duty ' to teach colonial peoples ' order and self-control ' and to ' impart to them, if it be possible . . . the drill and habit of law and obedience which we long ago got out of . . . English history '.[3]

---

[1] See Bert James Loewenberg, ' John William Burgess, the Scientific Method, and the Hegelian Philosophy of History ', *Miss. Valley Hist. Rev.*, XLII, Dec., 1955, pp. 490–509.
[2] Quoted by Howard K. Beale, *Theodore Roosevelt and the Rise of America to World Power*, Baltimore, 1956, p. 24.
[3] Woodrow Wilson, *History of the American People*, 5 vols., N.Y. and London, 1912 ed., V, pp. 255, 274–5, 294–6. William E. Diamond, *The Economic Thought of*

But the most mature exposition of American integral nationalism comes from the pen of Herbert Croly, born in New York of British parentage and educated at Harvard. Croly was attracted to the Progressive movement in the United States, which flowered after the Spanish war and which concentrated on the national government as the medium for leadership and reform. In 1909 he published a book, *The Promise of American Life*, which American Progressives accepted as their text. Eschewing the dialectic of German philosophy, Croly nevertheless developed much the same point of view in an argument that ' the national tradition ' was a basic spiritual force pushing the nation along and resulting in ' progress '. Traditional American democracy, he wrote, has been national in feeling, but not in idea and purpose. More concretely, he pleaded for an application of the ideas of Alexander Hamilton.

In a vigorous chapter recommending a national foreign policy, Croly criticized the habit of proclaiming ' doctrines and policies, without considering either the implications, the machinery necessary to carry them out, or the weight of the resulting responsibilities '. He put his finger on the fallacy of popular beliefs regarding the Monroe Doctrine, namely, the notion of incompatibility between America and Europe. ' That idea,' he wrote, ' has given a sort of religious sanctity to the national tradition of isolation; and it will survive its own utility because it flatters American democratic vanity. . . .' The key to Croly's thinking is to be found in his recognition that the power position of the United States had changed, and in his emphasis upon national responsibility. A. T. Mahan had written in this same vein, and had decried the Monroe Doctrine as a useless ' political abstraction '. Geographically, said Croly, the United States was so situated in relation to Europe that it would always have a profound influence on the strategic situation. And, he continued, the American responsibility for keeping the peace was similar to that of any peace-preferring European power. ' Peace will prevail in international relations, just as order prevails within a nation, because of the righteous use of superior force. . . .' Theodore Roosevelt, in his later and more mature years, concurred in this viewpoint and made ' responsibility ' the watchword of his foreign policy. And in 1910 Roosevelt said reflectively to Herr von Eckhardstein: ' We ourselves are becoming, owing to our strength and geographical situation, more and more the balance of power of the whole world '.[1]

Croly praised the forward policy that the United States had undertaken in China, justifying it in terms not of commercial advantage but of national responsibility. ' The chief advantage of possession of the Philippines ', he wrote, ' is the keeping the American people alive to their interests in the grave problems which will be raised in the Far East by the future development of China and Japan '. China should be protected—this was according to tradition —but the task could not be performed without ' a great deal of diplomacy and more or less fighting '. Assumption of this responsibility, he concluded, is ' an inevitable and a wholesome aspect of national discipline and experience.' Of similar mind was Willard Straight, a young man in his twenties who was serving as Consul-General in Mukden while Croly was writing his book in New York. Straight had come under the influence of Henry Morse Stephens, an American historian of English birth, and had got his first job under Sir Robert Hart in the Imperial Chinese Customs. Chinese culture fascinated him, as it had his fellow New Yorker William Rockhill; and, observing with distaste Japanese encroachment in Manchuria, he grew anxious for the United States to champion the open door and defend China's territorial integrity.

Straight had both drive and imagination, and he also had the contacts with J. P. Morgan & Company and other bankers in New York that resulted in bringing American business interests back to China with the express purpose of thwarting Japan. But of course he could not have done this single-handed. He had influential support from many Americans in the diplomatic service and in business. He and Thomas F. Millard, the Far Eastern correspondent of the *New York Herald*, stimulated William Howard Taft during the latter's visit to China in 1907; and Taft, upon becoming President in 1909 threw the full support of the government behind the banking group. Herbert Croly's *mystique* of national responsibility finds its best illustration in the character and activity of men like Willard Straight; and in its endeavour to convert the idea into a programme, the government under Taft celebrated a marriage with business. Years later, after the First World War and after the Washington

[1] Quoted in Beale, op. cit., p. 447. The quotations from Croly are taken from the 1912 edition of *The Promise*, pp. 306, 309–10, 312.

treaties had gone into effect, temporarily stabilizing the peace of the
Far East and supposedly safeguarding the open door and the territorial integrity of China, Croly reiterated his belief in the traditional
policy. 'America had a legal and a moral right,' he wrote, ' to resist
Japanese penetration, and to increase her own influence in that part
of China and by so doing to assist China in preventing the aggression
from taking place.'[1]

With the advent of Woodrow Wilson to the presidency this
concept of national responsibility reached its apogee. The nation's
responsibility, however, was the President's. Only the leader could
define it and direct it. Theodore Roosevelt had thus conceived it: he
was, as he himself said, the ' steward of the people '; and in his efforts
to be a good international steward, Roosevelt followed the rules
of nineteenth-century European statecraft. In the Caribbean he
played the role of a policeman; in Europe he attempted to restore
the concert system with himself as ' honest broker '; in the Far
East he worked for a balance between Russia and Japan. Actually
Roosevelt was a good European. An outspoken American nationalist,
he recognized and fostered the American kinship with Europe. He
believed in the system of national states and tried to conserve it.
He rejected the notion of American world domination, whether
moral or physical, and became impatient with the Kaiser and dis-
trustful of Germany. He had a fine comprehension of fundamental
international currents and an impressive number of close personal
friends abroad with whom he constantly exchanged ideas. He is the
American Bismarck, without the arrogance and the aloofness of the
Prussian statesman.[2] And as with Germany, where ' the pilot ' was
dropped in 1890, so it was with the United States in 1909 when
William Howard Taft, lacking Roosevelt's urbanity, knowledge and

[1] Herbert Croly, *Willard Straight*, N.Y., 1925, p. 275. Straight and his wife,
née Dorothy Whitney, who inherited wealth, chose Croly as editor in chief of *The
New Republic*, the weekly publication they established in 1912 as the organ of
American progressive thought. The Straights were imbued with the ' gospel of
wealth ', best explained by Andrew Carnegie, the Scottish-born steel magnate.
See David W. Noble, *The Paradox of Progressive Thought*, Minneapolis, Minn.,
1958. A detailed and fully documented account of American China policy in this
period is to be found in Charles Vevier, *The United States and China 1906–1913.
A Study of Finance and Diplomacy*, New Brunswick, N.J., 1955.

[2] Beale, op. cit., is the best book so far published on Roosevelt's diplomacy. A
scintillating essay on Roosevelt's personal friendships with European diplomats is
Nelson M. Blake, 'Ambassadors at the Court of Theodore Roosevelt ', *Miss. Valley
Hist. Rev.*, XLII, Sept., 1955, pp. 179–206. But for a first-hand acquaintanceship
with this highly individual and in many respects unique American Chief Executive,
the reader should turn to Mr. Roosevelt's own fascinating and voluminous letters.
See Elting Morison, op. cit., especially vols. IV–VIII.

experience, took over the presidency. Taft drew away from Europe, adopted at the bidding of Congress a policy of selfish discrimination against Europe in the use of the Panama Canal, and resumed the American 'mission' in the Orient which Roosevelt had wisely abandoned. Taft's policy is a return to traditionalism, but with the forces of industrialism in the seat of command.

With Wilson the United States climbed the heights in 1918 to the utopia of 'world leadership', only to see its idol come crashing to the ground and its dreams of 'saving' the world shattered. Wilson wrapped himself in the garments of an Old Testament prophet and proceeded to act out the role of a nationalist statesman. In education he was a product of nineteenth-century English liberalism. His intellectual masters were Walter Bagehot, John Stuart Mill, J. R. Green and Charles Darwin, but he had the Puritan's egoism and desire for salvation. In principle he was a Manchester free trader, but in practice he was a mercantilist, ambitious to employ the power of the State to obtain control of the world's commerce. A paper which he wrote, but did not publish, in 1907 reveals his inner thoughts. In it he declared:

> Since trade ignores national boundaries and the manufacturer insists on having the world as a market, the flag of his nation must follow him, and the doors of the nations which are closed against him must be battered down. Concessions obtained by financiers must be safeguarded by ministers of state, even if the sovereignty of unwilling nations be outraged in the process. Colonies must be obtained or planted, in order that no useful corner of the world may be overlooked or left unused. Peace itself becomes a matter of conference and international combinations.[1]

With the outbreak of the war in 1914 Wilson lost no time in an attempt to make these ideas national policy. He sponsored a shipping bill in Congress with the intent of taking over the interned German merchant vessels and running a government-supported merchant marine, and he declared that 'the Government must open these gates of trade, and open them wide'. He was thwarted in this measure by Senator Lodge, leading the opposition; but he antici-pated that the war would give the United States an economic stranglehold on Latin America and leave Britain and Germany so weakened that they would fall behind in the scramble for the world's markets. In 1917, we recall, he returned to the New York banks

[1] Diamond, op. cit., p. 141.

in the hope of driving a wedge into the growing Japanese monopoly of the Manchurian economy. America, he once wrote unctuously, ' was born to exemplify that devotion to the elements of righteousness which are derived from the revelations of Holy Scriptures '.[1]

Wilson had the evangelizing passion of Josiah Strong, but his missionary aspirations were political more than religious. He aimed at ' republicanizing ' the world, making over the nations in the graven image of America. His eager recognition of republican China in 1913 and of republican Russia in 1917, without prior study of the nature of the upheavals in those countries, are instances of his zeal and immaturity in international affairs. For Latin America he reserved his best schoolmaster's condescension. He would, he said, ' teach ' the Latin Americans to have good governments.

Wilson is the quintessence of American imperialism and of its tragedy. His imperfections are far from personal. They reflect historic national patterns of thought and the immaturity of a nation that materially had been highly privileged but intellectually had made little progress since the days of its founders. For a very short period in 1917–18 Wilson succeeded in building the presidential office into a personal absolutism, which was punctured by the Congressional elections of November 1918 and then shattered on the jealous rocks of senatorial rebellion. At the Peace Conference he personified the national legend of righteousness and republican virtue, proclaimed the United States the 'liberator' and the supreme judge of the world's political morals, and finally trapped himself in the ambiguous phraseology of Article X of the League Covenant.[2] According to Wilson this innocuous pledge ' to respect and preserve as against external aggression the territorial integrity and existing political independence' of the members of the League would absolutely stop 'ambitious and aggressive war '. According to the sceptics, who took Article X seriously or at least pretended to, it was an invitation to chaos because it laid down, or seemed to lay down, an inexorable law against change in the future relationships of states. The subsequent repudiation and humiliation of President Wilson was an ironic negation of the historic American national mission.

[1] Ibid., pp. 136–7, quoting from Wilson's essay on ' The Bible and Progress '.
[2] No attempt can be made here to enumerate the considerable literature on Wilson. For the Constitutional aspects of his wartime government consult Carl Brent Swisher, *American Constitutional Development*, Boston, Mass., 1943, pp. 596–689. Alexander L. and Juliette L. George, *Woodrow Wilson and Colonel House. A Personality Study*, N.Y., 1956, is an incisive criticism of the President by professional psychologists who have made careful use of historical materials.

With the downfall of Wilson, the United States entered a period of stagnation coupled with supreme self-assurance. Its position in the world seemed secure. No other nation could approach it, either in economic wealth or in massive political power. Merely by doing nothing—or almost nothing—it appeared able to impose its will upon the rest of the world. A hint of economic reprisal, or an implied threat of capitalizing the lead in naval power which it had gained during the war, was enough to force a compromise, if not a capitulation. It did not need the League of Nations; nor did it, for twenty years, venture far beyond the formalities of conventional diplomatic intercourse with foreign powers. Toward Western Europe it felt no obligation; it laughed at French fears of Germany, and sought to instruct Europe in the lessons of disarmament; and it concentrated on collecting old debts with one hand and, with the other, proffering new loans as a means of financing new markets overseas for the surplus of its swollen economy at home. Toward Soviet Russia it assumed an attitude of downright scorn, and took for granted that sooner or later the hated Bolshevist regime would be overthrown.

From Japan indeed came a faintly challenging voice. That nation too had gained in stature during the World War, and preened herself as the new and rightful champion of the Orient against the West. It was not long, however, before the Japanese found themselves cut down to size. Almost single-handedly, American diplomacy under the direction of Charles Evans Hughes brought them to Washington where, at the Arms Conference of 1921, they subscribed to a series of international agreements which, from their standpoint, set back Japan to the rank of a second-class power. The Five Power Naval Limitation Treaty had this effect through its requirement that Japan's capital ship tonnage be subordinated to American and British respectively in the ratio of three to five.

The Washington Conference rescued the powers, including the United States itself, from a costly naval race which none desired; but beyond that it established a paper league of nations system for the Pacific area, designed to keep Japan in check and to bestow upon China a sort of international bill of rights which, if events followed a logical pattern, would ultimately put China in first place among the nations of East Asia. At this conference Secretary Hughes assumed the mantle of Woodrow Wilson and showed a determination to promote by means of these treaties, a *pax Americana* for the

Pacific area. The nine Power Treaty relating to China was American inspired and American written; and the Four Power Pact was an ambiguously worded agreement binding the parties ' as between themselves to respect their rights in relation to their insular possessions and insular dominions in the region of the Pacific Ocean '. More adroit than Wilson, and more lucid in defining his objectives, Hughes worked to salvage something from the wreck tossed up by the senate in 1919. His Four Power Pact even contained a clause providing for mutual consultation regarding ' any Pacific question '. But his triumph was short-lived: as the price for its approval, the senate wrote in a reservation stipulating that ' under the terms of this treaty there is no commitment to armed force, no alliance, no obligation to join in any defense '.

This reservation, rather than the treaty itself, represented the spirit of the postwar period and, except as paper documents, the Washington treaties passed into oblivion. A chance to use them arose with the Far Eastern Crisis of 1931–32 but, despite appeals from both London and Geneva, the uncooperative government of Herbert Hoover held strictly to the line of inaction and mouthed the high-sounding moral phrases that the nationalist Republican leaders of the senate had taken over from Woodrow Wilson. But a further retreat into the inner sanctuary of neutrality was soon to follow through the enactment by Congress of a series of laws designed to fulfill the passionate demand of the decade to ' keep out of war '. These frenzied efforts to escape, while at the same time retaining the lofty post of the world's moral preceptor, encountered the inevitable debacle of 1941.

It goes beyond the purview of this volume to explore, or even comment upon, the second American attempt, under the direction of Franklin D. Roosevelt, to carry on the national mission. Like Wilson, Roosevelt was a crusader—an inveterate crusader. Indeed, if Wilson and his Fourteen Points are to be regarded as idealistic, what is to be thought of Roosevelt's flight into the dream world of the ' Four Freedoms '? Again, in a different context, the United States in 1945 scaled the heights to Utopia. In Roosevelt's dreams and crudely-drawn plans for a new world order, the familiar Wilsonian pattern is all there: the eradication of evil, the abolition of spheres of influence and ' imperialism ', the propagation of democracy, this time with the aid and cooperation of China—the 'policeman' of the Far East—and of Soviet Russia.[1]

The ideological extravagance of such a 'programme' puts it beyond the pale of criticism for any who have respect for history. Wilson and Roosevelt alike cut loose from all rational considerations, and surrendered themselves to the passion for making over the world in the fanciful image that they had constructed for the United States. But it was only an image, not a real life figure, an idol set up for the masses to worship and symbolizing the national legend. This is the great illusion, the supreme irony of American history which is self-defeating: the assumption of an historical innocence too good to be true, the hereditary belief that, *because* the United States is not like other nations but, rather, exceeds them in virtue, all mankind are bound to accept its lead.

[1] Much of Wilson's Utopian world had its counterpart in the teachings of Lenin. See Arno J. Mayer, *Political Origins of the New Diplomacy, 1917–1918*, New Haven, Conn., 1959. Willard D. Range, *Franklin D. Roosevelt's World Order*, Athens, Ga., 1959, admiringly discusses Roosevelt's ideology. Wendell Willkie, the Republican candidate, was as prodigal as F. D. R. in constructing his dream world of the postwar years. See his now forgotten, but once widely read tract, *One World*.

INDEX

WITHDRAWN